D1558881

Female Genital Cutting
in Industrialized Countries

FEMALE GENITAL CUTTING IN INDUSTRIALIZED COUNTRIES

Mutilation or Cultural Tradition?

Mary Nyangweso

AN IMPRINT OF ABC-CLIO, LLC
Santa Barbara, California • Denver, Colorado • Oxford, England

Library of Congress Cataloging-in-Publication Data

Nyangweso, Mary, author.
   Female genital cutting in industrialized countries : mutilation or cultural tradition? / Mary Nyangweso.
        pages cm.
   Includes bibliographical references and index.
   ISBN 978-1-4408-3346-5 (hardcopy : alk. paper) —
ISBN 978-1-4408-3347-2 (ebook)   1. Female circumcision.   2. Female circumcision—Social aspects.   3. Female circumcision—Government policy.
4. Female circumcision—Prevention.   5. Developing countries—Politics and government.   I. Title.
   [DNLM: 1. Circumcision, Female.   2. Culture.   3. Developed Countries.
4. Emigrants and Immigrants.   5. Ethics.   6. Social Values.   7. Women's Health.
GN484 .N93   2014]
   392.1—dc23   2014021611

ISBN: 978-1-4408-3346-5
EISBN: 978-1-4408-3347-2

18   17   16   15   14   1   2   3   4   5

This book is also available on the World Wide Web as an eBook.
Visit www.abc-clio.com for details.

Praeger
An Imprint of ABC-CLIO, LLC

ABC-CLIO, LLC
130 Cremona Drive, P.O. Box 1911
Santa Barbara, California 93116-1911

This book is printed on acid-free paper ∞

Manufactured in the United States of America

Contents

Acknowledgments

Social welfare has always concerned me. Having always been interested in exploring social dynamics as these relate to human behavior, I am often puzzled by how social institutions work together to promote certain ideals, attitudes, and general behavior. I am fascinated by the role of values in generating social behavior, whether this role is implicit or explicit. The transfer of these values into family settings, politics, health matters, and society in general demonstrates how social institutions interconnect in the process of social formation. This book is a continuation of my 20-year exploration of how a "simple" social practice such as female genital cutting illustrates the relationships between health care, religious values, culture, social behavior, legal and political nuances. This task has not been easy by any standard given that it was undertaken amidst my otherwise busy schedule. It was only possible to complete the writing with the support from friends and family.

All comments made intentionally or unintentionally went toward the progress of this work. I would therefore like to take this opportunity to acknowledge and express my deepest gratitude and regards to all that have contributed toward the completion of this project. I am grateful to East Carolina University for granting me the opportunity to do this research. I am grateful to my respondents and key informants for their generosity in sharing information toward the project. Because I promised all of them anonymity, all names used in this study are fictional. I am grateful to Catherine M. Lafuente, Lesley Reed, Traci West, Jacob Olupona and Susan

Pearce for reading the manuscript or some aspect of it, and my wonderful students Tyler Beasley, Rex Logan, and Tyree Barnes for reading through the manuscript. Lastly, I would like to thank my children Xylona, Tolbert, Brian, and Dennis for their patience and constant encouragement during the production of the manuscript. Without this very important moral support, the task would have been overwhelming. To all, I say thank you.

Introduction

Lali (not her real name) is a 15-year-old British-Somali girl and terrified. She is terrified of discussing her recent experience of genital cutting with a journalist. She is terrified not just because she will be breaking a taboo that could lead to her death; she also fears her parents will be arrested if she is discovered. "Promise you won't print my name or anything?" she pleads repeatedly. "Promise no one will ever know that I've spoken to you? If people in my community find out, they'll say that I've betrayed them and I'll have to run away. And anyway, I don't want my parents to be sent to jail" (Goodwin and Jones, 2008). Lali knows that to speak about genital cutting in her Somali tradition is taboo and that it is sometimes punishable by death. She is aware of a recent case in Norway, where a young Somali woman was beaten, almost to death, for narrating her experience to TV documentary program makers. Norway is one of several industrialized countries where female genital cutting is becoming prevalent among immigrants. And, in the United States, the experience of many young immigrant girls is no different.

Meanwhile, one cannot but be intrigued by the implication of the courageous letter of an 11-year-old whose desperate cries for help points to an underlying issue. Aisha (not her real name) is an immigrant girl in the United Kingdom desperate to avoid female genital cutting, a procedure that her unsuspecting sister was exposed to against her will. With the help of her teacher, she was directed to Equality Now, one of the few charity organizations in the country that advocates against this procedure. Luckily for her, she got the help she needed and is said to be safe from the procedure. Below is her courageous letter.

Dear Madam,

My name is XXX and I am 11 years old. I and my mum, sisters and brother came to England in 2005 when I had just turned 6 years old to join my dad who was at University. We come from Gambia in West Africa.

Three weeks ago we were watching a TV programme on African culture and as they were showing girls having their private cut, my older sister who is 12 years old started crying. After 2 days she told my dad that she also had her private cut.

Mum and Dad never knew about it and she was told if she ever tells anyone the spirits will come and kill her immediately. She said it was done one weekend by my aunties at my Nan's house. Last Friday, mum took her to our GP to have her checked and the doctor said it was done to her. . . . I went to school I told one of my teachers about it and together we went on the computer and found your group. . . . I don't want my private cut by anyone.

My dad loves us very much and he did not like what they done to my sister and he is very confused. We should be going back to Gambia any time after Eid and he is worried and upset that they would do the same to me. I don't what that too . . .

Please madam, help me, and my dad . . . I really hope you can help me, not to have my private cut. I am really confused especially seeing my dad so un-happy and not knowing want to do.

Thank you very much. (Maim, 2010)

In Washington, D.C., Mimi Ramsey, an Ethiopian immigrant, is heart-broken about what is about to happen to her friend Genat's baby. During a visit at Genat's, Mimi hoped to persuade her not to let her mother perform female genital cutting on her baby. As she spends several hours with her, they engage in conspiratorial whispers. "Mother says she will do it anyway, herself—when I'm out of the house—if I don't agree to get it done soon," Genat confides to Ramsey, hoping her friend can help her. "She says she will take a razor blade and do it." Ramsey, who has heard this story many times before, responds by reciting a long list of reasons why the older woman must be stopped. "You cannot let her do this to your child. Please. It is wrong. You know how painful it is. How damaging. Your daughter may hate you for life for what you allow to happen to her."

Genat shakes her head while expressing her dilemma. She doesn't want her baby girl—just born in this country—to be circumcised, as is customary in her native land, but her mother is adamant. "She believes in it so strongly," Genat says. "She said if I don't do these things, the girl will grow up horny. She'll be like American girls. And how will I be able to go back to work if my mother is not here to care for my child?" After several sleepless hours and a fruitless morning discussion with Genat's mother, Ramsey, discouraged, ends her visit. "Please send your mother home," she advises Genat. "Go on welfare if you have to, but don't let your mother stay in the house and do this to your baby" (Burstyn, 1995).

In Massachusetts, a 45-year-old immigrant, Fatima Mohammed, is faced with a question most American parents never worry about: "Should my daughter be circumcised?" Mohammed explains how difficult the decision is for her since she has been through this very painful experience herself as a child in Africa. She strongly opposes the idea of cutting her 11-year-old daughter, an American-born Somali girl. According to Mohammed, not every family in her African community in Massachusetts feels the same way. Most cannot swiftly make the decision not to cut their daughters because it is a cultural ritual. It is a practice that is integral to a woman's identity. According to Muhammad, "Some think I'm disrespecting my own culture. . . . Others say you act like an American now. You forgot about who you are" (Chen, 2010).

Female genital cutting is an issue of concern in the daily experiences of some girls and women within immigrant communities. Stories like the ones narrated above barely describe the experiences and struggles of immigrant women from female genital-cutting communities who live in industrialized countries.[1] Approximately 100–140 million girls have undergone genital cutting worldwide (WHO, 2010).[2] Although statistics indicate that there is a slow decline in the number of female genital-cutting procedures, at least 2 million girls remain at risk every year of experiencing genital cutting globally. In Africa alone, an estimated 92 million girls have undergone genital cutting, and approximately 6,000 new cases are reported every day—which amounts to five girls every minute (WHO 1997; Momoh, 2000). Although this practice is most prevalent in Africa—where it occurs in 28 countries, 18 of which have a prevalence rate of 50 percent or higher (Feldmans-Jacobs, and Clifton, 2010)—female genital cutting also occurs in some Middle Eastern countries, including Saudi Arabia, the Republic of Yemen, Oman, and Israel, as well as in Indonesia, Malaysia, Pakistan, Iraq, and India.

Female genital cutting (FGC), also known as female genital mutilation (FGM) or female circumcision (FC), is also increasing in industrialized countries. This sociocultural practice, often associated with African and Middle Eastern countries, is performed on girls and young women as a rite of passage. It involves the pricking, piercing, stretching, burning, or excision of the clitoris and/or the removal of part or all of the tissues around a woman's reproductive organ. In some cases, infibulation is performed—the stitching together of the vulva in order to narrow the vaginal opening.

While it is commonly performed on girls between the ages of 4 and 16, it is popularly performed as an initiation rite of passage into womanhood. Since most countries have outlawed the practice, parents who hope to evade legal consequences have performed it on unsuspecting toddlers and babies (Stanlie and Robertson, 2002; Spencer, 2002: 2).

It is apparent that as industrialized countries become culturally and religiously diverse, foreign values will increasingly exert their influence. Female genital cutting is one of many cultural practices that immigrants bring with them when they immigrate to these countries. Even though most industrialized countries such as the United States, Australia, Canada, England, and France have instituted policies to inhibit the practice, it has persisted among some immigrant communities. Although numerous cases go unreported, the frequency of female genital cutting-related cases in the media indicates a serious problem. In this study, I explore reasons for the increase of female genital cutting in industrialized countries despite its criminalization in some of these countries. I identify flaws and loopholes in existing intervention programs to recommend strategies for improving these. I argue that attitudes toward the practice have been influenced by controversial discourse on moral and cultural values, which manifest in the attitude of political correctness which is stalling efforts toward protecting the rights of girls who live with the risk and women who live with short-term and long-term health consequences of the practice.

The prevalence of female genital cutting in the United States is not fully known. However, studies indicate that the practice is increasingly common among immigrants (Keaton, 2010; Bashir, 2012). According to Guy Blake (1995: 159–162), many of the immigrant women from FGC communities in the United States have indicated that they intend to continue the practice of female genital cutting in their new country. If necessary, they will have to take their children to their native countries to get it done. Others have indicated that they will seek doctors to do it and this has indeed happened in such cases (Guy, 1995: 159–162). It is therefore not surprising that in 2002, it was estimated by the African Women's Health Center (AWHC) at Brigham and Women's Hospital (BWH) (Hundley, 2002) that of the 150,000 immigrant women from female genital-cutting communities living in the United States, approximately 228,000 have been cut or live with the risk of genital cutting—a rise in the statistic by 35 percent (AWHC, 2012; Lopez, 2013). Although female genital cutting has officially been banned in the United States since 1996, the pressure to succumb to the practice is very high and some parents who want to stay true to their tradition ask American doctors to cut their daughters. According to Terry Dunn, an obstetrician gynecologist in

Denver, Colorado, parents approach physicians, saying, "I want to have the procedure that makes my daughter like me" (Odigie, 2012).

In Seattle, Washington, internist Carol Horowitz testified to having treated more than 20 Somali refugees, most of whom had been exposed to the more severe form of genital cutting—infibulations (Gregory, 1994). Doctors have also reported witnessing the effects of genital cutting among refugees from Somalia and Sudan who live in Dallas, Texas (O'Connor and Yearwood, 1994). In Georgia, at Grady Memorial Hospital, a mother asked the head of obstetrics to perform genital cutting on her little girl (Guy, 1995: 162). In the same year, Meserek Ramsey, an immigrant nurse, was stunned to meet an 18-month-old Ethiopian American girl recovering from a genital-cutting wound resulting from surgery performed in Washington (Crossette, 1995). In June 2010, Pema Levy reported that female genital cutting was even being practiced in the United States at Cornell University's New York Presbyterian Hospital, one of the nation's major hospitals, where Dr. Pix D. Poppas of the hospital's pediatric urology department performs it under the guise of "corrective surgery" (Levy, 2010). Commenting on this practice, Barbara Crossette (1995) observes, "It is becoming apparent to health workers and lawmakers in the United States that the practice of female genital cutting goes on here among immigrants from several of the forty or more countries in Africa and the Middle East where mutilation is prevalent."

There are reports of female genital cutting in other industrialized countries as well. In Europe, it is estimated that 7 million women (The Department of Health CMO Estimates, 2004; Zero Tolerance, 2011) have been subjected to female genital cutting, with about 500,000 girls living with the risk (EU Parliamentary Estimates, 2011; Dirie, 2005: 16, 77–85). In the United Kingdom, it is estimated that 279,500 women have been exposed to female genital cutting, with about 33,000 believed to live with the risk (Leye, 2001, 2004, 23–24). In England and Wales alone, *Equality Now* reports, 66,000 women have been subjected to female genital cutting, with about 23,000 living with the risk (Equality Now, 2012). In fact, 2,100 were treated in London hospitals since 2010 for female genital-cutting injuries. Of these, 300 required surgeries to repair damage caused (Robinson, 2013). A report from the French National Institute for Democratic Studies indicates that more than 60,000 women living in France have been exposed to some form of female genital cutting, with about 20,000 at risk of exposure (Webster, 2004). In Germany, 60,000 have been exposed to female genital cutting, with 20,000 at risk (Tritze, 2012). In the Netherlands—a country with many immigrants due to its history of tolerance and trade, but where female genital cutting is illegal—39,000 have been subjected to the practice and 14,000 live at risk. In Austria, about 8,197 females have been subjected to the practice illegally (Poldermans, 2006: 64). In a small city of Norrkoping, Sweden, school health services found 60 cases of female genital cutting among school girls since March 2014. In a class of 30 girls, 28 had been exposed to the most severe form of female genital cutting (Synon, 2014; Hastings, 2014).

The list is long—a proof of irrefutable fact that female genital cutting is being performed in industrialized countries. But although these numbers may seem alarming, the actual numbers of women living with the risk of and consequences of female genital cutting are unknown, given the sensitive nature of the subject in communities concerned. In the United Kingdom, for instance, the All Party Parliamentary Group on Population, Development and Reproductive Health acknowledged in 2000 that there was a severe shortage of data on the practice in the country (BMA, 2004: 3). The fact that female genital cutting is also criminalized in most developed countries makes it even more difficult to access information. The secrecy that shrouds this practice inhibits efforts to prosecute because it is difficult to ascertain whether a girl or woman has been circumcised. Immigrant women find themselves confronted with the challenge of trying to uphold their cultural rights and maintain their cultural identity in a country that promotes human rights. This dilemma is made more difficult with the criminalization of female genital cutting in these countries.

The increase of the practice in industrialized countries is particularly disturbing to human and women's rights efforts because these countries have a history of promoting civil, human, and women's rights. As such, they are often viewed as a safe haven for girls who flee their countries to find refuge from demeaning cultural practices. As Lisa Wade observes, the West is perceived as the pinnacle of civilization and as an exemplar for the rest of the world. According to the theory of American exemplarism, for example, the United States is perceived as unique in its manifestation of ideals, including moral ideals (Wade, 2009: 294). For this reason, it is expected that industrialized countries such as the United States should have effective intervention programs to ensure the safety of girls and women.

Efforts to eradicate or transform attitudes toward female genital cutting have been challenging the world over despite the World Health Organization's and the International Federation of Gynecology and Obstetrics' (IFGO) position that the procedure is "medically unnecessary." WHO simply defines the practice as a process that alters or injures female genital organs for nonmedical purposes (WHO, 2014). But according to the human rights position, female genital cutting is a form of gender-based violence that makes it a violation of the human rights of children, girls, and women with respect to their health and bodily integrity. Feminists describe it as a symptom of patriarchal social systems that tend to control women's sexuality. Some modernists have described it as an indigenous, primitive practice that is incompatible with modern values. The central question of this study is this: Why does the practice persist despite efforts to resist it?

Although female genital cutting is criminalized in industrialized countries, studies indicate how difficult it is to enforce laws related to the practice. It is important to recognize the role of legal efforts in changing attitudes toward the practice. The dilemma of nonprosecution of culprits is intensified by those who argue in favor of the practice. Postcolonial discourse on cultural diversity has led some to defend the practice on the grounds of cultural rights. This position is clearly displayed in the American Academy of Pediatrics (AAP) policy statement released in May of 2010, arguing that some forms of female genital cutting are "harmless and less extensive than the routine newborn male circumcision commonly performed in the West" (AAP, 1089). Physicians who work with immigrant communities should be allowed to "'prick' or 'nick' girls' clitoral skin in recognition of the necessity to satisfy cultural requirements" (AAP 1091).

According to Douglas S. Diekema, a Washington physician and former chair of the bioethics committee at the academy, "The procedure could be effective in certain African communities in reducing harm, even though the pricking method is illegal in the United States" (Intact America, 2012). Such a position is not unique to the United States. In Australia, around the same time, the Royal Australian and New Zealand College of Obstetricians and Gynecologists (RANZCOG) was reported to be considering the sanctioning of medically performed ritual nicks to satisfy the desire of some culture for genital cutting of girls in a bid to protect them from more severe forms of the practice (Matthews, 2011: 139; Tatnell, 2010).

However, opponents of the practice are concerned about its increase, and especially, about those who advocate any form of it. "We are very disappointed," says Asma Donahue, senior program officer at the *Sauti Yetu* Center for African Women in New York, who explains that allowing a doctor to perform a modified form of female genital cutting "undermines the education and advocacy work being done to stop it" (Chen, 2010). According to Intact America, an activist organization for children's rights, AAP's position is motivated by "the blatant double standard it applies in its acceptance of infant male circumcision as a legitimate surgical intervention" (2012). Although it is clear that controversial positions on this practice continue to exist, both advocates

8   *Female Genital Cutting in Industrialized Countries*

and opponents of the practice agree that there is immense pressure for American girls in some immigrant communities to subject themselves to female genital cutting. AAP's actions are merely an indication of this pressure.

Soraya Mire, a Somali film director and activist who works with the African immigrant community in the United States, acknowledges that the pressure is immense. In 1994, she reported that she was aware of six girls who had been cut while in the United States and that the cutting took place in a U.S hospital (Guy, 1995: 159). This claim was followed by a declaration by experts at the International Conference on Population and Development—which took place in Cairo in the same year—that the practice was becoming increasingly common in immigrant communities in the United States, Canada, Europe, and Australia (Guy, 1995: 159–160). In her documentary, *Fire Eyes*, she chronicles her experience with female genital cutting when she was 13 years old. As Stephanie Chen reports, "From her Los Angeles, California home, she has counseled hundreds of genital cutting survivors and immigrant parents by letters and phone calls, including a few who have contemplated sending their daughters abroad to be cut. She sleeps with her cell phone tucked under her pillow so she can answer calls at all hours. When asked what she tells these immigrant communities, she responds, 'You don't have a right to do this to your children. . . . You are continuing the abuse'" (Chen, 2010; 2012). In response to suspicions of genital cutting being planned in the United States, Representative Joseph Crowley, a Democrat from New York, and Representative Mary Bono Mark, a Republican from California, proposed an amendment to close a loophole in the 1996 federal law banning female genital cutting. The legislation introduced would criminalize parents who force their daughters to have the procedure abroad.

The demonstrated prevalence of female genital cutting in industrialized countries poses certain theoretical concerns. First, it highlights the significant role of values, particularly cultural and religious values on social behavior. Second, it alludes to the efficacy of intervention programs. In this study, I argue that cultural or religious practices must be brought to bear upon contemporary values. By documenting the experience of girls and women who live with the risk and consequences of genital cutting, I highlight the need for cultural appraisal to promote social welfare. I argue that current attitudes toward cultural diversity and multiculturalism are responsible, in part, for the persistence of female genital cutting in industrialized countries. These attitudes, which embrace difference as a social group's right, have revived claims to cultural values, including those that have been defined as repugnant, archaic, primitive, and irrelevant in a modern society.

In the United States, for instance, the government's policies concerning diversity and multiculturalism are evident in educational programs that seek to help immigrants assimilate in the American society while maintaining their own culture and religion. Recognizing unique cultural values within a diverse country such as the United States is bound to reveal a conflict in values and principles. Yet, as I also argue, a reinforcement of a cultural lifestyle without critical appraisal of its norms and values can be problematic. While efforts toward respecting all cultural views, norms, and ideas must be applauded, continuous reports of genital cutting call this strategy into question.

In *Female Genital Cutting in Industrialized Countries*, I also engage the general assumption that primitive practices are incapable of adapting to modern scientific and civilized societies. In my analysis of the reasons behind the tenacity of female genital cutting, I observe that female genital cutting is a social and religious phenomenon that has survived in modern society because it addresses issues of meaning in the communities where it persists. In my conclusion, I argue for a cultural appraisal in efforts to adapt values that affirm human agency and dignity to our changing society. I caution against the trend in cultural diversity discourses toward romanticization of cultural and religious values. Social values must be first and foremost based on human rights values in order to protect the welfare of all.

STUDY FRAMEWORK

This study makes an important contribution to the scholarly literature in its exploration of the knowledge gaps that inform the persistence of female genital cutting in industrialized societies. Previous studies on female genital cutting in industrialized countries such as the United States have not documented the voices of women and girls who live with the risk and consequences of this practice. Similarly, no study has explored the influence of the discourse on multiculturalism on attitudes toward female genital cutting.

This study is informed by a number of theoretical perspectives—namely, cultural relativist, and moral universalist perspectives—along with the diffusion of innovations theory and empowerment theory. According to the cultural relativist theory, notions of right, wrong, and what is moral differ because the cultures in which they are found differ. Cultural relativism informs current popular positions on cultural diversity and multiculturalism, which has been used to defend female genital cutting as a social group's right. It is based on the argument that notions of right, wrong, and morality differ because the cultures in which they are found differ. According to the moral universalist theory, all humans are equally entitled to inalienable rights such as liberty, equal protection of the law, and freedom from being subjected to torture (Steiner and Alston, 1996). Moral universalism informs human rights values, guaranteeing everyone basic rights, even culturally sanctioned ones. These perspectives help in exploring the influence of two controversial moral positions on attitudes toward female genital cutting in industrialized countries. In *Female Genital Cutting in Industrialized Countries*, I transcend the bifurcated ethnocentric and imperialist approaches that characterize these two irreconcilable positions by introducing women's voice into this discourse.

The diffusion of innovation theory argues that social networking is important for social transformation. In essence, it is claimed that social networks contribute significantly to the dissemination of new ideas. Since most people are likely to adopt an idea that has received favorable evaluations, it is important that such evaluations receive wide circulation. Further, the theory claims, an idea is likely to be accepted if it is communicated to community members by the most respectable individuals in the community's social networks (Kegele, 1996). Thus, I argue that community leaders and religious leaders have a significant role in influencing social behavior decisions, especially on sensitive issues such as female genital cutting. As revered members of the community, leaders are in a privileged position to disperse information that can transform attitudes toward female genital cutting.

While I draw heavily on secondary material, primary sources constitute a significant component of the study. During my survey, I utilized an ethnographic approach where both quantitative and qualitative design methods of analysis were used to highlight experiences of immigrant women in industrialized countries. Participants were recruited randomly through a respondent-driven snowball sampling technique derived from existing contacts. Most were drawn from different ethnic communities in the diasporic world, mainly the United States. Most of them came from the following communities—Kenya, Somali, Sudan, Gambia, Sierra Leone, Nigeria, Liberia, Mauritania, South Africa, and Ethiopia. A sample of 113 participants was recruited in total. Respondents in other industrialized countries were accessed through international communication tools, including e-mail, phone, and online surveys. Participants were asked to endorse statements ranging from 0 (strongly disagree) to 5 (strongly agree), mainly to solicit participants' opinions. Main topics include the following: (1) Whether female genital cutting is practiced in industrialized countries where they lived, (2) where and how the practice was performed, (3) knowledge about criminalization of the practice in these countries, (4) reason for the persistence of female genital cutting, (5) whether religious values were a factor in the persistence of the practice. In-depth interviews were conducted with key informants identified from the survey.

By introducing the agency of women in female genital-cutting discourses, I grant their voice a significant place in this discourse. I grant them an opportunity to express their real experiences, desires, and interests in order to directly inform decisions and policymaking. As Einstein has validly argued, "To really understand the impact of a practice on the body, it is important to ask women themselves what they feel—in both figurative and literal sense" (2008: 95). This is important because women who undergo genital cutting have varying opinions and experiences with the practice. In order to take into account these varied experiences, the study offers the reader a nuanced awareness of the many situations immigrant girls and women face.

Findings confirm the occurrence of female genital cutting among immigrant communities in the industrialized countries. They attest to the fact that the practice is gaining momentum due to recent calls for attention to diversity and multiculturalism. Increasing sensitivity to the needs of multicultural societies appears to reinforce discourses about the rights of social groups and the need for moral values and cultural practices. Although it is a challenge to perform female genital cutting openly in these industrialized countries for fear of criminal consequences, most parents cite cultural right as the reason for demanding less dangerous forms of female genital cutting for their daughters. Some respondents insisted on the practice as a way to protect their cultural identity. Where parents have shied away from breaking the law, vacation cuttings have been arranged for their daughters abroad, mainly in their countries of origin. To be effective, intervention programs must be geared toward the actual needs of these women. I argue that a community that is empowered about its social reality is enabled to address issues that it faces. In-depth discussions and analysis of these findings, alongside analytical illustrations, will follow in various chapters of the book.

ORGANIZATION OF THE STUDY

Female Genital Cutting in Industrialized Countries emphasizes the need to include the voice of women in a discourse that concerns them. This approach allows women in genital-cutting communities to share their own experiences, concerns, and recommendations about this practice. It is envisioned that the approach will initiate a conversation on the subject in immigrant communities and help to promote solidarity between women and the rest of the immigrant communities. The use of testimonies allows for a discourse on female genital cutting to be captured alive both for the reader and for experts on this practice. Select testimonies included in the book represent the voices of a majority of women who live with the consequences and the risk of genital cutting. In addition, the voices of experts who work with these women are brought to bear and affirm their experience.

While it should be noted that female genital cutting may not have serious health effects on all women who are exposed to it, research indicates that there are health risks associated with this procedure. Health risks associated with female genital cutting vary by type, from situation to situation, and from woman to woman. I do not record these experiences to exploit or romanticize their experience. My goal is to put their experiences into perspective so that policymakers can address the insider's perspective. Since most of these women and girls sought refuge in these industrialized countries to escape genital cutting and other unhealthy or undermining cultural practices, it is only fair that their situation is examined in relation to these expectations.

In the chapters that follow, I explore reasons for the practice of female genital cutting in industrialized countries to highlight possible remedies with regard to intervention processes. After giving a general overview of the practice and highlighting issues of concern related to human and cultural rights, I immerse the reader in specific experiences, as voiced by women and experts on the subject. While the reader is likely to empathize with these women, and thus, appreciate their experience first-hand, my main concern is to allow the actual experience to inform effective intervention that will minimize the practice in industrialized countries.

In the following chapter, I engage with the question of multiculturalism as a consequence of postcolonialism and the emergence of much more diverse, less homogenous societies than were previously the norm. I explore the claims of human rights advocates and the rights of social groups to highlight the influence on the debate, attitudes, policies, and intervention efforts against female genital cutting. This is followed by an exploration of the role of religion in the persistence of female genital cutting. The question of social change is interrogated within modernist theories just as cultural appraisal is examined as a process of social transformation.

I end the book by exploring existing policies on female genital cutting in industrialized countries with the aim of highlighting flaws and loopholes in these policies. A case is made for the need to enact clear and enforceable laws. I also discuss the need to supplement legal policies with community-based initiatives that are sensitive to cultural and religious values that inform female genital cutting. Citing successful examples, it is argued that these values should complement legal strategies to combat the practice in a respectful manner. I argue that understanding cultural values that inform the practice must precede any strategy to intervene.

While female genital cutting raises concerns due to health consequences associated with the practice, efforts must be made to protect the
rights of the girls at risk and care for the women who live with the consequences. In order to protect the rights of the girls and women who live in
industrialized countries, health care intervention must be part of the program. This argument is made in Chapter 8. It is argued that medicalization of the practice should be encouraged where the practice is desired in
adults over 18 years. It is recommended that medical professions in industrialized countries should be trained in order to provide special health services, including reconstructive surgery to those women who desire such
services. A list of centers where such help can be sought is included.

The book concludes with the argument that female genital cutting
should be recognized as a serious human rights violation and health issue
in immigrant communities. It is recognized that serious efforts need to be
made to understand values that influence its persistence as effective intervention of the practice is pursued in efforts to protect the human rights of
girls and women who live with the risk and consequences of the practice
in industrialized countries.

NOTES

1. These countries are also known as Western and developed countries.
   I will use these terms interchangeably. Also, more life experiences of
   girls and women who live with the risk and consequences of female
   genital cutting will be presented in Chapter 2.
2. WHO estimates that 100 to 140 million girls and women worldwide
   are currently living with the consequences of female genital cutting. In
   Africa, an estimated 92 million girls of ages 10 and above have undergone genital cutting.

1

❖

Female Genital Cutting:
An Overview

Female genital cutting is an intentional, nonmedical modification of the female genitalia. It is commonly performed on girls between the ages of 4 and 16, although in some cases it is performed on infants as young as three months old. In this chapter, I give a brief overview of the practice, highlighting its origins and the reasons for female genital cutting in order to contextualize the practice in the broader historical and cultural values that inform it. Available statistics indicate that approximately 100–140 million girls have undergone genital cutting worldwide, with millions living with the consequences of the practice.[1] In Africa, where 23 countries practice some form of female genital cutting, it is estimated that 92 million girls have been cut (WHO, 1997; Momoh, 2000). Reports indicate that in countries such as Sudan, Somalia, Djibouti, Ethiopia, Eritrea, and Sierra Leone, about 75 to 98 percent of the population is exposed to female genital cutting (UNICEF, 2013: 2–3). In countries such as Burkina Faso, Chad, Ivory Coast, Egypt, Gambia, Guinea, Guinea Bissau, Kenya, Liberia, Mali, Nigeria, and Togo, the population range exposed to this practice is between 30 and 50 percent (UNICEF, 2013: 2–3).

In the Middle East, female genital cutting is practiced in Oman, South Yemen, Libya, Algeria, Lebanon, Iraq, and Palestine. The practice is prevalent in Yemen and the Kurdish region of Iraq, with rates exceeding 80 percent in areas such as Garmyan and New Kirkuk (UNICEF, 2013: 31). It is also found in Bahrain and Iran (UNICEF, 2013: 31; Najm, 2012;

IRIN, 2008). In Iraq, it is estimated that 65 percent of those exposed to the practice are Kurds, with only 26 percent of these being of Arab descent. Of these, 41 percent were Sunni Muslim and 23 percent were Shiites (Burki, T., 2010; Yasin et al., 2013). In Asia, the practice is found on a lesser scale in countries such as Indonesia, Malaysia, Pakistan, and India, especially in those communities that have sizable Islamic populations. Some reports indicate that the practice also occurs in individual ethnic communities in some South American countries such as Argentina, Chile, and Brazil.

Although the prevalence of female genital cutting in industrialized countries is not fully known, statistics indicate that the practice is gaining prevalence in countries such as the United States, France, Australia, Austria, Norway, Sweden, and many others, especially among immigrant communities (Keaton, 2010; Bashir, 1996; UNICEF, 2013: 23). For instance, in the United States, approximately 228,000 girls live with the risk of genital cutting (AWHC, 1999). In Europe, it is estimated that 500,000 girls and women live with the lifelong consequences of female genital cutting, with about 180,000 girls and women at risk of this practice each year (Amnesty, 1997). In the United Kingdom, it is estimated that 86,000 women have undergonefemale genital cutting, with about 7,000 girls at risk annually (Powell et al., 2000: 5). According to Miller (2007), 27 females in the London borough of Haringey have sought medical treatment after being sexually mutilated. Down the road, in Waltham Forest, more than a thousand women, girls, and female infants have experienced female genital cutting. The group Forward, which campaigns against this practice, estimates that as many as 66,000 women living in Britain have been exposed to female genital cutting, and explains that the practice is especially popular in the growing Somali community (Miller, 2007).

In Australia, immigration data show that from 1999 to 2009, Australia received 38,299 Africans, with 24,082 emigrating from Sudan, 6,258 from Egypt, 5,223 from Ethiopia, and 2,736 from Somalia (Australian Government Department of Immigration and Citizenship, 2009). In France, it is estimated that 27,000 girls and women have undergone female genital cutting. In Belgium, data show that of the 12,415 women from African genital-cutting communities, about 2,700 have been exposed to female genital cutting (Leye, 2008). In a small city of Norrkoping, Sweden, school health services found 60 cases of female genital cutting among school girls since March 2014. In a class of 30 girls, 28 had been exposed to the most severe form of female genital cutting (Synon, 2014; Hastings, 2014). This is clear evidence of the practice in industrialized countries. In a survey administered inquiring about the existence of female genital cutting in the industrialized world, 60 percent of the 113 respondents expressed knowledge of the practice in the country they live. Only 40 percent expressed no such knowledge. Fifty-six percent expressed knowledge of a girl or woman who was at risk of female genital cutting in the country in which they live. The following is a table of responses to other related questions, followed by maps and tables showing the prevalence of the practice in the world, particularly in Africa and in some industrialized countries.

Table 1.1: Survey of Attitudes toward FGC in Industrialized Countries

Attitudes toward FGC in Industrialized Countries	N = 113	
	Yes (%)	No (%)
FGC is found in the West	60	40
Knows a girl/woman at risk of FGC	56	44
Immigrants know that FGC is illegal	70	30
Consider FGC a human rights violation	81	19
Religion recommends FGC	25	75
Want FGC to be eradicated	81	19
Involve clerics in intervention	89	11
FGC is group's right	30	70

Table 1.2: Prevalence of Female Genital Cutting in Africa

Country	Source/ Year	% Approx.
Benin	DHS 2006	13
Burkina Faso	MICS 2006	72
Cameroon	DHS 2004	01
Central African Republic	MICS 2008	26
Chad	DHS 2004	45
Cote d'Ivoire	MICS 2006	42
Djibouti	MICS 2006	93
Egypt	DHS 2008	95
Eritrea	DHS 2002	89
Ethiopia	DHS 2005	74
Gambia	DHS/MICS 2005/06	78
Ghana	MICS 2006	04

(Continued)

Table 1.2 (Continued)

Country	Source/ Year	% Approx.
Guinea	DHS 2005	96
Guinea Bissau	MICS 2006	45
Kenya	DHS 2008	27
Liberia	DHS 2007/09	58
Mali	DHS 2006	85
Mauritania	MICS 2007	71
Niger	DHS 2006	02
Nigeria	DHS 2008	30
Senegal	DHS 2005	28
Sierra Leone	MICS 2006	94
Somalia	MICS 2006	98
Sudan (Northern)	MICS/DHS 2006	90
Tanzania	DHS 2004/05	14
Togo	MICS 2006	5.8
Uganda	DHS 2006	0.6

Source: Extracted from Behrendt (2011) and Population Reference Bureau (PRB) (2010).

Table 1.3: Prevalence of Female Genital Cutting in the West

Country	Cut	At Risk	Source
Europe	7,000,000	500,000	Dirie (2005)
U.K. (Britain)	279,500	33,000	Leye (2001)
U.K. (England & Wales)	66,000	23,000	Equality Now (2012)
U.S.	168,000	227,887	AAW
France	60,000	20,000	France24 (2013)
Netherlands	39,000	14,000	Poldermans (2006)
Belgium	2,700		Leye (2008)
Austria	8,197		Poldermans (2006)
Germany	60,000	10,000	Titze (2012)

Prevalence of Female Genital Cutting
Scaled 2011

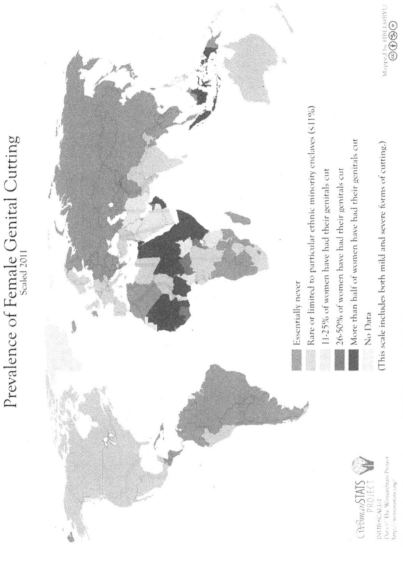

Essentially never

Rare or limited to particular ethnic minority enclaves (<11%)

11-25% of women have had their genitals cut

26-50% of women have had their genitals cut

More than half of women have had their genitals cut

No Data

(This scale includes both mild and severe forms of cutting.)

WomanSTATS PROJECT
INTRASCALE 1
Part of The WomanStats Project
http://womanstats.org/

Mapped by HBH LatBYU

Map 1.1: Prevalence of FGC in the World

Table 1.4: Prevalence in the United Kingdom

Year	From FGC Communities	Exposed to FGC	At Risk
2001	13,328	6,256	
2002	14,666	7,109	
2003	16,890	8,090	
2004	19,356	9,032	
2005		66,000	23,376

Table 1.5: Prevalence and Risk in the United States by Individual States as of 2000

State	Total	Under 18	18 +
U.S.	227,887	62,519	165,638
Alabama	657	118	539
Alaska	96	–	96
Arizona	2,741	999	1,742
Arkansas	157	–	157
California	38,353	9,631	28,722
Colorado	1,885	516	1,369
Connecticut	1,008	272	736
Delaware	375	237	139
District of Columbia	2,619	418	2,201
Florida	4,894	919	3,975
Georgia	9,531	2,404	7,128
Hawaii	103	–	103
Idaho	528	386	141
Illinois	6,420	1,307	5,114
Indiana	1,480	446	1,035
Iowa	828	213	614
Kansas	114	–	114
Kentucky	1,052	67	985
Louisiana	1,239	434	805

(*Continued*)

Table 1.5 (Continued)

State	Total	Under 18	18 +
Maine	–	–	–
Maryland	16,264	4,466	11,798
Massachusetts	5,231	1,318	3,912
Michigan	5,175	1,578	3,596
Minnesota	13,196	3,691	9,505
Mississippi	46	23	23
Montana	4	–	4
Nebraska	497	274	223
Nevada	604	–	604
New Hampshire	92	83	9
New Jersey	18,584	5,605	12,978
New Mexico	123	–	123
New York	25,949	7,675	18,274
North Carolina	4,297	973	3,325
North Dakota	1,134	837	298
Ohio	4,834	1,680	3,154
Oklahoma	410	43	368
Oregon	3,524	766	2,758
Pennsylvania	6,508	1,357	5,151
Rhode Island	1,271	214	1,057
South Carolina	680	261	419
South Dakota	1,344	866	477
Tennessee	2,823	1,275	1,549
Texas	13,100	3,790	9,310
Utah	377	232	145
Vermont	97	–	97
Virginia	17,980	4,312	13,669
Washington	7,292	1,943	5,349
West Virginia	257	159	98
Wisconsin	791	291	499
Wyoming	–	–	–

It is clear from the numbers cited above that the practice of female genital cutting is alive in industrialized countries. The American Academy of Pediatrics (AAP) alludes to the prevalence of the practice in its journal *Pediatrics*, while the American Medical Association (AMA) has officially recognized the practice as a challenge to many doctors in the United States (Kelton, CSA Report 5-1-94). Due to pressure from genital cutting communities, this international medical organization attempted to recommend a policy that would allow pediatricians to perform the safer form of the procedure commonly known as *sunna* or the ceremonial ritual nick. The American Academy of Pediatrics' proposal was based on the perceived need to be sensitive to the cultural and religious reasons that motivate parents to seek this procedure for their daughters. It was argued that allowing a ritual nick—a form of female genital cutting that is less extensive—will also keep families from importing traditional experts or sending their daughters overseas for a full circumcision.

As Adhikari and Salahi (2010) observe, many physicians who consider female genital cutting a horrifying experience are faced with a dilemma. If they turn down a patient, she is likely to be transported abroad for vacation-cutting, where most girls are often cut using crude and unsterilized instruments, such as a broken glass or razor blades, and more often than not, without anesthesia. According to Dr. Doug Diekema, a pediatrician at Seattle's Children's Hospital and former chairman of the AAP's bioethics committee, by refusing to cut girls in the United States, many doctors may be putting these girls' lives in jeopardy. "It's very easy to take the high road in cases like this," said Diekema. "But when you're dealing with religious or cultural beliefs, saying no sometimes is not sufficient for people and it will not necessarily eliminate the practice" (Adhikari and Salahi, 2010).

At the time of AAP's statement, there was no law in the United States protecting girls from being taken overseas for the procedure (*New York Times Editorial*, 2010). Interesting to note is the fact that the statement coincided with the United States Congressional Representatives introduction of the Girls Protection Act (HR. 5137), a bipartisan federal legislation that would make it illegal to transport a minor girl living in the United States to her native country for female genital cutting. Around the same time, the Royal Australian and New Zealand College of Obstetricians and Gynecologists (RANZCOG) was reported to be considering the sanctioning of medically performed ritual nicks for the same reasons (Matthews, 2011: 139; Tatnell, 2010). As expected, in the United States, the proposed AAP policy triggered controversy among opponents of the practice. The fact that female genital cutting is also criminalized in most developed countries makes it difficult even to access information on the subject. It should be remembered that because of the secrecy that shrouds female genital cutting, available statistics are mere estimates. Further, current studies on the subject do not provide up-to-date statistics. As Celia Dugger (1996) rightly observes, cultural values surrounding the practice inhibit efforts to study, report, or even ascertain whether a girl or woman has been circumcised. Talking about this practice is considered a profound invasion of privacy.

TYPES OF FEMALE GENITAL CUTTING

As indicated earlier, female genital cutting is often performed between the ages of 4 and 10 years, although in some communities, it may be practiced on infants or postponed until just before marriage. When performed on infants and young girls, a portion of or all of the clitoris and surrounding tissues may be removed. In cases where only the clitoral prepuce is removed, one may not be able to notice this unless a careful examination is carried out.

The World Health Organization (WHO) classifies female genital cutting procedures into four typologies to reflect its severity. Type 1, *clitoridectomy*, refers to the excision and removal of the prepuce (clitoral hood) with or without removal of any part of the clitoris (aka *sunna* circumcision). Type 2, *excision*, refers to the removal of the entire clitoris together with part or all of the labia *minora* (the inner vaginal lips). This type of genital cutting accounts for 80 percent of female genital cuttings in the world. Crude stitches of thorns may be used to control bleeding from the clitoral artery and raw tissue surfaces. Sometimes, mud poultices may be applied directly to the perineum.

Type 3, *infibulation*, refers to the excision of part or all of the external genitalia (clitoris, *labia minora*, and *labia majora*). Type 3 is the most severe form of female genital cutting. Excised *labia minora* and *labia majora* create raw surfaces that are stitched together, narrowing the vaginal opening, leaving a very small opening to allow for the flow of urine and menstrual blood. Often, the stitching together of the labia is done while the girl's legs are bound or tied together from the hip to the ankle to immobilize her for up to six weeks, in order to allow the formation of the scar tissue that is often referred to as Sudanese or Pharaonic circumcision. Infibulation involves a repetitive process of deinfibulation (the cutting open of the scar tissue that forms around the vaginal opening to allow penetration during intercourse or during childbirth) and refibulation (the sewing up of the vaginal opening after childbirth or periodically throughout a woman's life, whenever the opening becomes too big or loose). Infibulation has been compared to a chastity belt and is said to account for 15 percent of genital cuttings. It is common in Somalia, Sudan, parts of Egypt,

Ethiopia, Kenya, Mali, Mauritania, Niger, Nigeria, and Senegal. Type 4 is designated as *unclassified*. It refers to procedures that involve inflicting pain on the female genitalia. These procedures include the pricking, piercing, or incision of the clitoris and/or labia as well as symbolic rituals, including the application or insertion of corrosive substances into the vagina. This type usually accounts for 5 percent of genital cuttings in the world (WHO, 2012).

In most communities, the practice is performed by traditional excisers or circumcisers, usually older women (aunts and grandmothers), midwives, or healers, who are often understood as keepers of the tradition. Typically, the procedure is carried out without anesthesia. Traditionally, no steps are taken to reduce the pain; instead, the girl is held down by several women with her legs open. In such circumstances, the procedure is performed using a variety of instruments, including knives, razor blades, broken glass, or scissors. In developed countries, physicians may be sought to perform the practice under sterile conditions, often with the use of anesthesia. Because of modern influences, in some countries, medical professionals are increasingly contracted to perform the procedure.

Some wonder why women are the strongest advocates and defenders of this practice. It should be understood that women, like men, are socialized to accept the practice as the norm and the right thing to do. As Gerry Mackie (1996) rightly observes, the mothers who expose their daughters to cultural practices such as these love their children and want what is best for them. Because the uncircumcised girl is considered unacceptable for marriage, most mothers insist on their daughters being cut so that they will be considered eligible for marriage. These women do not hate their children—as is often assumed. An uncut girl is likely to pay a terrible social price, including not finding a marriage partner. Male expectations create such a market. Mothers are often fearful of the stigma of having an unmarried daughter. Most women are unaware of the dangers of the practice on the health of their daughters. This is because, compared to men, women in these regions are mostly uneducated, and therefore, ignorant of the health implications and other consequences associated with the practice.

CIRCUMCISION OR GENITAL MUTILATION?

The controversy over female genital cutting is also expressed in the disagreement over terminology. Historically, the term "female circumcision" was preferred because cultural values associated with the practice are similar to those associated with male circumcision. As Cardwell Urubuloye (Urubuloye, Cardwell and Cardwell, 2000) observes, explanations and justifications for both are similar. In fact, several dictionaries, including medical dictionaries, have defined circumcision to include cultural female genital cuttings. However, some feminist and medical scholars have argued that this terminology ignores the serious health and social effects associated with this practice. Male circumcision is nonmutilating in the sense that the removal of the penis foreskin does not damage the male reproductive organ, in contrast to female genital cutting.

In 1990, the term "female genital mutilation" was officially adopted at the third conference of the Inter-African Committee on Traditional Practices Affecting the Health of Women and Children (AIC) in Addis Ababa, Ethiopia. In 1991, the WHO recommended that the United Nations (UN) adopt this terminology. The terminology remains in use as the official term in the WHO documents in order to reinforce the harm associated with female genital cutting and to distinguish the practice from male circumcision. This position helps to justify and to promote national and international efforts to eradicate the practice on the grounds that it is a violation of the human rights of girls and women.

In spite of this, criticism has ensued regarding the use of this terminology, mainly from cultural relativists. It has been argued by some that the term "mutilation" is insensitive to genital cutting communities because it fails to recognize the cultural values associated with the practice. It communicates the erroneous assumption that parents who expose their girls to female genital cutting do not love their daughters. It is also argued that the term reinforces the imperialist social stigma associated with non-Western cultures. These criticisms led to a joint statement by WHO, UNICEF, and UNFPA, who admitted that the term was insensitive, judgmental, and demonizing in relation to cultural values of the communities involved.

In response to these criticisms, numerous alternate terminologies emerged, including "female genital surgeries," "female genital operations," as well as the now-popular "female genital cutting," a term that was adopted in 1996 by the Uganda-based initiative REACH (Reproductive, Educative, and Community Health). This terminology is often used because it is nonjudgmental and does not misrepresent the reality surrounding this practice. Scholars continue to be wary, however, about what term to use to describe the practice, as well as the context within which the term is to be used. Whereas policymakers prefer the term "mutilation," some scholars prefer the use of both "female circumcision" and "female genital cutting"—both of which, they believe, express their sensitivity. In this study, I adopt the term "female genital cutting" to recognize the sensitivities and concerns that have been raised, as well as to avoid any cultural biases associated with other terms. Understanding all the procedures that have been categorized by the WHO as female genital cutting within their social context will enable one to appreciate the values behind these procedures, even if one does not agree with the practice.

REASONS FOR FEMALE GENITAL CUTTING

Female genital cutting occurs in all social classes—including the educated class—and at all levels. To understand why it persists well into the 21st century, it is important to reflect upon the cultural and religious reasons for the practice, which are related in several ways. The most common reasons for performing female genital cutting are social and cultural. Female genital cutting is viewed in many communities as a way of socializing the female into her social roles. Often performed as a rite of passage, at puberty or just before marriage, this practice is viewed as a way to initiate a girl into womanhood. It is therefore a cultural practice that is linked to gender identity. In African settings, its role must be understood within the African concept of the individual—the idea that "one is not born into a woman or a man. He/she is made into one" (Gyekye, 1997: 38). A renowned African scholar, John S. Mbiti, validly observed, "an individual does not and cannot exist alone except corporately" because one owes one's existence to others in one's community, including those of the past generation, the family, and the clan, and one's contemporaries (1969: 106). This African sense of community draws from the perception that humans are naturally social and that organic relations are necessary for the general well-being, or as Gyekye puts it, "for the realization of the human potential" (1997: 38). It is, therefore, a practice that is viewed as a necessary part of raising a girl properly and ensuring her marriageability.

Female genital cutting is an important part of the initiation rite because during this ritual, girls are taught about female hygiene, sexual life, and other issues that prepare them to lead a successful life. Girls are also educated in matters pertaining to their role as women, wives, and mothers in their community. Alongside the social standing that a girl acquires, she is taught to display endurance and perseverance whenever she is faced with difficult situations in her life journey. During the procedure, she is to demonstrate courage as an expression of her ability to persevere in painful situations. The physical act of genital cutting and the pain the girl is exposed to are symbolic of the pain adult women face in their life journeys, especially during childbearing. By conducting herself appropriately during the ritual, she demonstrates her preparedness to assume difficult, painful, and often challenging adult roles. In addition, by allowing herself to be the subject of ridicule during the initiation process and the act of genital cutting, she demonstrates her total submission to her society, to her elders, and to the cultural and religious norms of her community.

In most communities, girls who are initiated at the same ceremony tend to develop a strong sense of solidarity and sisterhood. Conjoined pain fosters a sense of social cohesion and bonding among initiates. In Sierra Leone, for instance, female genital cutting is part of an initiation process into a women's secret society known as *Sande*. This secret society, which constitutes a form of resistance against male dominance, offers women a sense of comradeship. Women develop a sense of comradeship arising out of the memory of experiences shared during initiation. Because female genital cutting is a condition for social acceptability, initiated girls receive rewards, including public recognition, celebrations, and gifts. They are recognized as potential candidates for marriage who must be respected and granted the opportunity to engage in adult social functions. The girl is sworn to secrecy. She is not to speak about her experience to outsiders, especially to any uncut woman, making a solemn pledge that is necessary for the protection of her community's cultural dignity. A girl who is thus socialized learns to accept her gender and sexual role in society. Most importantly, she learns not to exhibit and express her sexual desires, including pleasure, because this is prohibited for chastity's sake. Any expression of sexual activity is considered a display of animal-like behavior, which amounts to a lack of control over her desire.

Marriage is a social virtue in most genital-cutting communities. Because marriageability in these communities has always been accompanied by chastity expectations, female genital cutting is viewed as a way to prepare a girl for a stable, chaste marriage. Most female genital-cutting communities require virginity as a prerequisite for marriage, and because virginity is certified during the procedure, most families believe that it helps to certify their daughters' marriageability. Since the procedure is believed to decrease a woman's sexual desire, her marital fidelity is ensured as well. The clitoris is viewed in these communities as an aggressive organ, the seat of sexual desire, which threatens the male organ and even endangers the baby during delivery. Infibulation, especially, is intended to dull a woman's sexual enjoyment—even to discourage and prevent it all together. Extramarital relationships are often prohibited in these communities and may be met with severe penalties, so it is considered important that sexual longing on the part of women be minimized.

Families of genitally cut girls tend to receive high bride prices, as men in these communities are encouraged to marry only circumcised brides to ensure marital fidelity. Conventional wisdom in these communities asserts that intact female genitals are dirty, and that genital cutting ensures better marital sex, improved women's fertility, and the safe delivery of babies—assertions that science refutes. A genitally cut woman is therefore connected to her family and the community at large through this procedure, which grants her a social status that enables her to participate fully in her community. It is for this reason that most parents encourage their daughters to undergo genital cutting as an act of love that ensures the stability of their marriage. Such parents fear that uncut children will have unstable marriages, thus becoming social outcasts and misfits. Although it was acknowledged among some Arabs that the practice could reduce the husband's own sexual sensation, it was accepted anyway as a small price worth paying to ensure the rewards that come with chastity.

Related to chastity expectations is the notion of aesthetics. Female genital cutting is often described in these communities as an aesthetic procedure. In some communities, the clitoris is considered to be unpleasant to sight and touch. A mature woman must remove her "ugly genitalia." The practice is categorized along with other cultural beauty enhancements, such as facial scarring, tattooing, piercing, and costumes—all marks of ideals of femininity and modesty. These ideals often include the notion that a girl will be rendered clean, feminine, and beautiful after the removal of some body parts. Some body parts are believed to be masculine, and thus dirty and defiling, and female genital cutting is believed to be one way of purifying, sanitizing, and beautifying a woman's body.

Some also believe that female genital cutting is a way of maintaining mental and physical health in a woman—a belief that was once shared by Western physicians. As indicated above, female genital cutting was used in the West to treat obscure nervous disorders such as hysteria, neurasthenia, and epilepsy. Victorian doctors performed the procedure to shield children from the "dangers" of masturbation (Shryrock, 1968; Sheehan, 1997; Lightfoot-Klein, 1989: 180).

Female genital cutting has often been associated with religion. While the practice is found among many religious groups (Muslims, Christians, Jews, and indigenous peoples), it is important to note that it is not mentioned in any of the major scriptures such as the Qur'an, the *Tanakh*, or the Bible. Female genital cutting is practiced by people of varied cultural, religious, and political affiliations. In Egypt, for instance, it is found among Muslims and Coptic Christians. In Ethiopia, it is practiced among Muslims and Ethiopian Jews. Myths and religious parables and stories are sometimes associated with the practice. In some indigenous communities, it is believed that children are naturally born as bisexual—a condition that must be rectified by genital cutting. The androgynous expressions of male and female bisexuality are found in the penis foreskin for boys and in the clitoris for girls. During the initiation ritual, genital cutting is viewed as necessary procedure to modify this condition of sexual duality in order for the initiate to assume an adult body and a specific gender role. For this reason, it is considered a purification rite in some religious communities. In some indigenous communities, the clitoris is viewed as a dangerous organ that can kill a man during the sexual intercourse or harm a baby during childbirth. Some believe that the child of an uncut woman may die during childbirth. Yet others claim that the genitals of an uncut woman will grow too long and hang down between her legs and that the food she cooks will smell bad (Spencer, 2002: 3). Jewish, Christian, and Islamic myths have also been used to sanction female genital cutting. All these mythical beliefs are explored in detail in Chapter 5.

Where the practice is required to guarantee a woman's acceptability as a marriage partner, peer pressure and the threat of social rejection can be significant factors in its persistence. In some communities, an uncut woman is considered a slave, an outcast, a prostitute, unclean, and unworthy of continuing the family lineage. She is not viewed as credible in participating in any recognized societal structures. She can only secure her status in society through genital cutting, a precondition for securing a high bride price for her family. When a girl's family insists on female genital cutting for tradition's sake, she may succumb to it out of her love for them. Even in the absence of pressure from her family, a desire to conform has led many girls to seek genital cutting on their own. Social pressure techniques include advising men not to marry uncut women. Such pressure, which often leads to isolation, leaves many women without any other choice but to negotiate for social acceptability through genital cutting. Social pressure is said to be most effective in illiterate communities. Statistics indicate that women with more education are less likely to practice female genital cutting (Population Reference Bureau, 2001). Unfortunately, most women often undergo female genital cutting too early for education to influence their decisions on this matter.

ORIGIN OF THE PRACTICE

Although female genital cutting is currently prevalent in Africa, historically, the practice is not an exclusively African or Arab phenomenon. At many points in history, including the present, it has been practiced in other parts of the world. The origins of female genital cutting are not specifically known. Studies indicate that this practice is ancient, dating back 4,000 to 5,000 years. Some studies have dated the practice to 163 BCE, but it also appears in historical texts from 450 BCE (Bastow, 1999). Early accounts of the practice are recorded in the works of Herodotus in the fifth century BCE. He is said to have attributed female genital cutting to the Phoenicians, Hittites, Ethiopians, and Egyptians (Coquery-Vidrovitch, 1997: 207; Wassuna, 2002: 104). The Greek geographer Strabo also mentions female genital cutting in connection with Egyptians around 25 BCE.

It is argued that the practice originated in Egypt and the Nile valley region during the time of the Pharaohs, which dates the practice to the sixth century BCE. Greek papyrus mentions that both female and male genital cutting occurred in Egypt, where genital cutting for both males and females was connected to cleanliness and hygiene. Male circumcision was reported among Greek philosophers during the time of Pythagoras. During his visit to Egypt, it is argued that Pythagoras was compelled to be circumcised before being admitted to study in the Egyptian temples.

In Rome, genital cutting was widely practiced on slave boys and slave girls to keep them from engaging in sexual activity (Coquery-Vidrovitch, 1997: 207; Wassuna, 2002: 104). Two doctors, Soramus and Aetius, who worked in Alexandria and Rome in the second and the sixth centuries BCE are also said to have left behind fairly precise descriptions of the operation and the instruments used to perform the ritual (Coquery-Vidrovitch, 1997: 207). According to historian Catherine Coquery-Vidrovitch, female genital cutting probably originated in Egypt and then spread to other parts of the world such as Rome, where it was widely practiced.

In some pastoral societies, according to Coquery-Vidrovitch, female genital cutting was also practiced, including infibulation, to prevent the rape of shepherd girls during the long periods of time when young people tended animals in faraway fields (Coquery-Vidrovitch, 1997: 207). She attributes infibulation or pharaonic circumcision to ancient Egypt and claims that this practice may have been performed on girls of the aristocracy during the first millennium—an assumption that is further evidenced by mummies showing that both Type 1 and 3 of female genital cutting was performed during that time (Coquery-Vidrovitch, 1997: 207; Skaine, 2005).

Some have argued that genital cutting, both male and female, originated with ancient practices of emasculation of enemies or phallic worship—a practice that was common in ancient cultures of the Phoenicians and Hittites. In these ancient cultures, the circumcised phallus was symbolic of national and religious honor. Just as Christians swore using the Bible, the Ancient Egyptians swore by raising the circumcised phallus. This practice soon migrated to the Red Sea coastal tribes through the Arab traders, eventually spreading to eastern Sudan and the surrounding regions (Paula, 2008). Although this practice is often associated with Islam, it is important to note that it predates Islam. The Victorian author,

Richard Burton, describes female genital cutting as an ancient custom among the Arabs. He explains how the operation was performed on girls at puberty in Egypt several centuries before Strabo and cites Sheikh al-Nawazir, who describes the practice as universally performed both in Egypt and Hijaz even among the Quraysh tribe where Islam originated (Burton, 1855).

In developed countries, female genital cutting is traced to the 19th century, when it was justified as a medical procedure. As Charles Forster explains, Isaac Baker Brown (1812–1873), a renowned surgeon in England, used it to cure "the vexing mental disorders of women" (Foster, 2011).

Australia and the United States also endorsed female genital cutting in the 1960s as a cure for excessive masturbation. American physicians who adopted the practice also extended the scope of the operation to include oophorectomy (i.e., removal of the ovaries). Lesbian practices, suspected lesbian inclinations, and an aversion to men were all treated by clitoral excision, as were hypersexuality, hysteria, and nervousness. Until 1905, labia were infibulated—a procedure used in the United States to prevent masturbation. This operation was reportedly performed in mental hospitals as late as 1935 (Foster, 2011). In 1968, Dr. Harold Shryock wrote:

> There are teenage girls who, impelled by an unwholesome curiosity or by the example of unscrupulous girlfriends, have fallen into the habit of manipulating these sensitive tissues as a means of excitement. This habit is spoken of as masturbation. . . . There is an anatomical factor that sometimes causes irritation about the clitoris and thus encourages a manipulation of the delicate reproductive organs. . . . Oftentimes the remedy for this situation consists of minor surgical operation spoken of as circumcision. This operation is not hazardous and is much to be preferred to allowing the condition of irritation to continue. (1968: 38)

While the origin of female genital cutting cannot be specifically pinpointed, it is clear from this discussion that the practice has existed for over 5,000 years. Where it has existed, there are cultural and social reasons for its existence.

In spite of this, female genital cutting is associated with health and moral concerns, which have led to its categorization as a human rights violation. It is for this reason that human rights and feminists have called for its eradication. Since industrialized countries have led this mission of protecting the civil and human rights of all individuals, there is cause for concern. It is for this reason that the main objective of this book is to examine possible explanations for the increase of the practice in order to reexamine the existing intervention programs so as to better protect the rights of girls and women who are at risk.

NOTE

1. Although WHO estimates that 100–140 million women worldwide are currently living with the consequences of female genital cutting, this estimate has remained the same over a decade. A serious evaluation of the prevalence is needed and an update of statistics.

2

❖

In Their Own Words

The subject of female genital cutting has often been presented from the outsider's perspective. Often, one is left wondering what the insider thinks about the practice. In this chapter, I grant the insider a voice on the issue in their own words. By listening to the experiences of women who live with both the risk and the consequences of female genital cutting, it is hoped that familiarity with the insiders' perspectives will inform judgment about the practice. Since it would be cumbersome to outline entire interviews of 113 respondents here due to space constraints, select excerpts that have been included are thought to be representative of central themes, concerns, and questions regarding living with the risk and consequences of female genital cutting. The chapter is divided into two sections: responses from primary sources—from surveys and interviews, and responses from secondary sources—excerpts from the media.

Responses from the survey and interviews were centered on the following open-ended questions: (1) Whether female genital cutting was practiced in industrialized countries where they lived, (2) Where and how the practice was performed, (3) Whether they or fellow immigrants had knowledge about criminalization of the practice in these countries, (4) Reason for the persistence of female genital cutting practices, (5) Whether religious values were a factor in the persistence of the practice, (6) Perceived flaws in existing intervention programs, and (7) Whether a religious component ought to be incorporated in intervention programs for effectiveness. While it is acknowledged that selected responses do not necessarily represent the opinions of all women who live with the risk or have experienced female genital cutting, their opinion are representative of perceptions of many women in these communities. The main argument in the chapter is to demonstrate that the increase of female genital cutting in developed countries is implied in the ongoing discourse about the practice, as clearly illustrated in the opinions of those who live with the risk and consequences of the practice.

OPINIONS OF FEMALE GENITAL CUTTING[1]

Miriam, a Kisii woman from Kenya moved to the United States seven years ago. Married and employed as a nurse, Miriam is a Christian, belonging to a Seventh Day Adventist denomination—a common denomination in her community, she adds. In her community, female genital cutting is an acceptable practice. "Every girl is expected to undergo circumcision if she is to be married," Miriam explains. "It is our tradition. Most parents insist on it because it is a serious tradition among the Kisii. They believe that benefits of female genital cutting hold water." Miriam describes her experience thus: "I was young and did not have an opinion about the practice. I did not know why I had to be circumcised and the health risks associated with this practice. My father did not want me to have the procedure performed on me. But the peer pressure was immense, so my mother arranged for us to be cut. She feared that we would be exposed to the social stigma associated with women who were not cut. They were treated as outcasts and called '*Ekisagane*' which means 'one who has not been cut.' She wanted us to fit in the community and to be accepted," Miriam explains. "I cannot say with certainty about it being performed here. But I know most immigrants from my community transport their daughters to Africa for this procedure," Miriam responded to the question whether female genital cutting is performed in the United States.

She is, however, aware of girls and women in the United States who are at risk, or are living with the consequences of the practice. She explains, "Yes. I know many women in the United States who have been exposed to this procedure and those at risk of being cut. My friend who is also cut is planning to have her four-year-old daughter cut when she turns nine years old. She plans to take her to Kenya where she will be circumcised when she turns nine. Unfortunately, her daughter is too young to know what female genital cutting is all about, not to mention the health risks associated with the practice. She can't have an opinion on something she does not understand. All she knows is that her parents plan to take her to Kenya to visit, and she is excited about that. Her mother believes in this tradition very strongly, and unfortunately, parents are the ones who make most of these decisions."

Miriam believes that immigrants in the United States are aware that female genital cutting is illegal. She explains, "Most of them are aware, but they do not really care about the law. If they want to, they will ensure that their daughters are cut. They do this even if it means transporting their daughters abroad for the practice." In her opinion, female genital cutting is practiced because "it makes one less hyperactive in the sense that it controls one's sexual desires." This is why they time it just before one reaches teenage, a time when you are likely to become sexually active. They believe that it helps prevent promiscuity among girls. It is also believed to be a necessary ritual in preparation for marriage or womanhood. During genital-cutting rituals, a group of women are secluded for three weeks and taught how to behave as a woman. "You are essentially taught your roles as an adult woman at age nine. The other reason is tradition. The Kisii believe in upholding their tradition. They do not question their tradition. To be considered a good Kisii, you must uphold your tradition. But the most pressing reason today is peer pressure. It was because of peer pressure that I was cut. Peer pressure is too much in my community. My deacon's daughter who was not cut was exposed to ridicule, and she became the whole village's laughing stock. I felt sorry for her. Every one mocked her, singing horrible songs to make her break down. She was lonely because no one wanted to be associated with her. It was sad. But I envy her courage. She did not succumb to the pressure."

Miriam believes that her religion has nothing to do with female genital cutting. In fact, she believes that her religion condemns the practice. She explains, "My religion condemns the practice. That is why my deacon's daughter was spared the cut. However, even though my religion—Christianity—Seventh Day Adventist is against female genital cutting, some Christian ministers support the practice. Those who support the practice ignore the Christian teachings about it." Female genital cutting should be eradicated, she declares. "This practice is mutilating to girls. It is irrelevant. It should be stopped." She continues, "I would like for opponents of the practice to work at eradicating the practice at the grass root level. Although most governments have criminalized the practice at the national level, a lot of work should be done at the grass-root level. Speaking against the practice at the national levels and enacting rules at that level without reaching the grass-root communities is ineffective. Most people at the grass-root level do not listen to politics or news in the media. We need people at the ground level to engage women and men on this issue. This is the only way to effectively curb the practice."

"It is important that those who have been cut are involved in speaking against the practice in order to highlight the health effects they have faced as a result of the practice," Miriam insists. "They should speak about various infections they have suffered and how these have affected their fertility and other sexual issues. They should explain it as torture to girls who do not need the practice in order to be good women. If there was anything I could do to reverse circumcision, I would. Also, it is important to impose a penalty on those who expose their daughters to the practice. Enforcing this will make people think twice. Parents who force their children to undergo this practice should be penalized. Girls from these communities should be provided with safe havens and educated on how to seek these safe havens. If girls know where to turn to evade this practice, many would run away from home to evade the practice. Education curriculum should include discussions of this issue in order to educate immigrant children about the possibility of being exposed to this practice. Most immigrant women know nothing about this practice. Because they are ignorant of the practice, it is often too late for them to resist it. It is important that we have teachers talk about the practice in schools or speakers to inform them about the risk of being exposed. They should be told what to look for and whom to turn to in case they suspect anything. I seriously think there should be a hotline number created and given to every immigrant community as a way to seek help in case one is at risk of female genital cutting. They should be encouraged to report their parents in case they suspect this practice in their home or community. Unfortunately, some children love their parents so much that they may not want to report them to the authorities."

Miriam believes that religious leaders should be involved in intervention programs. She argues, "I believe that local churches will make a huge impact if they speak against the practice. Because they reach these local communities, they are likely to be effective. It is only unfortunate that some of these leaders believe in upholding this tradition. These leaders should be educated on the risks associated with female genital cutting so they can communicate the right message about this practice."

According to Miriam, her community values female genital cutting, because "for them, tradition matters more than the law," she explains. "I hate to say [it], but some immigrants in the United States are ignorant. They are not as enlightened as people would want to assume. They are not especially exposed to health issues, especially those associated with female genital cutting, and some do not know the benefits that a woman gets when she remains uncut. They need to be exposed to this education in order to enlighten them so they can change their attitudes toward the practice." Miriam does not think those who value the practice should be left to perform it as their cultural right because, "I do not believe that female genital cutting is a cultural right. It is torture that is justified by culture. It should be stopped. Women should be given the right to live their life well and to the full. These women are deformed. Because the clitoris is taken out during circumcision, it certainly affects one's sexual desire and pleasure. These people do succeed in making you chaste and less hyperactive during teenage years. However, when you need the desire later during marriage, it is not there."

"As one who has been cut," she argues, "I will tell you that yes, this procedure affects sex. Sex is not a priority for me. It is not on my mind at all. It is a duty that I perform for my husband. I do not look forward to it and do not enjoy it. It takes me too long to get there. It is hard work because there is no sensitivity. Therefore, sex is not something I am interested in." Miriam describes how her husband struggles with sexual challenges emerging from this practice. She explains, "My husband once told me, 'These people really did you injustice.' He is against the practice and wishes it could stop."

It is her argument that the only way to protect girls in her community in the United States from exposure to this practice is through establishing a hotline so girls can call for help when they sense danger. She explains, "Criminalizing the practice is necessary but not enough. Most immigrant girls do not know that the practice is illegal. It is therefore important that the girls are educated about the practice in their schools to help provide options of how to resist the practice. It is important for these girls to know that there is the option of a safe haven. It is important that immigrant communities are taught about health risks associated with this practice and how they can protect their daughters from it. As I said earlier, it is important that a hotline is set up for these communities to help girls and parents who are against the practice to report it in case they suspect it." She continues, "In fact, I have a friend who took her daughters to Kenya for genital cutting. The practice was performed in Nairobi city. Most people think that this practice is only performed in rural communities. Not necessarily. Modern communities take their daughters to hospitals for the procedure."

Before concluding her interview, Miriam had this to say, "I also know a friend who lives in this country—Texas—whose mom performs the practice among immigrant communities. This lady is a nurse at the hospital. Because of this, many immigrant women trust her expertise with this procedure. Some immigrants who cannot afford to take their children abroad for female genital cutting make trips to Texas to have her perform female genital cutting on their daughters. What is interesting is the hypocrisy she displays with regard to this practice. In the public, she condemns the practice, yet in secret, she performs it. And because she is in the hospital system, it is very difficult to control what she does because it is all under the guise of the hospital." Although Miriam promised to put me in touch with her friends in Texas for an interview on this issue, she has since not been forthcoming. Asked why, she cites the pressure of being accused as a betrayer of her culture.

Habiba, a Gambian woman, is a Muslim. She arrived in the United States eight years ago. She considers herself an insider because she lived in a community that embraces the practice, and has several friends who have been circumcised. Although she is not sure whether female genital cutting is practiced in the United States, she is aware that it is practiced in other developed countries. She explains, "I know my friend who lives in Sweden has gone through situations in that country and it is definitely prevalent over there. African immigrant communities in Sweden perform the practice." Miriam also knows women in the United States who have been cut as well as girls who are at risk of being cut. She explains, "These women believe that circumcision protects women's virginity and chastity. Because it is their culture, they believe it is necessary to go through it," she adds. "There are, however, some women who have gone through this procedure but would not want to expose their children to it. Men are the ones who insist on it. But women want to give up the practice." Habiba is confident that her religion does not support female genital cutting. In her opinion, the practice should be eradicated because "It is harmful to girls. My friends have told me how difficult it is to give birth when you are circumcised. It also takes away the pleasure a woman is supposed to experience in her marriage," she adds.

She, however, acknowledges the difficulty in eradicating the practice. She explains, "It is difficult to eradicate it. Even girls who run away find it difficult to avoid it. Among our neighbors, the Hausa, female circumcision is a major ceremony. It is performed alongside annual festivals which require that most members of the community come home. Because of this, many African immigrants from this community arrange to attend these vacations. When they travel home with their daughters, they are then circumcised alongside other girls. It is because of the importance associated with these festivities that I think it is difficult to stop female circumcision. When girls are not taken home for circumcision, experts are brought from abroad to perform the practice for their girls in their houses. These women, usually aunts and grandmothers to the children, are trained to hijack and immobilize a girl through hypnosis so she cannot resist. By the time she recovers, the procedure is complete."

She explains further, "I have a friend whose name is Amina. She lives in Sweden. Although she comes from a community that does not perform female genital cutting, she is married to a man from this community. She vowed that she would protect her daughter from circumcision. So, she avoided gathering with African communities because some women in these communities were traditional experts who had been brought by some immigrant members to circumcise girls and babies of African immigrants. Because circumcision is a community issue, these women would show up at a gathering and hijack a baby or a woman and circumcise her. My friend thought she would protect her daughter from them. Unfortunately, one day, her daughter went to play in one of these women's house. By the time she realized it, it was too late. Her daughter was cut by these women. She could not go to the house to retrieve her baby because she would also be a target of circumcision. Asked whether her friend reported the incident to the authorities, she explains, "She thought about it, but then she decided against it. First, she knew it would not save her daughter, who was already cut. Second, she was afraid to turn her own relatives to the authorities. Incidentally, her own sister, who was visiting that same week from the United States with her children, arrived and heard about the incident. She left the following day for Dakar, Senegal, to protect her daughters from going through this procedure. You cannot fight culture." Habiba believes that religious leaders should not be involved in intervention programs. She explains, "Female circumcision is a cultural practice, and no one will listen even to religious leaders about eradicating it." Habiba believes that immigrants in the United States are aware that female genital cutting is illegal because "Often, when Africans arrive in this country, this is the first thing they learn through rumors. They are told that female circumcision is illegal. They know that they cannot talk about it in the open or practice it in the open. They know they can go to jail for it."

Asked whether those who insist on performing female genital cutting should be left to do it as their cultural right, Habiba responds, "No. It is a harmful practice. It is unfair to expose girls and women to a practice that is going to give them health issues for life. Women should also be left to enjoy life. They are human and need to be appreciated as well. Also, attempts to educate traditional experts on the importance of sterilizing their instruments have been resisted. They believe that this practice should be performed in traditional settings in order for it to be effective. As a result, many girls get infections, and sometimes, die in the process. This practice should be stopped. It is not necessary."

Habiba explains further, "My friends tell me about concerns such as infections, cervical cancer, and kids dying during the procedure. This is not right." It is her opinion that girls who live in the United States should be protected from this practice. She explains, "The most important responsibility falls on the child's parents. Parents need to learn more about the consequences of the practice, and they should take a role in protecting their daughters from this practice. Children should also be educated to speak out when they fear that they are at risk of exposure to the practice. They should tell their neighbors, and neighbors can find a way to protect them."

Asma, originally from Senegal, is Muslim as well. Although female genital cutting is not practiced in her community, she lived among the Soce and Djola community where the practice was prevalent, so she considers herself an insider. In fact, the pressure from her community to get cut was immense. She explains how everyone in her community expected "us to be circumcised. It was my mother who insisted that we should not be circumcised. I am grateful to her. Given that we were living in a circumcising community, it was courageous for her to resist the pressure in a community where the practice was common. My mother was a hero for protecting us." Asma believes that female genital cutting is performed among immigrant communities in the United States. She explains; "There are people from communities that practice female genital cutting who have immigrated to the United States who insist on maintaining their culture and they see female genital cutting as an important aspect of that."

Asma does not believe that her religion sanctions female genital cutting. She thinks that female genital cutting should be eradicated, even though she is quick to add, "It is important to remember that it is difficult to eradicate the practice as long as male circumcision is practiced. It is true that men do not lose sexual sensation after circumcision. And it is difficult to compare the two. However, it is not necessarily right to condemn female genital cutting on the basis of culture. As long as male circumcision is glamorized in the name of culture, it is going to be difficult to stop female genital cutting, because it is also rooted in culture. It is difficult to stop male circumcision because Jews will not be compelled to stop a cultural practice that makes them Jews. You know, it is all about double standards. Male circumcision is not condemned just because it is associated with Jews—very powerful people in the world—and yet, female circumcision is condemned because it associated with Africa, a continent that is often associated with anything barbaric, primitive, archaic. It is true!!" she exclaims. "How come numerous forms of plastic surgery are allowed in this country except female genital cutting? Look at the Amish community and their lifestyle. If they were Africans, that lifestyle would be condemned. But because they are white, they are explained away as weird but should be respected. The same applies to the Mormons and their polygamous lifestyle. It is for this reason that I think female genital cutting should not totally be eradicated. It should be placed in the category where girls are educated about the procedure and asked if they want to undergo it. But is it really a choice?" she adds.

Asma explains, "It is about social coercion. Female genital cutting has nothing to do with religion. In most African communities, female circumcision is coerced on girls. They have no choice in the matter. Among the Wolof, for instance, face tattooing was not required of all women. Yet, there was some kind of social coercion that made most women to want to be tattooed. Those who did not tattoo their faces were called wimps or considered outcasts. Because most women did not want to be called wimps or be considered outcasts, they succumbed to face tattooing. This is what I call social coercion. Most girls seek circumcision because they are socially coerced. They do not want to be considered outcasts. They want to be eligible for marriage. Most mothers expose their daughters to female genital cutting because they are dependent on their husbands, who demand that their daughters be cut. It is because of all these factors that it is difficult to eradicate female genital cutting."

"By the way," she adds, "Social coercion is also felt in the West. You see what women do to their bodies in order to attain 'good bodies'? Plastic surgery, weight loss, and all other 'crazies' women are made to do in order to please the desirable image of a woman for man. It is important that myths surrounding female genital cutting are lifted among immigrant communities in order to change attitudes toward this practice. It is easier to convince men to get away from this practice, but it is hard to convince women." Asked if there are more effective way to eradicate this practice, Asma responds, "Maybe waiting until the girls are adults so they make their own informed choices whether they want to go through the procedure or not." She believes it is a good idea to involve religious leaders in female genital cutting intervention programs. She explains, "Muslim clerics need to engage communities about what the Quran says about female genital cutting in order to eliminate myths associated with the practice." Although she believes that immigrant women are aware that female genital cutting is illegal in the United States with "all the campaigns against the practice," she insists that those who want to retain the practice should not be forced to abandon it. She explains; "I think it is more complicated and that negotiation is the best approach." It is important to identify the communities first, and engage them in a respectful way.

Rahab, an Arab Muslim woman is also an American citizen whose community embraces female genital cutting. Although she does not believe that female genital cutting is performed in immigrant communities in the United States, she feels most immigrant women do not know that the practice is illegal "Because it is never talked about." She strongly condemns the practice and thinks it should be eradicated because "it is not fair for women to lose their sensual feeling and for what? I don't believe in it." She adds, "It should also be a woman's choice." In her opinion, the most effective way to protect girls from female genital cutting in developed countries is to educate them. Rahab thinks it is important that religious leaders be involved in female genital cutting intervention programs because they have the ability to change attitudes toward this practice. She explains, "They can play an important role in educating the public about this practice."

Salma, also Muslim and Arab, is also an American citizen. In her opinion, the decision whether to practice female genital cutting or not should be left to the women. She does not think immigrant women in the United States are aware of the illegality of female genital cutting because "Female genital cutting is never talked about." She believes that religious leaders should be involved in intervention programs because they can help change attitudes toward the practice. To Salma, the most effective strategy to employ in protecting girls from female genital cutting in developed countries is to educate both the girls and their parents about health issues associated with the practice.

Aisha, a Ghanaian American is Muslim and a member of the community that embraces female genital cutting. She explains how she was lucky not to be exposed to the practice because it "is degrading a practice to women because it is all about power." She does not think that this practice is found among immigrants in the United States. She also does not know any woman in the United States who is cut or lives with the risk of being cut. She believes her religion sanctions the practice by requiring it as a necessary practice for protecting the youth. In her opinion, female genital cutting should be eradicated and religious leaders should be involved because of their ability to transform attitudes toward the practice. She explains, "They are not only respected in these communities, they possess the authority and power to change minds about beliefs, especially those that support the practice."

She believes that immigrant women in the United States are aware that female genital cutting is illegal. She elaborates, "This is not an issue of debate. Most are aware of the fact that female genital cutting is not condoned in this country." She, however, argues that those who embrace the practice should be left to practice it as their cultural right because "It should be their freedom of choice." Aisha believes that the most effective intervention strategy for protecting girls from exposure to female genital cutting in developed countries must involve a protest.

Salyma is African and Muslim. She is from a community that embraces female genital cutting as a cultural lifestyle as well. She resisted female genital cutting because "I feel as if it is unnecessary practice. It is unjust for humans to go through that procedure and to endure labor." She agrees that some fellow immigrants are very proud of their culture and would like to ensure that their children retain their culture. She, however, does not think the practice is performed here in the United States. Yet, she knows girls and women who are at risk of genital cutting in the United States. She explains, "I know a family friend. She has been going through that conflict with her family. She is not interested but her family is interested in her being circumcised. In her opinion, female genital cutting is performed when girls travel abroad for vacation and it is 'performed so females can remain virgins until they marry.'" Salyma believes that immigrant women in the United States and in the West are aware that female genital cutting is illegal. However, she argues, those who embrace female genital cutting as their culture should be left to practice it as their cultural right because "people should be left to practice their own culture and tradition when they choose to."

Salyma does not think her religion supports female genital cutting, and for that reason, she thinks the practice should be eradicated. She believes that the most effective way to eradicate the practice is through education. She explains, "If education on female genital cutting can be integrated into birth control education, most girls will be made aware of the practice. It is important that these girls are advised to stay away from places and communities that embrace female genital cutting." In her opinion, religious leaders should not be involved in female genital cutting intervention programs because "it is difficult for leaders to preach against it."

Leila, a native of Senegal, is a Muslim who arrived in the United States three years ago. Although her community embraces female genital cutting, she does not think the practice is found among immigrant communities in the United States because she does not know anyone in the United States who has been circumcised or is at risk of genital cutting. She thinks immigrant women in the United States are aware that female genital cutting is illegal. "Those who embrace the practice 'choose to' because they want to maintain their culture."

According to Leila, Islam does not sanction female genital cutting. In her opinion, the practice should be eradicated, and religious leaders can play a significant role in changing attitudes toward the practice. It is important that these leaders be educated as well since "some actually think the practice is religious. We don't want leaders who will reinforce the practice," she adds.

Opoku is a native of Ghana and a Christian. She arrived in the United States in the year 2000. She likes it here but she prefers her home country and her culture, "except female genital cutting," she adds. She was cut when she was very young. She describes her experience as unpleasant and painful. She does not think female genital cutting is performed among immigrant communities in the United States, but she knows several women who have been cut and live in the United States. Asked whether she thinks immigrant women in the United States are aware that female genital cutting is illegal, her response is, "No . . . I don't think many people know." She thinks those who embrace the practice should be left to practice it as their cultural right. She explains, "Women should be able to be circumcised, if it is okay with them."

In her opinion, her religion sanctions female genital cutting. She elaborates, "I was taught that it is only natural and normal to be cut." Asked whether the practice should be eradicated, she pauses and says, "I don't know." She offers no further explanation for her answer. Interestingly, she does not think that religious leaders should be involved in female genital cutting intervention programs, even though she does not elaborate why. In Opoku's opinion, the best strategy for protecting girls from female genital cutting is to remove them from their family situations.

Rehema, a Muslim woman from the Gambia, is proud for declining to undergo the female genital-cutting procedure even though her community embraces the practice. She explains, "It was out of my comfort zone . . . It takes away your human rights." According to her, female genital cutting is embraced in her community as a way to "keep girls safe from older males and for control." She thinks that her religion is very much a part of the process because it sanctions the practice.

In her opinion, female genital cutting is performed among immigrant communities in the United States and other developed countries because it is a cultural practice. She explains, "Some people who are used and well accustomed to it can continue their beliefs in the United States." Although she does not know any woman in the United States who has been cut or is at risk of genital cutting, she thinks there are. She believes that most immigrant women in the United States are unaware that female genital cutting is illegal because "they may be foreign and expect it to be okay here because they are already adapted into it."

Rehema believes that female genital cutting should be eradicated. In her opinion, the most effective way to eradicate it is by "standing up and making it against the law everywhere." She does not think religious leaders can be effective in intervening against the practice because it is a personal matter. She explains, "It's a life choice of someone and a leader should stay out of it." She believes that those who choose to be cut should be left to practice it as their cultural right. She explains, "If they believe in it, they should speak and act by it."

Rahman is a native of Senegal and a Muslim. Although she was born in a community that embraces female genital cutting, she considers herself lucky for not being subjected to the practice. She was not subjected to the practice because her family did not approve of it. She does not believe that the practice is performed among immigrant communities in the United States because, in her opinion, immigrant women are aware of the illegality of the practice since this is "undisputed knowledge all immigrants should know."

In her opinion, female genital cutting is performed to protect girls and to make them pure. She believes that while her religion sanctions the practice, female genital cutting is all about culture. Some cultures do, and others do not approve of it. That is why, she argues, some Muslims practice it and others don't. Rahman is undecided regarding the need to eradicate female genital cutting because she believes the right of others to practice their culture should not be interfered with. She explains, "Those who embrace female genital cutting should be left to practice it as their cultural right simply because it is their culture and I don't think there is anything wrong with people practicing their culture if they feel secure about it." According to her, the only way to protect girls from female genital cutting in the United States is by empowering their communities, especially women.

Jane is a Ghanaian and a Muslim who comes from a community where female genital cutting is embraced. She considers herself as one of the lucky few Ghanaian women who is not cut. She believes that female genital cutting is degrading to women and that the practice ought to be eradicated. She explains, "It is not an issue or a debate topic." She does not think immigrant women practice female genital cutting in the United States because she believes that they must be aware of the illegality of the practice. She does not know any woman who has been cut or who is at risk of genital cutting, but "won't be surprised in case there is one or several." She believes that her religion sanctions female genital cutting and that religious leaders should definitely be involved in efforts to intervene against the practice because they are likely to be respected and listened to. According to Jane, those who embrace the practice should be left to practice it as their cultural right because "it should be their free choice whether to be cut or not." Jane believes that one way to protect girls from female genital cutting in the United States is by protesting against the practice through advocacy.

VOICES IN THE MEDIA

To supplement primary sources, secondary sources were consulted as well as representative of women's experience in female genital-cutting communities. A brief description of the background and origin of the material is presented to help contextualize their positions on female genital cutting. For instance, Sue Lloyd Roberts, a newscast on BBC *NewsNight* gives us an insight into the prevalence of female genital cutting in France and the United Kingdom. According to Roberts, about 20,000 children in England and Wales and about the same number in France, are deemed "at risk" of female genital cutting every year. Laws criminalizing the practice in France and England were instituted in the mid-1980s. Although over 100 parents and practitioners of female genital cutting have been convicted in France, not a single prosecution has been made in the United Kingdom (Roberts, 2012). In her article, "Hidden World of Female Genital Cutting in the United Kingdom" aired on *BBC News Night* on July 23, 2012, she introduces her readers to Ayanna, a 23-year-old Sierra Leonean woman who was taken to her Sierra Leonean home at the age of 14 for female genital cutting. She now lives alone with her 11-month-old baby in the Red Road district of Glasgow. This area is home to a wave of refugees under the government's dispersal program. Ayanna claimed political asylum to escape forced marriage and to spare her daughter from undergoing genital cutting. Ayanna told Roberts, "I am so happy here. . . . I no longer suffer the pain of sex with my husband. The pain was worse than childbirth."

Ayanna explains that other mothers in Glasgow allow their daughters to be cut. "There were two children on her block, one aged three years and the other two weeks, who were cut recently by the elder women. They use razors, scissors, and sharp knives." Roberts explains how she also met a group of Somali women, all of whom had been mutilated. "If the authorities could help us to make these people stop it, we would be very happy," says one of them. "Since I arrived two years ago, I have heard nothing," says another. "There should be announcements, classes so people understand what's right and what's wrong."

Roberts reports how, five miles from Bristol, a group of girls told her about female genital mutilation (FGM) parties. These are parties organized for girls who have undergone female genital cutting to celebrate the occasion as well as reduce costs. "At first, the girls are all excited because it's a party, until they realize what is going to happen, and then they get frightened. It is done by the elder women, or the Imam, whoever is expert at cutting," Amina, a 17-year-old explains.

In this article, Roberts explains how, during an interview meeting with Isabelle Gillette–Faye at the Gare du Nord in Paris, the seasoned campaigner against female genital cutting described to her how two little girls were about to board the train headed for St. Pancras to be mutilated in the United Kingdom. "It was a Friday. We heard just in time. They had tickets for Saturday. A member tipped us off. We told the police and they were stopped from making the journey," Gillette-Faye explained. The parents were cautioned that had they gone ahead with the mutilations and been found out, they would have been imprisoned for up to 13 years. "We simply will not tolerate this practice," Gillette-Faye reiterates further.

Asked whether many French children have been cut in the United Kingdom, Isabelle responds, "Yes, because you do not care," she tells Roberts (referring to the British)—a comment that Simon Foy, a Scotland Yard specialist in child abuse cases, disagrees with. According to Foy, "I am not necessarily sure that the availability of a stronger sense of prosecution will change it (female genital cutting) for the better." In his opinion, "What Isabelle calls our 'respect' and what others call 'cultural sensitivity' make detection in the United Kingdom almost impossible. In France, the case is different because the mothers and babies attend specialist clinics up until the age of six. The genitalia of baby girls are routinely examined for signs of mutilation." Dr. Amellou, who works in a clinic in a Paris suburb, explains that after the age of six, responsibility is handed over to school medical teams, who continue to inspect girls, especially those coming from those high risk ethnic groups (Roberts, 2012).

Roberts introduces the reader to another Somali woman, Muna, who also moved to Bristol from Sweden in 2003. Muna believes that the government is doing little to stop the practice. In her opinion, the government is terrified and tends to use cultural sensitivity as an excuse to not do anything. "What would you do if the girl had blue eyes and blonde hair?" "Would FGM still be carrying on in the UK?" she asks. Asked whether she has a message for David Cameron, the Prime Minister of the United Kingdom, Muna responds, "Yes, do something about FGM. . . . And if you can't handle the issue, then there is no point in you doing your job" she adds (Roberts, July 12, 2012).

In an article, "Slain Mom, Daughters Sought Asylum," published in the *Atlanta Journal Constitution* on August 2, 2007, Yolanda Rodriguez and Tom Opdyke introduce us to the sad story of Jane Kuria, a Kenyan woman who fled her native country in 2001 because she feared that her daughters would be subjected to female genital cutting. She left after the death of her husband and the destruction of her home. According to her asylum application, the couple was targeted in Kenya because of their opposition to female genital cutting. The Catholic Church helped Jane move to South Africa to escape persecution. She returned to Kenya but later moved to Tanzania before seeking refuge in the United States. She arrived in Boston in March 2001 and later moved to Atlanta, Georgia in February 2002. As a licensed practical nurse, Jane worked as a nurse assistant at the Well Star Paulding Hospital.

The bodies of Jane Kuria—who was 45 years—her two daughters Isabella Kuria, 19, and Annabelle Kuria, 16, were found at their Powder Springs home. Jane Kuria's sons, Jeremy, 7, and cousin Peter Thande, 10, were also found unconscious, but alive. The boys were taken to the Children's Healthcare of Atlanta in Scottish Rule. According to her lawyer, Charles H. Kuck, an immigration attorney from Atlanta, "I am shocked. It's scary to think this could happen to anyone, especially to anyone who came here seeking the protection of the United States. Her fear was of [the] horrific practice of female genital mutilation and it happening to her daughter." Jane had applied for asylum in the United States, but her case was denied. Kuck was handling her appeal when the news of her murder was reported. Hearings for her two daughters' asylum cases were scheduled for August 29, 2007

Commenting on Jane's plight, Glory Kilanko, the executive director of Women Watch Africa, said female genital cutting "is one of the reasons women flee Africa, among a host of other reasons." Women Watch Africa is a nonprofit organization that works with immigrant and refugee women from Africa (Rodriguez et al., 2007).

In her article "What is Genital Mutilation?" (1997), Hannak Koroma describes the experience of Heather Abraham who was subjected to female genital cutting at the age of 10. In her own words, Abrahams describes her experience. "When the operation began, I put up a big fight. The pain was terrible and unbearable . . . I was badly cut and lost blood . . . I was genitally mutilated with a blunt penknife. After the operation, no one was allowed to aid me to walk . . . Sometimes I had to force myself not to urinate for fear of the terrible pain. I was not given any anesthetic in the operation to reduce my pain, nor any antibiotics to fight against infection. Afterwards, I hemorrhaged and became anemic. This was attributed to witchcraft. I suffered for a long time from acute vaginal infections" (Koroma, 2010).

In an interview with Lisa M Hamm of Associated Press, we are introduced to the surreal experience of Waris Dirie, a human rights defender and a survivor of female genital cutting. Dirie, who currently lives in Australia, describes her experience with female genital cutting thus: "It's like being crippled . . . the rest of your life, crippled, that section of your body." She explains how she looked forward to the practice when her sister told her about it. She narrates, "She used to tell me, 'Oh, I'm a woman now. I'm not a girl anymore.' I said, 'Mama, when are you going to do to me what you did to her? I want to be a woman!' Of course, my time came and it wasn't the greatest like I thought it was going to be." She pauses. "It was nothing but torture." On the day the procedure was done, Dirie's mother woke her before dawn. The two met an old gypsy woman and walked into the desert to a large, flat rock. She describes, "My mother looked at me and said, 'I haven't got the strength to hold you down. Don't fight me.'" She recalls how her mother stuck a piece of root between her teeth and told her to hold onto it for controlling pain. As Lisa explains, the gypsy woman took out a small, dull blade, and suddenly, Ms. Dirie felt a searing pain, followed by seemingly endless agony. "I didn't move," Ms. Dirie murmurs. "I just shivered. There was no painkiller, no anesthesia, no nothing. I don't really know when it was over. I passed out . . . I am sure my mother thought she was doing me a favor, and in any case, I don't believe she had much choice. It was a society where what the man says goes—my mother was simply obeying. It was the norm there" (Lisa, 2011; BBC News, 2007).

Dirie was exposed to infibulation, the most severe form of female genital cutting. Commenting on her scar, she says, "There's nothing I can do but live with it, heal myself . . . You know, thinking about it, looking out, there're little girls it's happening to today, right now, as we're speaking, somewhere," she says, ". . . It's definitely got to stop! It's just got to stop" (BBC News, 2007). A native of Gaalkacyo, Somalia, Dirie left her country for England in 1978 at the age of 13 to avoid being married off by her family to a much older man in exchange for five camels. Here, she was lucky to develop her modeling career. In 1997, she spoke out against female genital cutting for the first time. Her interview received worldwide media coverage culminating in her becoming the United Nations ambassador for the abolition of female genital cutting the same year. In 2002, she founded the Waris Dirie Foundation, an organization based in Vienna whose goal is to raise awareness regarding the dangers surrounding female genital cutting.

Dirie believes that female genital cutting should be eradicated. She observes, "There are laws, but people also need to be punished—that still doesn't happen often enough. School girls need to be checked after the holidays. Everyone needs to be involved . . . But most of this is something men and women have to work together to stop. The men need to know about it. They need to talk to their mothers, sisters and daughters. But it's not something one person can do something about alone. People ask me, 'How's your work doing?' or [say,] 'Good luck with your work!'— and I think, it isn't just my work; this should be everybody's work" (BBC News, 2007).

In an interview with *Frontpage*, Lucy Mashua, the Global Ambassador for fighting FGM and standing up for women's rights describes her experience with the practice. "I was born 30 years ago in a small village in southern Kenya in Rift valley province. I come from the Maasai tribe, which is known for its cultural wearing of beads, red ochre and wraps. We are nomadic people and move with our animals from one place to another in search of pastures, as it's a semi-arid area. My tribe practices female genital cutting because they are ignorant and brainwashed since the days of Pharaoh in Egypt as they migrated to East Africa with this tradition. The philosophy is that women will be more tame and controllable . . . They also engage in early childhood marriage to control and tame women because if you are married off at 12, by the time you are 18, you are just worn out and you will never see the need to explore life. The younger the girls are, the easier it is to control and manipulate them. It's also about wealth. The more wives and cattle you have, the wealthier you are and you have more property."

Mashua is happy that she did not suffer the control her community inflicts on women. However, she was cut alongside other girls in her community. She describes how. "One chilly morning in a group of 29 girls, we were mutilated. I was tied with a rope because I was screaming and begging them to stop. Some girls were considered brave for not crying aloud. But I know their heart cried out loud. I could hear their cry and still do. It is so hard for me to talk about this. It's so fresh. I am still so traumatized. They used the same knife on us, not caring about any infections. These are traditional mutilators and midwives that perform this savagery. My mom could not watch this. Up to now, I am scared of any human blood. I scream when I accidentally cut myself. I have never coped. I have very painful PMS. I have extra glands growing so I need surgery. I have scar tissues. That's why my vagina muscles hurt. I will live with this for the rest of my life. I will never cope, but one thing for sure, I will never stop voicing out against FGM. One day, I will reach the World Court and criminalize globally FGM. I swear I am going to reach there. I am now building a very big network of very committed people. I aspire even to be a human rights movie documentary producer. I am going to get words out there and catch the attention of all kinds of good people."

Mashua explains the various challenges she has encountered as an advocate against female genital cutting. "First, I was rejected by my own society, relatives, and friends because of my strong uncompromised belief that women are human too and that no one should take a razor, knife, or sharp glass to cut off our clitoris. No man owns a woman and no one has the right to beat or hit a woman." Mashua began her campaign officially in 1999 in Kenya by holding demonstrations, speaking in seminars, radio and television programs, and in other East and Central Africans countries. She later on launched a worldwide campaign to stop FGM in Europe. She has braved resistance, including imprisonment. She has suffered beatings, rejection, sexual abuse, and separation from her children. She is disappointed that some activists are hypocritical. She narrates, "All they care about is opening their mouth or scribbling some words online or on paper to act as if they care, and so far, they have scooped several Grammies for best actors." She singles out Rukia Subow, the vice chair of the Women's

Development Organization in Kenya, for saying that "unlike other gender issues, such as access to education, FGM is viewed as cultural practice, which, if threatened, endangers the cohesion of an entire community." In her opinion, the vice chair of Maendeleo ya Wanawake Organization—or MYWO—a leading Kenyan women's rights group based in Nairobi that receives funding to help the cause of women should not be uttering statements like this. She also singles out Ricken Patel of AVAAZ for telling her that FGM is not an important issue since it "cannot beat climate change."

According to Mashua, religion sanctions female genital cutting. Although she is Christian, she believes that her religion has not done enough to discourage female genital cutting. She admits, "Yes my tribe is Christian and also full of traditional believers. I don't know why they practice it because there is no single Bible verse that says to mutilate women. As I said earlier, it's a way of controlling women. It has nothing to do with Christianity and they do not point to Christianity." Mashua believes that while her religion does not condone female genital cutting, Islam does. She elaborates, "My experience with Islam on FGM is very sad. As you correctly point out, a majority of people who practice FGM on women are of the Islamic faith, and in the Muslim countries that I have visited, their women and children have encountered the worst form of it, and many reconstructive surgeons can testify to this. It is a form of control and manipulation in the name of religion. The good news is that there many Muslims who are rising to end any form of torture against women."

Mashua believes that a lot can be done to help protect the rights of those who live with the risk of female genital cutting. She explains, "What we do here in this country has an effect on the entire world's view of women, on their status, on their role in human affairs. America, we are the hope of the world. Let's stand together and let's not be scared of the haters. When the world takes care of women, women take care of the world" (Glazov, 2011).[2]

Cleunse (not her real name) considers herself a survivor of female genital cutting because of her courageous actions that saved her daughter from this practice. She explains:

I met this man who was from Egypt. He was Islamic, divorced, and 6 years my junior. However, he was polite, respectful, and did not ask for my virginity before marriage. So, I married him in 1998! But, I had no idea that his mother was circumcised, nor his views on the subject. Hey, I was a 3rd generation Polish/American woman from Jersey! What [in] the world did I know about female genital mutilation? To me, it boggled my mind when I found out that I was 4 months pregnant with my eldest daughter and he tells me he wants her to be circumcised! I nearly killed him! . . . I ran as fast as I could to the airport. I proceeded to purchase a one way ticket to Georgia and have never looked back since . . . There was no way anyone would even try to mutilate my baby girl! Over my dead body! I am not saying that all Egyptian men or foreign-born men are female genital mutilating. . . . However, I am writing this . . . to warn you about marrying outside of your culture and problems that will arise from such a union. Before you tie the knot with a foreign-born man, remember to make sure that you understand the culture from which he comes and the customs of his culture. (Cleunse, 2010; Collins, 2010)

Cleunse wrote this blog as a way to educate others on the possibility of this happening to them.

Meanwhile, in their article, "Female 'Cut' Exported to Europe," published in the *East African Standard* in May 2007, Justo Casal and Linda May relate the story of Kadra, a young Somali Norwegian woman who stirred up controversy in Norway in the year 2000, when she revealed that female genital cutting is still alive among many migrant communities who have come to Norway from Africa. Kadra set out to expose this practice by wearing a hidden camera and a microphone while speaking to an Imam, a Muslim leader who tried to convince her to get circumcised. When television reporters sought out the Imam to verify his views on female genital cutting, his response was inconsistent with the advice he had given Kadra. When both his stated positions were aired on television, the Imam was outraged by Kadra's recording of an informant without prior consent. The Imam's outrage, however, was entirely drowned out by Norwegians' outrage at the revelation that female genital cutting was practiced in their country. As explained by Justo Casal and Linda May, the immediate reaction to the Imam's recommendation that Kadra should be circumcised was the assumption by many that female genital cutting was required by Islam. This misconception is held by many beyond Norway. For her courageous act to expose female genital cutting, Kadra was threatened and forced into hiding. When she thought that it was safe to return to her normal life, she was beaten by suspected Somalis (Casal, 2007).

Meanwhile, Casal and May introduce us to yet another Gambian woman living in Norway who filed charges against her husband after finding out that her young daughters had been circumcised during the holiday with their father to Gambia. Even though the doctors at The Ullevaal Hospital in Oslo confirmed that the girls were circumcised, the police dropped the case due to lack of sufficient evidence. The woman went into hiding after receiving death threats by outraged Gambian men (Casal,

2007). While these outcries have compelled the Norwegian government to take this issue seriously, a lot is yet to be done to protect children's and women's rights in the country. It is important, however, to recognize the fact that the outcry led the Children and Equality Minister Karita Bekkenmellem to declare the fight against female genital cutting her department's "new mission."

Ayan Hussein, a reporter with *Vox,* a newspaper serving teenagers in Atlanta, Georgia is a victim of female genital cutting. In her article, "My Personal Experience with Female Circumcision," she describes her opinion about this cultural practice. She was very young when she was circumcised. She decided to talk to older women in her community to understand why she was exposed to this practice and to share her opinion with her peers. Because her conversation on this issue is revealing of the experience of girls and women who live with the risk and consequences of the practice, part of her interview is included in here. Below is her conversation with other women on the subject.

Ayan:	I'll never forget what happened. I was only seven years old . . . My mama knew the pain I felt, so I'm wondering why she held me down. Why me? Now at 17, my views at this issue are clearing up (*sic*). I'm living in the U.S. I'm searching for answers. I can't get them from my mom, so I started asking other women from African cultures to explain, like Rasheeda Muhammad, who is from Sudan. But it's not easy getting answers. (Hussein, 2006)
Rasheeda:	It's really something we don't talk about. You don't discuss it. It's personal; it's taboo to talk about sex in general. And to talk about that subject, it's something you don't discuss it with your friends . . . It's part of the culture. It's just part of what they believe.
Ayan:	Our culture is different from American culture. Sex is an open discussion in the U.S. compared to back at home. No one among the community questions female circumcision. African women like Rasheeda say female circumcision is a right [sic] of passage . . .
Rasheeda:	My own opinion, it's like, now you are not a baby anymore.
Ayan:	Does that mean that a girl who is not circumcised is a baby?
Rasheeda:	Maybe, I'm not sure.
Ayan:	What makes one a woman and not a girl? Surely a part of their private part is not the answer.
Rasheeda:	I have a friend who's very well-educated . . . who has two daughters. She circumcised them because she said she

	talked to the physician there and she told her it's just the little things you have to do and it's healthy.
Ayan:	I don't agree that it's healthy . . . I'm not through looking for answers. (Hussein, 2008)[3]

In another interesting account of female genital cutting, Habibou Bangre (2008) introduces us to Hawa Greou, a woman from Mali, West Africa, who was jailed in 1999 for eight years for circumcising 48 girls in Paris. Her case was the first to be prosecuted in France against performing female genital cutting since the practice was outlawed in 1984. In this case, which was tried by a woman judge, Martine Varin, two dozen parents were also convicted and sentenced to prison terms for taking their daughters to Greou for genital cutting.

This case was triggered by the complaint of a victim, Mariatou Koita, a French woman of Malian origin. Ms. Koita, a 23-year-old law student in Paris, demanded to see a judge five years after Ms. Greou went to her parents' flat to circumcise her younger sister. Although she recognized Greou as the woman who had circumcised her at the age of eight a decade earlier, she remembered her mother concealing the practice by claiming to be taking them to hospital for treatment. She explains: "My mother said she was taking us to have injections," she said. "But then I heard Sira [another sister] scream."

"There were several women. Two forced me to lie down, one held my legs, the other my arms. The third bent down and circumcised me."

After filing her complaint, investigators identified dozens of girls between the ages of one month and 10 years who had been taken to "Mama Greou" for the operation. Among the items they found in her home were razor blades, creams, and compresses. In her defense, Ms. Greou reportedly told the police, "I do it the way my mother and my grandmother did it. I cut the clitoris, I take clean earth and I mold it into a charm that I place on the child's sex." Ms. Greou, who charged $30 to $80 for each circumcision, apologized at the beginning of her trial. "I am sorry if I caused any harm," she said. "It is a custom; I did not do it maliciously. Now I understand—now we must stop."

According to Bangre, Koita's mother, Cisse, was jailed for two years. Greou's lawyer, Jean Chavais, did not contest the facts, but agreed that circumcision was a deep-rooted African custom that the justice system was not well equipped to fight. Greou, who spent about five years in prison, is now an advocate against female genital cutting (Bangre, 2008).

Peter Viathagen Simpson, in his article, "Girl Receives Damages for Genital Mutilation" (2009) recounts the experience of Zainab, the Somali girl who lives in Gothenburg, Sweden, who received damages for being subjected to female genital cutting. Zainab, the 19-year-old girl was awarded compensation in the Swedish court for having been subjected to genital cutting in her parents' Somali home. The girl had been taken to Somalia by her parents on the pretext of a holiday in 2001. While there, she was held down by her mother and two other women while her clitoris and inner labia were removed by a man, in return for payment. The girl's vagina was then sewn up down to the opening of her urethra. The whole procedure was conducted without anesthesia. The girl's mother, who explained in court that the girl had been taken to Somalia for "cleansing," was convicted for the violation of the girl's rights and ordered to pay her daughter 450,000 kronor in compensation.

In its decision to award the damages to the 19-year-old, the Crime Victim Compensation and Support Authority wrote that the genital mutilation resembled torture and was intended to limit her possibilities to have a normal sex life. The girl was awarded 390,000 kronor, the equivalent of $52,000 in U.S currency, in damages for abuse and gross violation of integrity. The authority also considered the girl's entitlement to further damages for pain and suffering (Simpson, 2009).[4]

There are numerous stories and diverse opinions on this subject in the communities that practice female genital cutting, both local and abroad. It is important that all voices on the subject are represented in discussions about the practice.

NOTES

1. All names and identifying information has been changed to protect the identity of these women and their families.
2. Jamie Glazov is *Frontpage Magazine*'s editor. He holds a PhD in History with a specialty in Russian, U.S., and Canadian foreign policy. He is the author of *Canadian Policy toward Khrushchev's Soviet Union* and is the co-editor (with David Horowitz) of *The Hate America Left*. He edited and wrote the introduction to David Horowitz's *Left Illusions*. In his new book, *United in Hate: The Left's Romance with Tyranny and Terror*, he argues that the Left will not campaign against female genital cutting and take a stand on Islamic gender issues because it is in their political interest not to do so.
3. Ayan's experience, was produced, hosted, and aired by Farai Chideya of NPR Youth Radio in collaboration with VOX Newspaper in Atlanta, Georgia, on April 10, 2006 at 9:00 A.M.
4. Simpson's articles can be accessed in *The Local* at www.thelocal.se, November 24, 2011.

3

Health and Moral Concerns

Although the cultural practice of female genital cutting is not the most dangerous issue affecting women's health globally, research indicates that some women suffer serious adverse health effects. Health problems associated with female genital cutting vary according to the type and severity of the procedure, the cleanliness of the tools used in the cutting process, and the health of the girl or woman being cut. Women who undergo Types 1 and 2 of the procedure are at a lesser risk for obstetric complications than those who have undergone Type 3, which involves infibulation. Moral concerns about female genital cutting are informed by health consequences and the implication of cultural values on gender relations. In this chapter, I discuss the health consequences associated with female genital cutting and moral concerns as framed in the human rights and cultural discourses to highlight the reasons for the ban of the practice in industrialized countries. In addition, the position of the United Nations (UN), the World Health Organization (WHO), and other governmental institutions is described to demonstrate the weight of this concern at the international level.

HEALTH CONCERNS

In most countries of origin, female genital cutting is performed in unclean conditions by traditional practitioners who may use scissors, razor blades, knives, broken glasses, tin lids, thorns, sharp stones, or pieces of glass, all of which pose high health risks (Skaine, 2005: 11; WHO, 2004). Because most genital cuttings take place in a group setting, unsterilized instruments are often used on more than one person, increasing the risk of infection. Due to the health risks involved, those who live in modern countries, especially in urban cities, prefer to have the procedure performed in hospitals. In most industrialized countries, however, the procedure has been criminalized in an effort to protect children from its health consequences.

These health consequences can be immediate, long-term, or both. Immediate consequences include severe pain, urine retention, shock, hemorrhage, and infection (Dorkenoo, et al., 2007). The cutting of the clitoris is extremely painful due to the dense concentration of the nerves in the clitoral and the vulvar areas—most girls are routinely cut without anesthesia. The worst pain tends to occur the day after the procedure, when they have to urinate through the wound. Although some patients may experience shock, which often occurs from acute pain, the most life-threatening complications are hemorrhage, infections, urinary retention, and sepsis. Almost every girl or woman who is cut experiences hemorrhage, or bleeding which is caused by the amputation of the clitoris and the high-pressure blood flow from the clitoral artery. A further complication may result from ruptured blood vessels in the clitoris. In cases where there is limited access to immediate medical attention, especially where the practice is performed in rural areas, such hemorrhage may result in death. Even where medical facilities are available, deaths may occur because of the reluctance of families and practitioners to refer cases to hospitals, for fear of prosecution.

Long-term consequences of female genital cutting include damage to the genitalia, cysts, abscesses, keloids, scarring, damage to the urethra, dyspareunia, difficulties with childbirth, and sexual dysfunction. Women who undergo the most severe forms of the procedure are left with scars that cover most of their vagina. In some cases, the urethra, anal sphincter, vaginal walls, or bartholin glands may be permanently damaged, leading to slow or strained flow of urine or even dangerous urine retention. Scars can also develop into cysts, abscesses, or keloids that can cause severe pain during intercourse. Other forms of tissue damage make normal sex impossible or very painful, or can lead to tear during intercourse. Neuromas, which often develop where the dorsal nerve of the clitoris is divided, result in permanent and agonizing hypersensitivity. Vaginitis, sterility, and the frequent need for episiotomies during childbirth continue to be part of the lives of the women who suffer this practice (Coquery-Vidrovitch, 1997: 208; Dorkenoo, 2007; Boyle, 2002: 33–34). Statistics indicate that infertility rates among women who have had female genital cutting are as high as 25 percent to 30 percent (WHO, 2006). Most infertility cases among cut women result from intercourse difficulties and infections. Pregnancy problems, which include heavy bleeding and infection during delivery, can distress both the infant and the mother. In the United Kingdom, studies show that women who were exposed to female genital cutting required episiotomy for sustained perineal tears at the time of delivery (Dorkenoo et al., 2007).

Such women are also at high risk of infection due to unsafe conditions that surround most procedures. If the infection is not immediately taken care of, patients can get fevers or sepsis (a blood infection), or may even die. Infections such as septicemia and gangrene of the vulvar tissue may be caused by urine and fecal contamination of the wound. Unclean conditions and the use of unsterilized tools also subject these women to life-threatening infections such as tetanus and sexually transmitted infections, including HIV/AIDS and Hepatitis B and C. Their risk of these infections also increases due to the damage to the tissues around the female sex organ area, which is likely to tear during sex. Transmission of HIV and hepatitis is a long-term concern because such a patient must receive specialized services, including referral to HIV care services. Reproductive tract infections result from vaginal fluid retention and menstrual blood retention. In some cases, pelvic infections have led to sterility or prolonged labor, increasing the risk of back pain and painful menstruation. Untreated lower urinary tract infections may lead to bladder and kidney infections, resulting in renal failure, septicemia, and death (Dorkenoo et al., 2007; Wangila, 2007).

Infibulation is particularly harmful because it is designed to prevent vaginal intercourse (Dorkenoo, 1994: 14). For women in the cultures where it is performed, sexual organs may be damaged further when the vulva is reopened after marriage and re-infibulated after the birth of each child. Gynecological problems associated with infibulation include painful menstruation and recurring infections. A woman who has been exposed to infibulation is left with a narrow vulva, resulting in neointroitus, a condition that results in a slowed urinary stream, stagnant urine, and even the chronic ascendance of bacteria into the urinary tract, which can cause recurring infections. The small opening also often inhibits gynecological examination, especially if such women had a more severe form of the procedure. This is because the narrow entrance at the vaginal opening prevents health care professionals from using the tools required to perform pap tests and pelvic exams. Other complications relate to difficulties with menstruation, including the collection of menstrual blood behind the sealed vagina. This may cause dangerous urogenital tract infections, but there are also other deadly consequences. As El-Dareer (1983) explains, the accumulation of several months' menstrual blood and amenorrhea sometimes leads to an increase in the size of the abdomen—a condition that is sometimes mistaken for pregnancy. In communities where virginity and honor are highly valued, misdiagnosed girls suffering this condition have been killed for disgracing their families (El Dareer, 1983: 37).

Obstetrical complications include the difficulty in getting pregnant, concerns during pregnancy, and obstructed labor and excessive bleeding from tearing and de-infibulation during childbirth. For infibulated women, childbirth is prolonged, thus inhibiting fetal descent. Such women are at a greater risk during vaginal deliveries for perineal tears, wound infections, episiotomy separations, postpartum hemorrhage, and sepsis. Obstructed labor can also cause fetal brain damage—the reason for the many still births reported in these women. A clear case of this is presented by Tadeletch Shanko, an Ethiopian woman who herself performed female genital cutting on girls for 15 years. She declared before a panel of dignitaries and members of the Ethiopian National Assembly that "I lost seven of my children in childbirth. Because of the scarring that I sustained, I was not elastic enough. All seven of them suffocated inside my womb" (Tuloch, 2009).[1] Therefore, it is important that prior to delivery, a pregnant patient who has been infibulated be de-fibulated—a procedure that helps open the scar tissue in order for the birth to take place.

Recent studies associate the practice with a deficiency in amniotic fluid during childbirth, gestational diabetes, an increased need for episiotomies and caesarean sections, dangerous bleeding after childbirth, extended hospitalization following childbirth, the need for infant resuscitation, maternal illness, and sometimes, death after childbirth. Birth outcomes affecting millions of deliveries globally include elevated infant death rates during and immediately after birth (Australian National University, 2006).

Findings from a recent collaborative study by African and international researchers detail the adverse effects of female genital cutting on birth outcomes (*Science Daily*, 2010; WHO, 2006). Those who are exposed to the severe forms of female genital cutting have an average of 30 percent more risk of undergoing a caesarean section compared to those who have not. Seventy percent of these women are more likely to suffer hemorrhage after childbirth. During childbirth, their newborns not only require resuscitation more often, but death rates among these babies during and immediately after birth are also higher. Professor Emily Banks of the National Center for Epidemiology and Population Health at Australian National University, a member of the international research team described above, believes that the study provides the first reliable evidence of the impact of female genital cutting on complications during childbirth. She calls for an urgent need to address the practice because of the risk it poses to large numbers of infant deaths in the world, as well as the increased burden of maternal illness affecting millions of deliveries (*Science Daily*, 2010).

According to this WHO study, which involved 28,393 women in 28 obstetric centers in six African countries (Burkina Faso, Ghana, Kenya, Nigeria, Senegal, and Sudan), women who have been exposed to female genital cutting are significantly more likely to experience difficulties during childbirth, and their babies are more likely to die as a result of the practice (WHO, 2006: 367; 1835–1841). In addition, about 5 percent of babies born to women without female genital cutting were stillborn or died shortly after delivery. This figure increased to 6.4 percent in babies born to women with female genital cutting.

In another study, T. Adams observed that women who are exposed to female genital cutting have an elevated risk of serious health consequences, including infertility, susceptibility to STIs, psychological trauma, and obstetric complications. In addition, their infants are at higher risk for perinatal death. Adams also notes the effects of female genital cutting on a country's economy. He estimates that medical costs associated with obstetric complications related to female genital cutting amounted to about $3.7 million for the 53 million women living in the six countries studied (Burkina Faso, Ghana, Kenya, Nigeria, Senegal, and Sudan)— an immense economic burden on these nations' health systems. He also reported that a 15-year-old who undergoes the most severe form of female genital cutting (infibulation) is likely to have only 75 percent of the life expectancy of noninfibulated women (Adams, 2010).

As Adams noted, female genital cutting is also associated with psychological and emotional stress. This is because it is typically performed on very young girls, some of whom do not understand what the procedure involves and why it is necessary. The psychological effects of female genital cutting include anxiety and phobic behavior, with recurrent flashbacks of the pain and trauma of the procedure, especially during intercourse. The disfiguring scar tissue that often grows at the wound site can be psychologically distressing. Personal accounts of genital cutting reveal feelings of anxiety, terror, humiliation, and betrayal, all of which are likely to have long-term psychological effects that are among the criteria for a diagnosis of post-traumatic stress disorder. In addition, although this is not so common, some girls and women who have been cut have problems with insomnia and depression.

Studies have verified the health consequences associated with female genital cutting. In 1994, Dr. Rosemary Mburu, a Kenyan gynecologist, estimated that 15 percent of all females who are exposed to genital cutting die from bleeding or infections (Mann, 1994). Other reports estimate that out of every 1,000 females who undergo female genital cutting, 70 women die as a result (Kahiga, 1994: 3–5). In an ABC News documentary interview, Dr. Mark Besley of the Division of Family Health of the WHO in Geneva observes that "There is no single practice which has such a dramatic negative effect on health in the broadest sense as female genital mutilation" (ABC News, 1993). This is not to mention the psychological effects as discussed by Toubia (Rahman and Toubia, 2001). Commenting on the effects of female genital cutting on sexual satisfaction, and the assumption that the practice will make women more faithful, Esther Kawira, a medical officer in charge of the Shirati Mennonite Church of Tanzania Hospital observes:

> It might do the reverse as far as making women think that men don't care about them, don't care about them having undergone this pain, or don't care that wives are sexually handicapped as a result. Men and women start out unequal already in the area of sexual relations. Women's sexual response is slower than men's to begin with and circumcision is giving her an added handicap. If you're talking about mutual fulfilment in sex, circumcision would make it much harder for a woman to reach orgasm or for a man to produce that in his partner. In fact, I wasn't sure myself, if a circumcised woman, at least one who had the clitoris removed, actually reached orgasm. A person I talked to said that a circumcised woman can have orgasm but it is much less likely and it takes a lot longer. So, it seems that one effect would be that women would have an inherent dissatisfaction (or even anger) because she knows it has been done to her by a man or may be the male society. It would make her and women collectively feel that men didn't care about them, didn't care about what was happening to them, the effect might be to diminish what we hope would be the natural affection across the genders and make it more difficult, instead of at least starting out the way we were created physically and hoping that the affection can increase over time. (Nigeria Demographic and Health Survey, 2003; Skaine, 2005: 21)

In my previous study, *Female Circumcision: The Interplay of Religion, Culture and Gender in Kenya* (2007), one informant, Wanyama, a nurse, had the following to say about female genital cutting-related health risks on women's experience:

> I have met and interacted with these women who are circumcised and their experience is pathetic and painful. I am a nurse and so I have tried to assist those who are circumcised, during delivery, for instance, and it is not easy either for the mother or the midwife. There are more complications such as perineal tears, bleeding, delayed second stage leading to still births, infections, et cetera. (Wanyama, Interview, July 2003)

Unfortunately, due to the secrecy that shrouds the practice, the traumatic results of the practice, both physical and psychological, often go unreported, sometimes with tragic results. It is because of these serious medical complications that the WHO has officially described the practice as female genital mutilation (FGM), a terminology intentionally adopted to communicate the harm that a girl child or woman is exposed to during the procedure. To emphasize the violation of sexual reproduction rights, WHO defined female genital cutting as the removal of part or all of the clitoris, a procedure which maims the main female genital organ, an equivalent in anatomy and physiology to the male penis (WHO, 1997: 8). Based on this description, WHO opposed any medical intervention or modification to the practice claimed to minimize perceived health risks and pain for women who are exposed to the procedure. It is argued that medicalization of female genital cutting would undermine their key position that any form of this practice severely compromises a woman's right to sexual health.

Expert Opinions

Expert opinions on the subject help to contextualize health experiences of female genital cutting. In this section, therefore, opinions of professionals such as obstetrician gynecologists, activists, and those with expert knowledge on the subject are brought to bear on raised concerns. Ted Weaver, for instance, is an obstetrics gynecologist affiliated with the Royal Australian and New Zealand College of Obstetricians and Gynaecologists, Australia. In an interview with Emily Bourke, of ABC News, on February 6, 2010, he affirms that female genital cutting is alive and well in Australia. He says, "There is some evidence to suggest that it does happen in certain parts of Australia. It's hard to gauge the actual numbers because it is prohibited by legislation and it is something that is performed in an underground way. . . . But certainly, there have been reports of children being taken to hospitals after having the procedure done with complications from the procedure. If we try and dictate and pontificate about this and not provide culturally appropriate care, we'll further disenfranchise those women" (Bourke, 2010). Weaver thinks that the only way to end the practice is to continue advocating against it. He explains, "I think all we can do is advocate against it, speak out, and try to educate women, try to empower women, certainly in this country, and we should do our best for international organizations that are also espousing the same message" (Bourke, 2010).

Martha Teshome is an expert from the Department of Health and Ageing, Australia. When asked about female genital cutting in an interview with *Inzert: International Understanding Justice and Peace* magazine,[2] she explained how she heard the cries of girls in the suburbs when "circumcisers performed the acts at home." She also narrates how girls are taken by parents to Singapore on holiday, only to find out that they were to undergo female genital cutting. She explains, "It surprised many that practices that we have so often thought of as being limited to African countries such as Somalia, Sudan, Eritrea and Ethiopia can happen to women living here in Western Australia." She continues, "When people migrate to Australia they usually bring their culture with them. If female genital mutilation (FGM) was practiced in their home community, then it is seen by some as being a necessary 'rite of passage' to adulthood" (*Inzert*, 2007). She compares female genital cutting to foot binding in Chinese culture and rib-breaking corsets in early Western cultures. She relates the painful experience of infections and the brutal opening of stitches on wedding nights and the severe urine retention that the sewing up of the labia can cause. In spite of these health risks, she explains that in Australia, there is no mandatory reporting of female genital cutting and that health professionals have no way of checking children who are at risk of female genital cutting (*Inzert*, 2007).

Zeinab Muhammad, a Somali woman who works in Melbourne, Australia, in the Family and Reproductive Rights Education Program at Royal Women's Hospital, has also encountered survivors of female genital cutting. Zeinab, when interviewed by *Inzert*, had the following to say: "One of the questions that we ask these women is 'why were you doing it?' And they will tell you, 'because of my religion'. . . . We bring Imams or priests to convince them that there is nothing from the books (*Quran, hadith or the Bible*) that says you have to do circumcision to girls. So why are you doing it?" (italics are mine). "You have to work with them, listen to them. You have to know where they are coming from in order to help them" (*Inzert*, 2007).

Petra Bayr is a Social Democrat Member of Parliament in Austria and a member of the Austrian platform against female genital cutting. Her group estimates that between 6,000 and 8,000 women in Austria have been forced to undergo female genital cutting. In an interview on this practice, she explains how "Many parents believe they are doing their daughters a favor by forcing them to undergo it." According to Bayr, this practice is a violation of human rights of girls. It leaves "its victims mentally and physically damaged for the rest of their lives." It should be curbed by challenging parents' thinking that it is good for their daughters. She calls for raising awareness in order to make it clear to parents that genital cutting was neither called for by religion nor a pre-condition for finding a husband (*Austrian Times*, 2010/2011). Bayr and her group are working with health personnel and other migrant organizations, including religious leaders to try to change the situation in Austria.

Terry Duhn is a medical doctor and the director of a women's clinic in Colorado, United States. She has observed that about four female genital-cutting cases are seen each year at the clinic. In an interview on female genital cutting, she explains, "Obviously, parents don't use the word female genital mutilation. What the mom of the patient says is, 'I want to have the procedure that makes my daughter like me.'" She continues, "I know of one patient where it was clear it was performed in this country" (Adhikaria, 2010/2011).

Pierre Foldes is a French doctor who has been working with victims of female genital cutting for almost 30 years. He began his work in this area while volunteering in Burkina Faso. Speaking on the subject, he had the following to say—"I met a population of women suffering from mutilation. Some of them asked me if I could fix things that were painful," he explained, referring to the scar tissue that frequently develops over the clitoris. "When I came back to France, I realized there was absolutely no data on this, no technique," he adds.

This motivated Foldes to develop a simple procedure that helps reconstruct the clitoris by removing the painful tissue by cutting the ligaments to expose the original root. Six to eight weeks after the procedure, the area "begins to appear normal," and in six months, sensual "feeling begins to come back." He explains to CNN, "The results are getting better and better," as 72 to 75 percent of his patients have reported normal sexuality after 18 months.

"We are working very hard on the evolution of the program and are involved in treating patients for up to two years," says Foldes. Currently, Foldes operates on approximately 80–100 women each month at a hospital outside Paris. He estimates that he has operated on more than 3,000 women in total there. The healing process is more complicated than just the physical healing. Foldes explains that "the surgical procedure is only a small part of the whole problem. We have a whole team with psychologists that follow up with patients for months." Since female genital mutilation is a crime in France, Dr. Foldes has found a way of getting the French public health system to reimburse the cost of the operation, which allows about 70 percent of his patients to receive treatment for free.

Foldes compares the trauma caused by female genital cutting to sexual assault. "It's like a rape," he says. "It's very important to deal with the aggression and emotions to progressively get back to normal sexuality." Foldes has encountered some resistance to his practice, including multiple death threats. Men with knives have confronted him at his office numerous times. In his view, these threats emanate from radical "Islamic people." In spite of this, he vows to continue to help women who have been exposed to this practice (Sterns, 2011).

MORAL CONCERNS

Efforts to recognize female genital cutting as a violation of women's rights meet roadblocks on all fronts. This is because female genital cutting is not only sanctioned by private actors (family members), but it also finds legitimacy in cultural and religious communities that see the procedure as a cultural right. As illustrated in the interviews and surveys discussed above, issues of identity continue to dominate cultural diversity discourses, making it difficult to challenge female genital cutting on the basis of human rights. Before exploring in detail the controversial discussion surrounding the practice—a task addressed in Chapter 4—it is important to highlight specific areas of moral concern.

Moral concerns about female genital cutting draw from the health consequences and cultural implications of the practice on gender relations. Where these values contradict those of communities that embrace the practice, controversies have ensued. In most industrialized countries, moral values are centered on questions of human rights, which are informed by a moral position commonly referred to as moral universalism—the idea that human beings are entitled to certain universal rights merely by virtue of being human. These rights, which are described as universal and inalienable, are believed to be held equally by all humans based on the human dignity they possess. Therefore, these rights must be assured in all societies. Human rights are considered a necessary condition for a good life because they guarantee the conditions required for personal development. If these basic human rights are denied, whether by the family, the community, the state, or society at large, individuals are encouraged to claim them. Consequently, the family, the community, and society are enjoined to allow them these rights (Ake, 1978: 94).

Cultural relativist values emphasize the need to recognize cultural values that inform a particular practice. As will be illustrated below, female genital cutting is a controversial issue among feminists, as it is among human rights activists. Feminism is the notion that women as individuals should not be disadvantaged due to their gender and that they should be afforded basic rights to freedom, justice, and peace. This perspective is also embedded in moral universalist values. As Susan Mohller Okin validly explains, it is the recognition that women "have human dignity equally with men and the opportunity to live as fulfilling and freely chosen lives as men" (Okin, 1997; 1999). The feminist movement arose in Europe and America in the 19th century, responding to social tendencies to exclude women from participation in political and public life. Exclusion of women was justified by references to their sexual differences from men. Feminists, both men and women, reject the ideology of sexual difference, and support instead women's rights to equal treatment. Feminists claim that because women are members of the human species, they deserve the same rights due to all humans. The general patriarchal assumption, however, is that women are objects of sexual desire and should be confined to a lifetime of subordination "within the limits of male needs" (Delmar, 1986: 18).

As a social movement, feminism aims at the establishment and defense of social rights and equal opportunities for women. Feminist activists have also campaigned for women's rights to bodily integrity, autonomy, and reproductive freedom. Most feminists follow a moral universalist position, therefore they consider female genital cutting a violation of women's rights. These feminists describe the practice as an expression of patriarchy (the unexamined conviction that male experiences and male values are the basis upon which societies operate), sexism, and male control of female sexuality (Gruenbaum, 2001: 133). To these feminists, female genital cutting is in violation of the UN's Declaration on the Discrimination against Women (CEDAW), a statement that calls for an end to all forms of gender discrimination (Steiner and Alston, 1996: 244–245; Shell-Duncan and Hernlund, 2000: 28). Although feminists differ in opinion about the source of such discrimination, the opponents of female genital cutting tend to view it as embedded in a patriarchal social structure that sanctions male dominance. These feminists perceive female genital cutting as a cultural practice designed in patriarchal cultures to control and oppress women.

Among members of this camp, female genital cutting is understood to be informed by patriarchal notions that male dominance and women's subjugation are legitimate and that women are incapable of restraining their sexual desires. Because the removal of the clitoris during female genital cutting is associated with the control of women's sexual pleasure, feminists see it as a patriarchal attempt to "police the womb," ensuring that a woman remains chaste to her husband, thereby protecting his honor. Nancy Bonvillain explains:

> Female genital mutilation is consistent with men's fear of and, therefore, the wish to control women's sexual behavior. Women who are subjected to the procedure have reduced sexual desire, both because of the loss of part of their sexual organs and because of their fear of the pain involved with intercourse. They therefore are unlikely to engage in premarital or extramarital sexual activity that evidently so threatens the patriarchal social systems that male-dominated ideologies legitimate. (Bonvillain, 2001: 277)

The practice therefore reinforces male dominance and the subjugation of women (Daly 1978; Bonvillain, 2001). As a result, it is often linked to other cultural practices such as polygamy, early and arranged marriage of girls, bride price, and widow inheritance, all of which are designed to limit women's self-realization and enjoyment of life in the name of chastity and family honor (Gruenbaum, 2001: 133).

Moral universalist feminists have critiqued the devaluation of pleasure within patriarchal communities. It is argued that the mindset that devalues pleasure is embedded in a dualist view of the world in which the body is seen as less important than the mind. This is especially true of the woman's body, specifically a woman's right to her body and to pleasure. Feminist Alice Walker has described female genital cutting as "the sexual blinding of women," a practice in which sexuality is literally destroyed (Walker, 1993: 15–19). Mary Daly describes female genital cutting as an "unspeakable atrocity, torturous and mutilative, aimed at depriving women their femininity, sexual sensitivity and pleasure" (Daly, 1978: 153–159). The Hite Report, which is frequently cited by these feminists, explains what is denied to women whose clitorises have been cut:

> Clitoral stimulation evokes female orgasm, which takes place deeper in the body, around the vagina and other structures, just as stimulation of the lip of the male penis evokes male orgasm, which takes place in the lower body of the male. (Hite, 1976: 99)

The effect of clitoridectomy on a woman's sexual desire is validated in the claims of some men who have reported lack of sexual fulfillment from their wives. According to Mahran:

> Excision is one of the causes of the ever increasing use of hashish among men who believe, albeit wrongly, that smoking it delays ejaculation, giving men their orgasms at the same time as their excised wives; 16 percent of excised women admit that their husbands smoke hashish for sexual reasons. (1981: 1–2)

The removal of the clitoris and *labia minora* destroys sensitive parts of the reproductive organ. Furthermore, the narrowing of the vaginal opening leads to painful intercourse, and the pain experienced during the procedure leads to the association of sex with pain. As Barbara S. Morrison explains, "The female body is a symbolic construct upon which power is inscribed. The clitoris is a site for pleasure. Although pure pleasure and its removal do not compromise the reproductive ability of the female, the removal serves to create pain in the female body and also to permanently obliterate one of the sites of pleasure that constitutes that female body"

(Barbara S. Morrison, 2008: 126). Because most cut women are taught not to initiate sex even in marriage and not to show that they are enjoying it during intercourse, female genital cutting is intended to protect them from a presumed promiscuous lifestyle. By diminishing sexual desire, female genital cutting inhibits sexual orgasm, thus preventing the enjoyment of sex for women. Thus feminists believe that female genital cutting should be outlawed and abandoned completely.

Also critiqued is the notion of honor that is often associated with this practice. Honor is achieved by brutal acts ensuring not only that a woman is chaste in her marriage, but that the children she bears are her husband's and no one else's (Coquery-Vidrovitch, 1977). This reasoning is evident in the fact that a woman was required to remain infibulated to ensure that she does not engage in sexual intercourse with anyone else in the absence of her husband. It is argued that this procedure, which leads to frigidity and the dislike of sex among cut women, is informed by cultural notions of female premarital chastity and passive sexual experience. The procedure is intended, therefore, to restrain women's sexual activities. Because these cultural concepts are imparted in the women during the socialization process, opponents of female genital cutting describe an adult woman who accepts the practice voluntarily as misguided and often acting out of fear, coercion, or peer pressure. She is compared to a battered woman who stays in an abusive relationship for fear of the stigma associated with divorce.

It is important to remember, however, that opposition to female genital cutting is not universal among all feminists. Some feminists embrace a cultural relativist position, which advocates the need to promote cultural sensitivity ahead of human rights. They argue that the cultural values behind the practice need to be recognized and appreciated. For instance, they view the practice as a form of aesthetic enhancement, not mutilation. They are concerned that female genital cutting has been portrayed by biased opponents of the practice as "savage, horrifying, harmful, misogynist, abusive, and socially unjust" without an attempt to present factual, "real, evidence-based argument that defeats the standards of critical reason and fact checking" (Goldberg, 2012). These individuals put forth the argument that the occurrence of reproductive and medical complications that are connected to FGC is minimal. For instance, the two types of female genital cutting that comprise 90 percent of procedures are harmless, since they involve the reduction of the clitoral hood and tissue and the reduction or elimination of the labia and the clitoris. Medical research, they explain, has found that a high percentage of women who have had genital surgery are able to have regular and fulfilling sex lives, with the ability to reach orgasm on a regular basis (Goldberg, 2012).

They also explain that in almost all societies where female genital surgery is performed, male genital surgery also takes place. Thus, it is erroneous, they believe, to argue that such societies "are singling out females as targets of punishment, sexual deprivation, or humiliation." They claim further that the practice of female genital surgery is not connected to the patriarchy. Very few patriarchal societies practice the procedure, and furthermore, female genital surgery is uncommon among the most sexually restrictive populations. They assert that because the practice is managed and controlled by females, the fault does not rest on men, and therefore, on patriarchy. Ironically, they also believe that any organization that tries to stop the practice is disempowering for women.

These supporters argue for a balanced examination of the practice. They particularly recommend that the media, activists, and policymakers stop speaking out against the practice in a manner that sensationalizes the families who practice female genital surgery on their daughters, as they believe that is does not cause harm to their sexual health and reproductive well-being. They also wish to have opponents to the practice acknowledge that female genital cutting is not strictly an African practice. They insist on likening the practice to the prevalence of genital piercing and vaginal rejuvenation surgery in the West. They recommend that activists who are demanding safe, hospital-based FGC be heard in public policy forums. At critique are approaches that advocate for Zero tolerance policies, which they argue are counterproductive because they limit dialogue about medicalized FGC, and often render the procedure more dangerous by forcing the practice to go underground. They also criticize the policies and regulations that make female genital cutting a crime for adult women, which they argue is discriminatory (Goldberg, 2012).

In spite of their differences, feminists agree that women's sexual freedom is necessary if women are to achieve equal rights.

WHO and the UN Position

Opponents of female genital cutting assert that the practice violates the human rights of those involved as articulated in Article 5 of the Universal Declaration of Human Rights. This article cautions against the subjection of anyone "to torture, or to cruel, inhuman or degrading treatment or punishment" (The Advocates for Human Rights, 2011).[3] Those who object to female genital cutting as a human rights violation, therefore, bring the weight of the UN to their argument. The human rights claim is endorsed by the UN's Universal Declaration of Human Rights, which states that "'Everyone has the right to liberty, 'all persons' are entitled to equal protection, 'no one' shall be subjected to torture, and 'everyone' has the right to an adequate standard of living" (Steiner and Alston, 1996: 192–193). Human rights are rights inherent to all human beings, whatever their nationality, place of residence, sex, national or ethnic origin, color, religion, language, or any other status. All are equally entitled to human rights, without discrimination. These rights are all interrelated, interdependent, and indivisible. The purpose of the UN is to "achieve international co-operation in promoting and encouraging respect for human rights and fundamental freedoms for all without distinction as to race, sex, language, or religion" (Steiner and Alston, 1996: 1148).

And the UN is not alone in its efforts to guarantee human rights. Other human rights conventions also seek to protect people from cruelty and violence, including The Universal Declaration of Human Rights (UDHR) of 1948; The United Nations Convention on the Rights of the Child (1959); The African Charter on Rights and Welfare of the Child (1990); The United Nations Convention on the Elimination of All Forms of Discrimination Against Women (CEDAW of 1992); The United Nations Declaration on Violence Against Women (VAW, 1993); The World Conference on Human Rights, Declaration and Programme of Action, Vienna (1993); and The United Nations High Commission on Refugees, Statement Against Gender-Based Violence (1996). These statements also ensure that bodily integrity is protected and that all have access to health care, education, and self-realization.

The international commitment to protect human rights was instituted early in 1948. This commitment is formalized in the following resolutions— the Universal Declaration on Human Rights (1948), the International Covenant on Civil & Political Rights (1966), and the Convention on the Rights of the Child (1989). Universal human rights are often expressed and guaranteed by law in the forms of treaties, customary international law, general principles, and other sources of international law. International human rights law lays down obligations that each government should follow in order to promote and protect the human rights and fundamental freedoms of individuals or groups. According to the UDHR, human rights are based on the "recognition of the inherent dignity and of the equal and inalienable rights of all members of the human family." These rights are the "foundation of freedom, justice, and peace in the world" (Steiner and Alston, 1996: 1156). The Universal Declaration of Human Rights states that "everyone is entitled to all the rights and freedoms set forth in this Declaration, without distinction of any kind, such as race, color, sex, language, religion, political or other opinion, national or social origin, property, birth or other status" (Article 2). Under Articles 55 and 56, all signatory members pledged "to take joint and separate action in cooperation with the organization for the achievement of the purposes of the United Nations, including the promotion of a universal respect for, and observance of human rights and fundamental freedoms for all" (United Nations Charter, 1945).

Specific to the topic at hand, the UN, in collaboration with other world organizations, such as the WHO, United Nations Children's Fund (UNICEF), and Amnesty International, has designated female genital cutting a violation of the individual's rights to physical and mental health, self-determination, bodily integrity, and freedom from sexual discrimination. A joint statement released by the WHO, UNICEF, and the United Nations Population Fund (UNPF) states:

> It is unacceptable that the international community remains passive in the name of a distorted vision of multiculturalism. Human behaviors and cultural values, however senseless or destructive they may appear from the personal and cultural standpoint of others, have meaning and fulfill a function for those who practice them. However, culture is not static but it is in constant flux, adapting and reforming. People will change their behavior when they understand the hazards and indignity of harmful practices and when they realize that it is possible to give up harmful practices without giving up meaningful aspects of their culture. (World Health Organization, 1996)

Since the UN endorses these values, all member countries of the UN implicitly agree to accept, elaborate, and ratify treaties regarding these rights. And because these rights are applicable to every human being, individuals in these countries have the right to claim them.

Clearly, female genital cutting is in violation of specific United Nations Human Rights articles. Every country and state is obligated to respect human rights, regardless of a person's race, color, sex (gender), religion, political opinion, language, or national or social origin. Therefore, female genital cutting is in violation of human rights as articulated in the UN's Article 5 and 24(3). Article 5 states that "No one should be subjected to torture, or to cruel, inhuman or degrading treatment or punishment." Article 24 (3) protects children's rights to good health and exposure to cruel and exploitative tendencies that endanger their health.

Defenders of the practice have often justified it based on its traditional cultural values. However, human rights advocates describe it as a violation of the right not to be subjected to torture or ill treatment, citing its serious health and social consequences. According to those in the human rights camp, the practice is a violation of the Convention Against Torture and other Cruel, Inhuman, or Degrading Treatment or Punishment (CAT), Articles 1 and 16; ICCPR, Article 7; ECHR, Article 3; Charter on the Fundamental Rights of the European Union Article 4; Declaration on the Elimination of Violence against Women, Article 3; CRC, Article 37; and African (Banjul) Charter on Human and People's Rights, Article 5. In a 2001 resolution of the Council of Europe, concerns were expressed regarding the fact that female genital cutting was practiced in member states of the Council of Europe. Female genital cutting was declared an inhuman and degrading treatment within the meaning of Article 3 of the European Convention on Human Rights even if the practice was carried out under hygienic conditions by competent personnel. Proponents of cultural relativism were denounced for justifying the practice.

Genital Cutting as a Violation of UN Convention

Feminists' efforts led to an international feminist movement, which was successful at protecting the rights of women in several international instruments. Female genital cutting was specifically designated as a violation of the right to health and to enjoyment of the highest attainable standard of physical and mental health in Article 12 of the International Covenant of Economic, Social and Cultural Rights, which was adopted and passed by the General Assembly in New York in December 1966 and entered into force on January 3, 1976. In 1990, the United Nations' CEDAW denounced female genital cutting in its general recommendation No. 14. CEDAW, whose mission is to promote women's rights and status, defines discrimination against women as any "distinction, exclusion or restriction made on the basis of sex, which has the effect or purpose of impairing or nullifying the recognition, enjoyment or exercise by women, irrespective of their marital status, on the basis of equality between men and women, of human rights or fundamental freedoms in the political, economic, social, cultural, civil or any other field" (Article 1). It calls for an end to all gender discrimination and requires that nation states modify their cultural and social patterns of conduct for both men and women with a view to eliminating prejudices and all other practices based on gender inequality and stereotyped roles (Minority Rights Group 1992: 11). Female genital cutting is declared to be an example of the general subjugation of women and a form of violence against women, in violation of the Declaration on the Elimination of Violence against Women enacted by the UN in 1981.

At the United Nations' Fourth World Conference on Women in Beijing in 1995, a resolution was passed granting International Women's Rights, which were seen as being part of the category of general human rights. At the United Nations' 23rd special session of the General Assembly titled "Women 2000: Gender Equality, Development, and Peace for the Twenty-First Century," held at the UN Headquarters in New York between June 5 and June 9, 2000, it was declared that the member states of the international community observe the basic rights of women as affirmed in the UN Charter and in subsequent resolutions. In its 2002 Resolution on Traditional and Customary Practices Affecting the Health of Women and Girls, the UN General Assembly called upon all states to ratify or accede to CEDAW and to adopt national measures to prohibit traditional practices such as female genital cutting.

The United Nations Declaration on the Elimination of Violence against Women describes female genital cutting as a form of violence against women and as a human rights violation that should incur individual criminal responsibility (Article 2a of UN General Assembly Resolution, 1993). The Declaration on the Elimination of Violence Against Women states that "violence against women means any act of gender-based violence that results in, or is likely to result in, physical, sexual or psychological harm or suffering to women, including threats of such acts, coercion or arbitrary deprivation of liberty, whether occurring in public or in private life" (Article 1). It further asserts that states have an obligation to "exercise due diligence to prevent, investigate and, in accordance with national legislation, punish acts of violence against women, whether those acts are perpetrated by the State or by private persons" (Article 4-c). The Resolution further states that "women who are subjected to violence should be provided with access to the mechanisms of justice and as provided by national legislation to just and effective remedies for the harm that they have suffered." States should also inform women of their rights in seeking redress through such mechanisms.

In its special report on VAW, the UN stressed the importance of the empowerment of women in the fight against female genital cutting in a 15-year review report of violence against women. The report elaborates that in meeting its responsibility, "the state must include not only legislative, investigative and judicial reform to end impunity, . . . it should also initiate empowerment approaches to build women's capacities and to facilitate the questioning of hegemony within cultures by women" (United Nations VAW). The report describes the rights of everyone to enjoy the highest attainable standard of physical and mental health and labels the right to control one's health and body as an important freedom. Female genital cutting is described as a "serious breach of sexual and reproductive freedoms" and is "fundamentally and inherently inconsistent with the right to health" (UN Special Rapporteur, 2004).

Female genital cutting violates the 1984 United Nations Convention against Torture and Other Cruel, Inhuman or Degrading Treatment or Punishment (CATCID), which defines torture as "any act by which severe pain or suffering, whether physical or mental, is intentionally inflicted on a person for purposes including any reason based on discrimination of any kind" (Shell-Duncan and Hernlund, 2000: 29). According to the Minority Rights Group International Report 92/3 of 1992, the procedure is a form of torture, given the panic, shock, and pain that children and young women are exposed to (Minority Rights Group International, 1992). The United Nations' Special Rapporteur on violence against women designates any cultural practice that involves pain, suffering, and the violation of physical integrity as torture. Under customary international law, strict penal sanctions and maximum international scrutiny must be ensured to prevent such practices. According to the 2008 Report of the United Nations' Special Rapporteur on Torture and Other Cruel Inhuman or Degrading Treatment or Punishment, a law that authorizes any practice that amounts to torture constitutes consent or acquiescence by the state to such a practice (Amnesty International, 2011).

Female genital cutting is viewed as a violation of the right to physical integrity of the child or woman who is subjected to it. Every human being has a right to freedom from violence and should not be forced to undergo any practice for any reason. To coerce any individual to undergo female genital cutting is to violate UDHR, Articles 1 and 3; ICCPR, Article 9; Paragraph 1; ICESCR, preamble; and ECHR, Article 8. It is also a violation of the Charter on the Fundamental Rights of the European Union, Articles 1 and 3; Declaration on the Elimination of Violence against Women, Articles 1 and 2(a); CRC, Article 19; African (Banjul) Charter on Human and Peoples' Rights, Articles 4 and 5; Protocol to the African Charter on Human and Peoples' Rights on the Rights of Women in Africa, Articles 3, 4, and 5; American Convention on Human Rights, Article 5, Paragraph 1; Inter-American Convention on the Prevention, Punishment, Eradication of Violence against Women, Article 1; Platform for Action of the Fourth World Conference on Women (Beijing 1995), Paragraphs 107(d), 118, and 232(h).

Female genital cutting is in violation of the right to health because of the health consequences a girl or woman may suffer after undergoing the procedure. Specifically, female genital cutting is viewed as a violation of Article 25 of UDHR, Article 12 of the International Covenant on Economic, Social, and Cultural Rights (ICESCR), Article 2 of the Convention on the Elimination of all Forms of Discrimination Against Women (CEDAW), Article 3 of the Declaration on the Elimination of Violence against Women (VAW) Article 24 of the Convention on the Rights of the Child (CRC), Article 16 of the African (Banjul) Charter on Human and Peoples' Rights, Article 14 of the Protocol to the African Charter on Human and Peoples' Rights on the Rights of Women in Africa, Article 14 of the African Charter on the Rights and the Welfare of the Child, Article 10, paragraph 1 of Additional Protocol to the American Convention on Human Rights in the Area of Economic, Social, and Cultural Rights, Paragraph 7.2 of the Program of Action of the International Conference on Population and Development, and Paragraph 89 of the Platform for Action of the Fourth World Conference on Women (Beijing 1995). Health is often defined in a broad sense to include the right to maturity and to reproductive and sexual health.

Female genital cutting is in violation of the right to life, because the procedure may result in death. A child's death from female genital cutting contravenes Article 6 of the Universal Declaration of Human Rights (UDHR), Article 6 of the International Covenant on Civil and Political Rights (ICCPR), Article 2 of the European Convention for the Protection of Human Rights and Fundamental Freedoms (ECHR), Article 4 of the African (Banjul) Charter on Human and Peoples' Rights, and Article 4 of the Protocol to the African Charter on Human and Peoples' Rights on the Rights of Women in Africa, all of which seek to protect the right to life of every child.

Since female genital cutting is often performed without the consent of the girls, it is also viewed as a breach of their right to freedom, which grants them the right to express their views freely (Article 12). In most cases, the girls undergoing the practice are not consulted and have no voice in the decision about genital cutting, which is often made on their behalf by members of their families. Even if the girl child is aware of and accepting of the practice, the issue of consent remains problematic because girls are usually too young to understand its implications for their future psychological and physical health. When adolescent girls and women agree to undergo the practice, often they do so for fear of nonacceptance by their communities, families, and peer groups. As I noted in my previous studies, the practice often involves social coercion and the kidnapping of unwilling children (Wangila, 2007).

In addition to violation of freedom of choice and expression, female genital cutting is also considered a violation of the right to the dignity and bodily integrity of women and children who are exposed to the practice because it involves the mutilation of healthy body parts. The committee on the Convention on the Rights of the Child has indicated that states parties to the Convention have an obligation "to protect adolescents from all harmful traditional practices such as early marriages, honor killings, and female genital mutilation" (CRC, 2003).

Since female genital cutting is socially constructed based on gender values, it is also viewed as a violation of the right to nondiscrimination. According to this argument, because it is performed on women as a way to control their sexual desires based on gender values, it is rooted in societal values that promote discrimination. In addition, because it is performed in patriarchal societies that assign gender roles based on the perceived superiority of men and the inferiority of women, it is a violation of social equality as stipulated in the United Nations Charter, Articles 1 and 55;

UDHR, Articles 2 and 7; ICCPR, Article 2; ICESCR, Article 2; ECHR, Article 14; CEDAW, Articles 1 and 5(a); the African (Banjul) Charter on Human and Peoples' Rights on the Rights of Women in Africa, Article 2; the African Charter on the Rights and the Welfare of the Child, Article 26; and the American Convention on Human Rights, Article 1. In particular, it violates their right to be free from discrimination (Article 2) and to be protected from all forms of mental and physical violence and maltreatment (Article 19(1)), as well as their rights to the highest attainable standard of health (Article 24) and to freedom from torture or other Cruel, Inhuman, or Degrading Treatment or Punishment (Article 37). According to the United Nations' Committee on CRC, "discrimination against girl children is a serious violation of rights, affecting their survival and all areas of their young lives as well as restricting their capacity to contribute positively to society." Article 5(a) of CEDAW specifically states: States Parties shall take all appropriate measures:

(a) To modify the social and cultural patterns of conduct of men and women, with a view to achieving the elimination of prejudices and customary and all other practices which are based on the idea of the inferiority or superiority of either of the sexes or on stereotyped roles for men and women.

Female genital cutting is also criticized because it is viewed as a violation of children's rights as stipulated in the Children's Rights Convention (CRC). The United Nations Declaration of Rights of Children was adopted in 1959. It stipulates that each child should be given the opportunity "to develop physically, mentally, morally, spiritually and socially in a healthy and moral manner and in conditions of freedom and dignity," and should be "protected against 'all forms of neglect, cruelty, and exploitation'" (Shell-Duncan and Hernlund, 2000: 27). Because female genital cutting is performed on girls who are usually under 15 years of age, it exposes them to cruel and exploitative tendencies that endanger their health and general development, thus violating children's rights as defined in the CRC. It is, therefore, a violation of CRC Articles 2, paragraph 1; CRC Article 24, paragraph 1 and 3; and African Charter on the Rights and the Welfare of the Child Articles 4, paragraph 1; 5, paragraphs 2, 10; 14, paragraph 1; and 21, paragraphs 1(a) and (b). The negative effects of female genital cutting in children's development contravene the best interests of the child (Article 3). According to Article 19, Paragraph 1 of CRC:

States parties shall take all appropriate legislative, administrative, social, and educational measures to protect the child from all forms

of physical or mental violence, injury, or abuse, neglect or negli-
gent treatment, maltreatment or exploitation including sexual abuse
while in the care of parent(s), legal guardian(s), or any other person
who has the care of the child.

In addition, it is stated in the CRC Article 24, Paragraph 3 that:

States parties shall take all effective and appropriate measures with
the view to abolishing traditional practices prejudicial to the health
of children.

This fact is also stated in the African Charter on the Rights and the Welfare of the Child Article 21, Paragraph 1(a) and (b).

It is clear from the discussion above that the central place of universal
human rights to social and health concerns associated with female genital
cutting is significant. It is also clear that health and moral concerns about
female genital cutting are genuine. Expert opinion on the subject helps
validate these concerns. It is important therefore that industrialized countries should be concerned with the increase of the practice in their countries and indeed elsewhere. As is demonstrated in the opinions of those
who live with the risk and consequences of the practice, the controversy
in opinion is significant and plays a role in the persistence of female genital cutting in industrialized countries. It is important to note, however,
that the controversial view of female genital cutting complicates attitudes
and behavior toward the practice as well.

NOTES

1. Some women experience severe tearing; in some cases, the whole
   perineum of the rectum, including the sphincter, is torn. These tears
   can result in vesico-vaginal and rector-vaginal fistulae (openings
   between the vagina and the urethra or rectum), which result in an
   unstoppable flow of urine and the passage of feces through the vagina)
   as clearly explained by Shell-Duncan and Hernlund, 2002: 14).
2. *Inzert* can be accessed at http://www.zontaperth.org.au/files/Download/
   070606inzertJune2007.pdf.
3. The Advocates for Human Rights, "What are Human Rights," *The
   Rights of Workers in the United States* accessed at www.ohchr.org, August 2, 2011.

4

❖

Is "Political Correctness" Condoning Female Genital Cutting?

The cross-cultural approach begins by presuming that universal human rights represent the desirable end-state. It then inquires how, in a global order characterized descriptively by cultural pluralism, one may effectively establish conditions under which, more often than not, international human rights receive respect. The cross-cultural approach's answer is to manipulate and redeploy each culture's internal resources in the service of human rights. . . . Rather, the objective seems to reside in amalgamating the most broadly-shareable mores of each society in an effort to achieve an overlapping consensus of basic values that most cultures will respect most of the time. (Sloan, 2001: 580–581)

As Western countries globalize, they become centers of value conflict. Values that are often considered foreign have become a part of the postcolonial discourse on diversity in these countries as elsewhere. This fact is evident in current discourses surrounding female genital cutting, one of the foreign practices that has drawn the most interest internationally. Due to the fact that female genital cutting is associated with serious social issues and health risks, efforts to protect women and families from the practice have thrived. Most industrialized countries view the practice as a violation of the basic human rights of girls and children. Thus, the practice is criminalized in these countries on human rights grounds. Yet, as human rights and feminist activists call for the eradication of this practice, cultural diversity activists insist on defending the practice on the grounds of culture, under the cloak of groups' rights. Varied positions on this issue are not only apparent in the controversy surrounding these practices, but they also translate into the dilemma that is expressed in attitudes toward the practice and the general experience of women. One is left wondering whether political correctness is leading to behavior that is condoning the practice even in the industrialized world? Leyla Hussein seems to think so in a recent article, "Londoners sign Fake Pro-Female Genital Petition out of 'Political Correctness,' Anti-FGM Advocate Says" (Anna Davis, 2013).

Hussein, a 32-year-old Londoner who was exposed to female genital cutting was speaking to Davis about her study on attitudes toward female genital cutting in the United Kingdom. She conducted an experimental study to test the influence of multicultural discourse, which she calls "political correctness" on attitudes toward this practice. With a signed petition supporting female genital cutting, she approached shoppers and told them that she wanted to protect her "culture, traditions and rights." To her dismay, 19 people signed the petition after only 30 minutes. Some of those who signed the petition admitted that female genital cutting was wrong but agreed to sign because "it was part of Ms. Hussein's culture." Hussein's conclusion to the study was "many were scared to speak out against FGM because they worried about criticizing another culture." Hussein's campaign against FGM is titled "The Cruel Cut" and has been featured on TV programs (Davis, 2013).

In this chapter, I explore the implications of cultural diversity discourse and human rights discourse on the rights of women, with a particular reference to the rights to health and freedom from discrimination. Drawing from these discourses, I highlight the rationale behind the persistence of the practice in industrialized countries. I argue that claims about social groups' rights that are rooted in cultural diversity discourse tend to affirm corporate values and are likely to undermine individual rights. Although diverse religious values inform the practice of female genital cutting, human rights values should be the basis of interpreting these values if basic rights of all are to be protected. I also analyze assimilation expectations to question the assumption that immigrant communities should assimilate to their current cultures.

MORAL UNIVERSALISM

Moral universalism asserts that human beings are entitled to certain universal rights by virtue of being human. Moral universalism promotes freedom, justice, and peace—a set standard that the United Nations General Assembly and its 48 affiliate countries sanctioned as universal norms. The United Nations' Universal Declaration of Human Rights (UDHR) endorses these ideals, declaring that "Everyone has the right to liberty, 'all persons' are entitled to equal protection, 'no one shall be subjected to torture,' 'everyone' has the right to an adequate standard of living" (Steiner and Alston, 1996: 192–193). Moral universalism and human rights are based on four theories: natural law theory, the theory of rationalism, the doctrine of positivism, and human capabilities theory (Zechenter, 1997: 320–322; Billet, 4–5). Natural law theory holds that human beings possess a certain degree of sovereignty with regard to ideals such as freedom and honor and that all human beings possess this sovereignty equally. Natural law tends to imply divine guidance, suggesting that imposing any restriction on human sovereignty is morally wrong. The theory of rationalism argues that all humans, as rational beings, are sovereign beings equal to each other. According to the doctrine of positivism, countries with representative forms of government should promote universal norms of behavior According to the human capabilities theory, fundamental characteristics that define what it means to be human occur across diverse societies. These include the recognition of one's need for food, drink, shelter, and mobility; and the capacity for pain and pleasure. As Martha Nussbaum explains, universal human rights have evolved to ensure that the basic needs of the entire human population across all cultures are fulfilled (Nussbaum, 1995a: 76–80).

Moral universalist defenders of human rights argue against cultural practices that violate human rights such as female genital cutting. Although some moralists would argue that a social group has no right to impose its morality on voluntary members of the group in a liberal democratic society, they tend to respect the cultural practices of any group as long as they do not violate any basic human rights. A democratic government—as a liberal entity—should be neutral, but it should be willing to protect the rights of all minorities. Some feminists have demanded that policies be established to ensure that discriminatory practices are condemned, discouraged, and even criminalized. Others have argued that such practices should be eradicated in order to protect women's basic human rights.

The theory of moral universalism is often viewed as morally complicated. First, because it is associated with the West, it is often viewed as a plan to destroy diverse cultures in order to homogenize the world. Insofar as it draws from the Western liberal ideology and religious faith, mainly Christianity, it is considered to be absolute, arrogant, and imperialistic. It is also suspect because it embraces a social norm generally associated with the West, which has had the tendency to universalize its own norms—political, religious, and ideological—without regard for those of other social groups. Furthermore, because human rights norms are based on the Western notion of the individual, they also reflect one set of values—primarily Western values, which as Winter argues, are "culture specific" (1997: 503–504). The concept of human rights espoused by moral universalists is also relative to a particular cultural environment and historical context—the West. It is, therefore, biased, and likely judgmental. Cultural relativists have described international human rights standards as another version of neocolonialism.

It is due to such criticism that standard discourses about human rights have been resisted by some cultural and ethical relativists. They believe that all cultures are different; therefore, they resist value judgments made by outsiders on any culture (Ierodiaconou, 1995). They also view any legislation based on culture as judgmental and inappropriate. A Nigerian feminist, Amede L. Obiora, has argued that cultural standards and values are specific to certain peoples because humans tend "to generalize from their situated perspectives and realities that are influenced by assumptions" (1997: 277–288).

In response to moral universalist claims that cultural practices such as female genital cutting are sexist and patriarchal, and therefore in violation of basic human rights, cultural relativists insist on the need to recognize unique cultural values in which this practice is embedded. Some have argued that although patriarchal societies are generally unjust, not all practices in such societies are sexist or wrong. It is important that the functional role of cultural values is understood as contributing to the moral norms that inform them. If understood in context, one will realize that some of these practices are intended to protect women's interests. Citing the example of the controversial Muslim veil, for instance, Bonnie Honig has argued that veiling enables Muslim women who might otherwise stay at home because of their religious obligations about female modesty to go out into the world, acquire an education, and participate in public life (Honig, 1999). Similarly, while female genital cutting is harmful, as is clear based on scientific evidence, the functional role of the practice in providing the community with an atmosphere in which to bond and socialize should not be minimized. In other words, although a cultural practice may appear distasteful to some, the functional role of the practice should be given some importance. In essence, therefore, cultural diversity discourses promote the multiculturalism ideology, which recognizes difference as a reality. The need to recognize the importance of particularity, especially unique circumstances that shape social behavior, is emphasized.

GROUP RIGHTS ADVOCACY

Cultural diversity is a term used in debates on multiculturalism to emphasize groups' differences or identity politics and antidiscrimination policies. It draws from the cultural relativist approach, which emerged out of a critique of moral universalism, both locally and internationally. Drawing from a moral position derived from cultural relativism, proponents of group's rights have accused moral universalism of ethnocentrism, imperialism, and ignorance of the norms and moral values associated with the traditions of other cultures, like female genital cutting. Their position, which is informed by the demands of cultural diversity, insists that difference between women should be recognized (Butler, 1990). Feminists—cultural relativists particularly—tend to equate moral universalism with Western feminism. Acknowledging that every culture has a unique moral system, they argue that not all cultures conceive of the individual as existing separately from other members in their societies. By implication, therefore, a cultural practice such as female genital cutting must be examined within its cultural context.

Central to the cultural relativist discourse is the need to correct and prevent the misconceived imperialist attitudes and behaviors that have previously been associated with colonial agents who have embraced universal moral ideals. Questions of difference, which shape the discourse, first arose in the 1994 at the Cairo Conference on Population and Development. Here, some Muslim and Christian fundamentalists, including representatives of some Asian governments and leading members of the Catholic Church, united to oppose the idea of women's universal human rights on both cultural and doctrinal grounds. As Kalev explains, they challenged the concept of human rights as a Western imperialist ploy (Kalev, 2004: 345; Afkharmi and Fridi, 1997). By invoking cultural imperialism and intellectual colonialism, the concept of human rights was questioned as a moral principle suitable to be adopted by other non-Western cultures (Kalev, 2004: 345; Afkharmi and Fridi, 1997).

In 2001, for instance, the Universal Declaration on Cultural Diversity was adopted by UNESCO as a legal instrument that recognized the "common heritage of humanity," demonstrating the United Nations' sensitivity to this issue. In 2007, the Convention for the Safeguard of the Intangible Cultural Heritage was ratified by 78 nations. It was agreed that:

The intangible cultural heritage transmitted from generation to generation is constantly recreated by communities and groups in response to their environment, their interaction with nature and their history, and gives them a sense of identity and continuity, thus promoting respect for cultural diversity and human creativity. (UNESCO, 2003)

The need for sensitivity to cultural diversity was also reiterated in the Montreal Declaration of 2007, and by the European Union the same year. The United States has introduced cultural diversity programs in its federal offices. In 1996, for instance, the Immigration Naturalization Services (INS) was instructed to establish programs that educate both old and recent immigrants on how to survive and assimilate in American society, while maintaining their own culture and religion.

The cultural diversity discourse is informed by the cultural relativist theory, which dates back to the Greeks and developed in the disciplines of ethnology and ethnography in the early 20th century as a response to the inherent bias against non-Western societies (Renteln, 1990: 62–63). According to the theory of cultural relativism, rights and rules about morality are encoded in and dependent on a particular sociocultural context. Relativists argue that notions of right, wrong, and morality differ throughout the world because the cultures in which they are found differ. Therefore, no culture should impose its ideas or ideals on another culture (Steiner and Alston, 1996: 192–193). In other words, as a theory, cultural diversity or multiculturalism is a form of moral relativism that holds that ethical truth is relative to a specific culture. To impose any culture's moral concepts on another culture amounts to imperialism.

The term "culture" is often used in a broad and diffuse way to encompass not only indigenous or customary practices, but also political and religious ideologies and institutional structures. The moral question raised by cultural relativists is this: On what basis should a cultural group be denied the right to engage in its long-held cultural traditions? Who grants anyone the right to do this? Those sensitive to issues of cultural diversity recognize the reality of difference as expressed in a variety of social groups and experiences, such as gender, culture, race, religion, ethnicity, language, tradition, and morality. Theoretically, the discourse on cultural diversity is rooted in cultural relativism, a moral position in reaction to moral universalism. These two moral positions are often difficult to reconcile. According to cultural relativism, it is not right to say simply that a certain kind of behavior is right or wrong for all, as a moral universalist would. Rather, as moral relativists contend, a certain kind of behavior is right or wrong relative to a specific society (Holt, 2006).

In the realm of policy, cultural diversity fosters multicultural ideals, social ideals that encourage the recognition and accommodation of social difference as manifest in coexisting cultural and religious social groups. According to Sebastian Poulter, policymakers who align with multicultural ideals claim that the cultural practices of minority communities need to be "recognized and respected in the interests of liberal democracy" (1985: 593). Arguments for this moral approach tend to pursue inclusive policies that reflect fairness, respect, and commitment to the dignity of every person, regardless of their origin (Gilbert and Ivancevich, 2002). The ultimate goal of multiculturalism is the promotion of harmonious interactions, uniqueness, and plurality of identities among various groups. Stress is placed on the need to respect the culture within which the individual develops. Multicultural ideals, therefore, occur when many subcultures exist within the same jurisdictional framework. The need to protect and preserve the special group rights of minority cultures is paramount.

Cultural diversity activists who defend female genital cutting have often adopted the groups' rights approach, criticizing moral universalists for disregarding the cultural symbolism of this practice. In arguing for the need to recognize cultural values associated with female genital cutting, they describe it as a rite of passage necessary for girls to transition into adulthood and become responsible members of society. Related to this issue is social coercion. A girl who chooses not to be cut may risk social alienation and ostracization and may be ineligible for marriage. In communities where girls are economically dependent on men, it is difficult to discern who is actually making the decision that a girl will undergo the procedure. The dilemma on which this assumption is based is that the triumph of cultural rights ensures the marginalization of individual rights. Adhikaria and Salahi have observed that the pressure on doctors to perform female genital cutting on girls is immense—a fact that explains why doctors would want to perform the pinprick/nick form of the procedure. To some parents, criminalization of the practice is unfair as it is about culture, a group right. When parents in such situations are turned away, they often choose to transport their daughters abroad for vacation-cutting (Adhikaria and Salahi, 2010), which, as we have seen, can lead to serious health consequences. ·

Cultural relativists have argued that health issues associated with female genital cutting have been exaggerated and can be minimized if the practice is performed in sanitary facilities such as hospitals, or if safer forms of genital cutting commonly referred to as ceremonial pinprick nick or *sunna* are performed. For instance, Fuambai A. Ahmadu, an ardent defender of this position who was raised in the United States before traveling to Sierra Leone as an adult for genital cutting in her *Kono* community, has argued that critics of female genital cutting have exaggerated the medical dangers and misunderstood the effect of the procedure on sexual pleasure. She claims that westernized feminists hold the mistaken view that female genital cutting denies "us this critical aspect of becoming a woman in accordance with our unique and powerful cultural heritage" (Ahmadu, 2000). She continues:

> It is difficult for me—considering the number of ceremonies that I have observed, including my own—to accept that what appears to be expressions of joy and ecstatic celebrations of womanhood in actuality disguise hidden experiences of coercion and subjugation. Indeed, I offer that the bulk of Kono women who uphold these rituals do so because they want to—they relish the supernatural powers of their ritual leaders over against men in society, and they embrace the legitimacy of female authority and particularly the authority of their mothers and grandmothers. (Ahmadu, 2000)

TO NICK OR NOT?

This cultural relativist position became prominent in the United States during discussions about female genital cutting in April and May 2010, when the American Academy of Pediatrics (AAP) issued a policy statement on ritual genital cutting of female minors, calling for changes in a federal ban of all forms of the procedure. This nationally recognized medical organization was calling for legal changes to allow pediatrician physicians to perform a ceremonial pinprick or nick on the clitoris of newborn girls from communities that embrace female genital cutting. This way, it was argued, the doctors would remain "sensitive to the cultural and religious reasons that motivate parents to seek this procedure for their daughters" (Committee on Bioethics, 2010: 1092; Belluck, 2010).

The report claims that the outright ban of this procedure disregards any form of accommodation to custom or ritual. In the statement, the academy defended its position, arguing that "it was a way to potentially forestall what it sees as the more dire consequence of outright prohibition, namely, encouraging parents to send their daughters outside the U.S, where they would be subjected to 'disfiguring and life threatening procedures in their native countries'" (Committee on Bioethics, 2010: 1092; American Academy of Pediatrics, 2010). In the report, AAP argued, "Some forms of female genital cutting are described as less extensive than the new born male circumcision commonly performed in the West" (Committee on Bioethics, 2010).

Needless to say, the American Academy of Pediatrics' move caused uproar among human rights activists. The uproar was based on a number of concerns: First, the difficulty of reconciling human and collective rights had been raised. Second, the academy's ethical position was questioned for recommending a medically unnecessary surgical procedure that is essentially declared illegal in over 50 states. The main argument was to resist any form of alteration that would likely create loopholes for continued performance of female genital cutting.

PATRIARCHY AND SEXUAL CONTROL

This question is connected to the feminist concern about patriarchal and sexual control—arguments that are vehemently critiqued by some as unfounded. It has been argued in part that the description of female genital cutting as a patriarchal phenomenon is shallow, uninformed, and a misrepresentation of reality because other cultural values associated with this practice are ignored. The patriarchal paradigm of male control is rejected for contradicting some cross-cut gender cultural variables in which men and women relate and are bound together in social units, institutions, and categories as found in some communities (Obiora, 1997). It is also argued that the claim that the practice is embedded in patriarchy is untenable because patriarchal institutions exist beyond cutting societies, and girls and women are the most ardent defenders of female genital cutting (Ahmadu, 2000: 292–296; Shweider, 2000: 7–8; Boddy, 1989: 53–58). This is a critique of the patriarchy argument that I find misinformed because it either ignores how the socialization process works or is ignorant of it.

One area of critique for these cultural relativist feminists relates to the claims about the loss of sexual desire and the non-enjoyment of sexuality because of female genital cutting. It is argued that assertions that relate female genital cutting to the loss of sexual desire or non-enjoyment of sexual pleasure are erroneous and exaggerated (Obiora, 1997: 295; Ahmadu, 2000: 284). For instance, Ahmadu refutes the claim that female genital cutting leads to a loss of sexual desire and enjoyment of sexuality. Further, they argue, cultural patterns tend to structure sexual norms and experience differently. A general assumption that women in all societies desire sexual fulfillment is misleading since sexuality must be understood within the social contexts within which it is defined (Ahmadu, 2000: 284). Similarly, Amede L. Obiora has argued that norms about sexuality and even enjoyment of sex are determined by different cultural moral systems. She explains:

Article 5 of the Universal Declaration of Human Rights . . . stipulates: "No one shall be subjected to torture, or to cruel, inhuman, or degrading treatment or punishment." The meaning of this provision, though, is not self-evident. Conceptions of human dignity tend to be indeterminate and contingent, and what may appeal to one school as torture, may be absolved or approved of by another as culture. An act one may condemn as depreciative of human dignity may have been enacted by its practitioners as an enhancement of human dignity. The very act that one may construe as cruel and in violation of Article 5 may be embraced in cultures where it is practiced as a "technology of the body." (Obiora 1997: 277)

To these feminists, cultural patterns structure the sexual experience such that what is defined in one culture as sexual fulfillment may not be defined that way in another. They condemn the promotion of Western norms of sexual fulfillment that go contrary to those acceptable in female genital-cutting communities (Ahmadu, 284). Dr. Richard Shweder has critiqued Westerners who try to impose a zero-tolerance policy on female genital cutting for ignoring the fact that female genital cutting as an initiation rite is generally controlled by women who believe that it is a cosmetic procedure with aesthetic benefits. He criticizes Americans and Europeans for outlawing the practice, while at the same time, they endorse their own forms of genital modifications, such as the circumcision of boys or the cosmetic surgery for women called vaginal rejuvenation. Some cultural feminists have argued that female genital surgery was performed in developed countries such as the United States and England in the 19th century as a cure for masturbation, promiscuity, and nymphomania (Bulbeck, 1998).

THE QUESTION OF DOUBLE STANDARDS

The question of double standards has arisen in the cultural diversity discourse surrounding female genital cutting. As mentioned above, some cultural relativists have equated the procedure to male circumcision, a practice that is widely accepted even in industrialized countries such as the United States. D. L. Coleman, a defender of the nick or pinprick form of genital cutting, has argued that the procedure is less severe than the circumcision of boys. Under the Equal Protection Clause, he argued, hospitals must either perform such a procedure on girls, if requested, or stop circumcising boys (Coleman, 1998: 717–783). The frustration of immigrant women with the double standard is clearly articulated by Layla Guled, a Somali immigrant who works with immigrant patients at the African Women's Health Center in the United States. Guled explains, "They felt like it's not right, and I don't blame them." The custom is "something they've known all their lives. Sometimes they say, 'Layla, I'm so worried. Who's gonna marry my daughter?'" (Tuhus-Dubrow, 2007). To cultural relativists, however, female genital cutting is a group's right that ought to be protected because it is already deemed culturally legitimate. In response to those who consider groups' right a form of social coercion, cultural diversity proponents have argued that consent should be prioritized if cultural practices such as female genital cutting are to be seen as legitimate. This position has however been criticized by advocates against female genital cutting as illusive since advocacy of group's rights rarely acknowledges individual rights.

To cultural relativists, therefore, the fundamental question is this: Should outsiders have the right to comment on a cultural practice that they do not subscribe to or understand? Defenders of the practice have argued for the need to recognize the complexity of cultural values and cultural practices embraced in some communities. It is important that these cultural practices are evaluated within their own cultural and moral framework. They emphasize the need for female genital cutting to be understood as a norm that is embedded in a given social structure.

SOCIAL NORMS OR ROMANTICISM?

There are problems, however, with the way cultural relativists defines a social norm. Cultural relativists have been criticized for assuming that everyone in a given community is acting on a unanimously held opinion. As Kalev validly observes, they fail to recognize that an individual can be oppressed in a social group by social norms that are acceptable in his or her community. As Alison Jaggar explains, some of these individuals may desire a cultural change that the larger community is not ready to accept (1988). In this regard, feminist cultural relativists are cautioned to be careful not to defend cultural difference at the expense of the rights of individuals in their communities. Kalev is right in observing that the feminism they espouse is likely to preserve the status quo in communities simply on the grounds of cultural norms. By "abandoning the original feminist goals of promoting equal rights for women," these feminists have found themselves justifying practices such as female genital cutting by making parallels with Western practices of cosmetic surgery (Kalev, 2004: 347). It is important to recognize that while the West has its own practices that undermine the rights of girls and women, these practices are not necessarily acceptable to Western feminists. They are also not culturally imposed on children, as is the case with female genital cutting.

This critique is often related to queries about the romanticism that surrounds the idea of cultures—a biased portrayal of cultural systems as good, pure, and devoid of immoral injustices. A position that resists critical appraisal of any social situation is likely to mask social injustices in a given cultural context. According to Francis Beckwith and Gregory Koukl, cultural romanticism as a form of extreme relativism can lead to a world in which nothing is wrong—nothing is considered evil or good, nothing worthy of praise or blame. It would be a world in which justice and fairness are meaningless concepts, in which there would be no accountability, no possibility of moral improvement, no moral discourse and no tolerance (Beckwith and Koukl, 1998: 69). As Beckwith and Koukl explain, a cultural relativist position presents one with a world in which moral questions are left to the social group and the critical interrogation of ethical justice, human rights, human integrity, freedom of choice, and modernity is not done.

RECONCILING LIBERAL AND CORPORATE VALUES

The other problem with cultural relativism as manifest in multiculturalism in the modern industrialized world lies with the direct conflict between liberal democratic values and corporate values. While democratic liberal values are essentially rooted in moral universalism in the sense that they protect individual freedoms, corporate values are rooted in the cultural relativist values in the sense that they protect groups' rights. Thus, while democratic values tend to promote individual freedoms in the sense of the right of choice, cultural relativist values have been critiqued for undermining these freedoms through social coercion. Some cultural relativists have insisted on cultural determinism in an effort to prevent any form of compromise. As Tilley observes:

> Relativists are likely to revise the ethnocentricism argument so that it avoids our criticism. According to the new argument, even if universalists are not ethnocentric in the usual sense, any list of precepts they produce is bound to be culturally biased. This is ensured by the well-established thesis of cultural determinism, according to which all of our beliefs, concepts and perceptions are culturally conditioned to such an extent that unbiased thoughts, choices, and inferences are impossible. (Tilley, 2000: 540)

By adopting the groups' rights approach, individual rights are, in essence, compromised, especially in a situation where these rights are granted and not asserted. In most female genital-cutting communities, for instance, corporate values dictate that the practice be imposed on the individual regardless of their own choice. It is because of this focus on a group's rights that some advocates of cultural diversity have been critiqued for neglecting individual rights and autonomy. In such a society, as John Rawls (1971) argues, the individual needs to belong to a rich and secure cultural structure in order to develop self-respect; a strong identity is valued over the ability to make independent choices.

Scholars such as W. Kymlicka have argued that any liberal democratic society should allow meaningful individual choice (1991: 169). A group's right should not entail the suppression of individual rights or liberty; otherwise, it contradicts the major purpose of group rights (Kymlicka, 1991: 169). As Poulter rightly observes, cultural tolerance should not be a cloak for promoting oppressive and unjust practices (Poulter, 1986: 593). Individual members of a cultural community must be voluntary participants, entitled to leave their social groups if they so desire (Kalev, 2004). Kukathas reiterates this argument when he proposes that the individual should have the right to choose even those cultural practices that others may perceive as oppressive. He explains, "Liberal political theories rest on the assumptions that while the interests given expression in groups, cultural communities, or other such collectives do not matter, they matter ultimately only to the extent that they affect actual individuals" (Kukathas, 1995: 234). It has also been argued that the cultural diversity debate often ignores the dynamic nature of all cultural phenomena, especially the role of social change. Although a cultural community should be allowed to pursue its own traditional practices, modern societies should recognize the importance of individual rights and freedom of choice. Social groups, as social phenomena, are bound to adapt as they encounter social change. As they adapt, they often discard irrelevant values, while retaining useful ones. According to Kymlicka, group rights should only be applicable to a social group that itself accepts liberal democratic principles. This is because liberal values require both individual freedom of choice and a secure cultural context from which individuals can make their own choices.

THE DILEMMA OF VOLUNTARISM

While proponents of group rights tend to argue for the voluntary participation of group members, the term "voluntary" is often difficult to measure, especially where children are concerned. Cultural relativists have argued that as social group rights are granted, the right to individual consent should be guaranteed in these groups. Membership must be voluntary in order to prevent social coercion. What is often ignored is the fact that a person can desire to remain a member of a community for a variety of reasons, including cultural affinity, family connection, or definitions imposed on them by the society. As Kalev validly observes, actions that may seem voluntary may result from processes of persuasion, indoctrination, and implicit or explicit threats carried out within the community

(Kalev, 2004: 342). This is often part of the socialization process that the individual is exposed to in a larger cultural setting.

In my earlier studies on female genital cutting, I encountered numerous cases where girls and women who were against female genital cutting ended up succumbing to the practice due to social pressure. They sought to impress parents-in-law and husbands-to-be, and to avoid being killed. Similarly, there were recorded cases where girls "consented" to polygamous marriages in order for her parents to collect a sizeable bride price to help alleviate economic difficulty the family might be facing. Arguments about consent also ignore the contradiction that this requirement poses for social groups. For informed consent to occur, it must be preceded by liberal education. Therefore, although multiculturalists have defended cultural values and practices by insisting that voluntarism or informed consent should be ensured, it is sometimes impossible to protect group members from social coercion. This is the perceived threat of the multiculturalism ideology to individual rights. As illustrated earlier, parents continue to make decisions for their children—a fact that is evident in the parental pressure placed on doctors to perform female genital cutting. To evade laws that criminalize the practice, some parents have resorted to having their young daughters cut in their younger age, even as infants. In addition, as we have seen, some Africans in the diaspora take their children on vacations abroad to have genital cutting done. In most immigrant communities, parents believe that it is their responsibility to make decisions for their children; as indicated earlier, this corporate moral responsibility is embedded in non-Western value systems. They are convinced that this practice is necessary because it is a cultural virtue. As a result, it is difficult to ensure voluntary participation or informed consent in cultural practices where coercion is likely to occur and especially where the discussion of issues such as female genital cutting is considered taboo.

Although it is important to embrace cultural heritage and the values associated with a specific culture or religion, cultural practices that have become irrelevant or even dangerous should be abandoned. For instance, while a practice such as female genital cutting was symbolic and relevant in the indigenous cultural settings of the communities in which it was originally practiced, as medical knowledge advances, underlying health concerns should force a community to reevaluate these values. To defend a cultural practice such as female genital cutting while ignoring the health and other social concerns the practice raises is not only hypocritical, it is a violation of the basic rights of those exposed to the deleterious effects associated with such practice. To protect girls and women from these discriminatory norms is not only to seek social justice for half of the individual members of the community, but it is to attempt to transform discriminatory cultural systems. Insisting on maintaining the practice in medicalized or transformed nick or pinprick form, while appealing to those who value cultural symbolism, is to expose girls to proven social and health consequences. As we embrace scientific and other modern values, we need to recognize this reality. Endorsing any cultural practice that undermines women's rights is not only immoral in a democratic society; it displays a lack of attention to real facts on the ground.

Clearly, respect for cultural diversity is important. Feminists should be careful, however, not to invoke cultural relativism if this means promoting the very oppressive values they fight so hard to eradicate. As they seek to defend cultures, they should defend women who do not want to be cut or to cut their daughters in the name of cultural tradition. Although differences of opinion should be recognized, feminism as a movement must continue to defend the basic human rights of women everywhere.

TOWARD CROSS-CULTURAL UNIVERSALS

Human rights claims and appeals to multiculturalism are therefore the manifestation of the perceived conflict between moral universalism and cultural relativism. The conflict is about an argument about individual rights and cultural rights, which may translate as individual harm and communal harm. These two positions—moral universalism and cultural relativism—can be dogmatic extremes, making it difficult to protect individual human rights. Several questions underlie this discourse, however: How is one to ensure that basic standards of social justice are upheld and defined in the provision of both individual and group rights? How are the differing values in the claims of both individual and group rights to be reconciled without infringing on the rights of the other? How is one to argue for controversial collective and individual rights in the social context in which women live with culturally legitimated practices such as female genital cutting, without undermining these women's basic rights to health and general welfare? Most importantly, what role does the state have in negotiating these values and rights? Sloan asks an essential question: By what criteria should it be determined that culture violates universal standards? (Sloan, 2001: 531). Although it may seem as though these two positions have no common ground, I demonstrate in this book that common ground does indeed exist. Borrowing Sloan's and Bret Billet's arguments on cross-cultural universals, I argue for a cultural dialogue that also recognizes cultural dynamism as a fact that centers on the welfare of the individual.

It is apparent from the foregoing that multiculturalism and cultural pluralism are often defended under the contemporary liberal multicultural model, a model that appreciates cultural difference and the rights of social groups. This argument has its virtues, but I argue here that cultural diversity as a discourse brings with it serious social implications for women (Parekh, 1999: 121; Grillo, 1998: 189). Commenting on the possibility of pursuing social justice in a multicultural situation, Iris Young reminds us that, whereas difference as displayed in multicultural values can be a source of power, recognition, identity, and emancipation for the marginalized social groups, it can also be an instrument of social exploitation, marginalization, violence, and especially cultural imperialism (Young, 1990: 39–63, 163). In fact, too much attention to multiculturalism can easily lead to romanticization of cultures and of cultural values that undermine social justice.

It has been established that female genital cutting is associated with serious health risks, including severe pain, hemorrhaging, shock, acute urine and menstrual blood retention, infection, abscesses, ulcers, septicemia, tetanus, birth complications, and sometimes, death (Australian National University, 2006). To deny this reality in order to uphold cultural traditions is a moral absurdity. In order to negotiate the seemingly unbreachable chasm between universalism and cultural relativism, cultures should evolve to the point where they can at least accommodate human rights standards. A middle ground must be sought, even though this may not be entirely satisfying to those on either side.

To reach this middle ground, we must identify general guidelines, which Sloan and Billet call "cross-cultural universals" (Sloan, 580; Billet, 183–185). These guidelines must be preceded by an acceptance of the fact that all cultures, both Western and non-Western, suffer from ethnocentrism and a commitment to preserving the values, beliefs, and morals that define their people. As Billet explains, the failure to recognize this fact is the reason for perennial conflict between moral universalists and cultural relativists and makes it difficult to apply human rights universals in diverse cultures (Billet, 184).

To resolve this conflict, all parties must work to achieve a deep understanding of diverse cultures. As a fundamental step toward cross-cultural understanding, we might ask the following questions:

1. Whose voices are being heard in a specific culture?
2. Who defines culture and who has the power to define it?
3. Who benefits from the said definition and who does not?
4. How can all voices be heard?
5. How can education be designed to empower those without power? (Reichert, 2006: 29)

Since cultural relativism challenges the logic behind acknowledging one set of values—international human rights as universal value—it is important that the proponents of universal human rights provide guidance about when and under what conditions international actors may justifiably intervene in the affairs of sovereign states to deter, terminate, or redress human rights violations. It is also important to review widely accepted human rights to ensure that they are relevant to a great number of cultures. A criterion should be developed to determine whether a culture violates universal standards before the international human rights community intervenes. But this criterion should be continually revisited; it should never be viewed as absolute (Sloan, 2001: 531). Although it is important to recognize difference as a social fact that defines all human cultures and societies, cultural relativists should not insist on the concept of tolerance at the expense of individual rights. Where individuals are likely to be harmed by cultural values, assimilation and enculturation options should be pursued.

Where a cultural practice such as female genital cutting is involved, it is important that a serious inquiry into the role of the practice in a culture be examined and understood. It is important, for instance, to examine the origin or history of the practice, the specifics of the practice, and its cultural relevance, noting areas of cultural clash and implications for local and foreign relations. It is particularly important that clear solutions are arrived at so that areas of conflict can be addressed. To return to female genital cutting, for instance, determining that it dates back to the sixth century and was practiced in ancient but powerful societies such as Greece, Rome, Egypt, Phoenicia, Babylonia, Syria, and Arabia helps one understand how widespread and resilient the practice has been, even in the face of external pressure. It helps to know that this practice predates some of the religions it is associated with, such as Islam. A deep knowledge of the specifics associated with the practice, such as the different types of genital cutting, along with the different values ascribed to the practice, enables one to understand whether to categorize it as a human rights violation or not. Understanding that the culture rationalizes the practice as a tradition helps one to discern the role of socialization and to note how a practice is defined and shaped within a given social structure. Once this is understood, efforts toward cross-cultural transformation can then be made by seeking common values to promote unity in diversity.

CULTURES AND SOCIAL CHANGE

Cultures are dynamic institutions that change as societies change. One way in which cultures are transformed is through assimilation. According to the assimilation theory, as generational transition occurs, the distinct ethnocultural characteristics tend to fade in strength over time (Gordon,

1964; Goldscheider and Goldscheider, 1989; Alba, 1995; Wilmolh et al., 1997; Abbas-Shavazi and McDonald, 2000; Arias, 2001). Assimilation as a cultural change phenomenon can also occur in an amorphous manner. This means, depending on characteristics of the population education, skills, culture, opportunities, and social discrimination—the assimilation path can result in either abandonment of ethno-cultural characteristics or reinforcement of these characteristics. Where discrimination is a factor, it can become a barrier to social acceptance. As a result, cultural values often become a shelter from corrosive social conditions.

Developed countries now home to immigrants whose cultural traditions include female genital cutting have taken varying stances on whether immigrant women should be allowed to continue the practice. In the Netherlands, female genital cutting is illegal. It is prohibited under general criminal law Articles 300–304 of the Dutch Pena; Code, title XX, where it qualifies as a form of abuse. In the Netherlands, a culprit is allowed to press charges regarding female genital cutting after she turns 18, just as in other cases of sexual abuse. In Australia, laws covering female genital cutting have been in force in six of the eight Australian states since 1994–1997. Although the Constitution does not include the Bill of Rights, it acknowledges rights and liberties in judicial and legislative efforts. It also considers female genital cutting a human rights issue. In Europe, female genital cutting was declared a human rights violation in accordance to the European Union Parliament Resolution on Female Genital Mutilation of 2001. Although there is no specific law outlawing female genital cutting, France has relied on existing criminal legislation to prosecute both practitioners of the practice and parents who procure the services for their daughters. French law calls for prison sentences of up to 20 years for parents who subject their daughters to female genital cutting as well as for those who perform the procedure.

The United Kingdom is the first European country to introduce a specific criminal law prohibiting female genital cutting. Although there is no constitution or bill of rights in the United Kingdom about female genital cutting, the 1985 Prohibition of Female Circumcision Act made it a criminal offence for any person to perform this procedure and for other persons to aid, abet, counsel, or procure the performance of these acts. Anyone guilty of this offense is liable to a fine or to imprisonment for a period not exceeding five years or to both. The penalty for performing genital cutting was increased from 5 years to 14 years imprisonment in 2003. In the United States, legislation criminalizing female genital cutting was enacted by the 1995 bill and provides for prison of up to five years for anyone who engages in the practice against anyone who has not attained the age of 18 years. These countries failed to foresee the persistence of cultural values among immigrants. The situation is similar to what is observed in the United Kingdom.

Although change is necessary in any society, it is often gradual, and historically, this has been for the good. Social change requires an educational process that slowly alters attitudes toward cultural behavior. For change to be effective and well received, it must seem to emanate from within. Real cultural transformation can only take place if community members recognize that they need to change. One hindrance to social change is the persistence of ethnocentric views. It is important that initiators of change find a way to address the power of those who hold these views. In the case of female genital cutting, this includes finding ways to address social ideas such as patriarchy that tend to promote attitudes that deny members of the society certain basic human rights. If those who hold power in these societies can be engaged, there is a chance that human rights can be upheld to the benefit of diverse cultural communities.

In concluding this chapter, I argue that multiculturalism as presented in the cultural diversity discourse fulfills a healthy and vital need for the invigoration of lost cultural heritage. Clearly, diversity is a social reality that should be embraced by all in our modern, pluralistic, and globalizing world. This discourse is an essential tool for countering colonial and imperialistic attitudes that have dominated our society for centuries. All cultural values have contributions to make to the wider knowledge base. But although cultural difference in all societies should be embraced, appreciated, and encouraged, cultural values should not be used to undermine human rights. Culture should not be a cloak that masks social injustices.

It is important that as cultural diversity is promoted, cultural appraisal should also be encouraged in order to promote a progressive form of cultural heritage. Cultural heritage should evolve and change in accordance with values that are embraced by each culture or group. Measures must be put in place, however, to ensure that basic human rights are not violated. It is particularly important that women's rights, both in industrialized countries and elsewhere, are respected and protected at all levels. As social groups' rights are advocated for in modern societies around the world, the notion of basic human rights must also be embraced as a defining variable. While most industrialized countries acknowledge the plights of specific social groups and grant them the right to practice their culture, they must assert these rights with attention to ethical and social justice issues. By promoting an environment within which basic human rights of children, girls, and women are protected within a cultural community, all are encouraged to abide by the values that prevail in these countries.

It is in recognition of this fact that those opposed to female genital cutting, such as Taine Bien-Aime, the president of the international human rights organization, *Equality Now,* have discouraged any form of female genital cutting, including pinprick or *sunna.* Activists against the practice have argued that allowing any form of the practice may legitimate abuse and suffering for many women. Aime explained her position in reference to the AAP's initial proposal that a nick or pinprick should be considered for the female genital cutting communities. He argued, "What the AAP is in fact doing is 'wink wink, nod, nod' in order to protect patients from a possible worse form of female genital cutting. The reality is that such a statement perpetuates female genital mutilation in all forms" (ABC WorldNews, 2010). While it is important to discourage the practice by resisting any form of modification, it is important to be sensitive to the needs of immigrants and to approach the subject in a sensitive manner. Dr. Nawal Nour, the director of the African Women's Health Center at Brigham and Women's Hospital in Boston, Massachusetts, takes a softer approach, explaining that it is important not to vilify the immigrant community (Adhikai and Salahi, 2010).

5

❖

Religious Side to Female Genital Cutting

Although female genital cutting is considered by many to be a cultural practice, it is also associated with religion. While adherents of specific religions practice female genital cutting, some believe the practice is sanctioned by their religious values.[1] To understand how religious values contribute to the persistence of female genital cutting, it is important to explore the relationship between culture, religion, and the historical origins of the practice. In this chapter, I argue that religious values are in part responsible for the persistence of female genital cutting in industrialized countries such as the United States. In my analysis, I engage the discussion that indigenous values and practices are uncivilized or static, and therefore unable to adapt to social change. I argue that while female genital cutting is indigenous to native cultures and religions, its persistence in modern society is indicative of its tenacity and ability to adapt and find relevance.

Of the 113 respondents interviewed, over 60 percent connected the persistence of female genital cutting in immigrant communities with tradition or culture.[2] Often, it is difficult for some Africans to distinguish between tradition, culture, and religion because in the African worldview, these mean the same. Although 25 percent considered religion to be a factor, this is significant. The fact that some of these respondents believe that the practice is a religious injunction is crucial ᵢf religion in the practice. One of my infor-

, and foremost Africans. Therefore we are not
ιcestors' tradition just because we live in the
merica. We must continue to pride ourselves in
ιgion of our forefathers. They followed it for a rea-
soɪ.   /ith Kofi, 2003)

Gitobu, another informant, argued, "Since Abraham was circumcised as a sign of his faith in God, we also should emulate him if we want to be righteous before God the way he was" (Interview, 2005).

Similar sentiments about the practice have been expressed by people interviewed in the mass media. In an interview aired on Al-Mihwar Television on May 10, 2007, Egyptian villagers link female genital cutting to Islam.

Investigator: In the Islamic religion, and in the villages and neigh-borhoods, it is always said that girls should be circum-cised just like boys. Does it come from the *Sunna*, or is it a custom of yours?

Female Villager: Circumcision is part of the *Sunna* of the Prophet. We used to bring a *daya*, and she would circumcise the chil-dren, but when the role of the *daya* was abolished, we stopped. Now we take our children to the doctor, and he circumcises them.

Investigator: So it is the doctor who circumcises the girl?

Female villager: Yes. If a girl is not circumcised, she can't stand it. When she is circumcised, she is calm and has self-restraint. The circumcision protects the girl and makes her calm.

Investigator: So you think all women should be circumcised to pro-tect their honor.

Female villager: The Prophet said that the men go and wage Jihad for a year. He said that girls should be circumcised so they can bear it for a whole year until the men return. (Sheikyermami, 2007)

In an interview aired on Al-Mihwar TV on May 10, 2007, Al-Azhar cleric Farahat Said Al-Munji explains that female circumcision is a choice, but clearly associates it with religion:

The Prophet said that circumcision is obligatory for men, and is noble for women. This means that for the sake of her honor, a woman can be circumcised. This noble act can be either carried out or not. (Farhat, 2012)

Syarief Hamid, the treasurer of the Assalaam Foundation who also runs several Islamic schools in Jakarta Bandung, suggested that religion was the main reason for circumcisions, but also cited health reasons. "I understand that a girl who is not circumcised would not have clean genitals after she urinates and sometimes that can cause cervical cancer. The religious view is, if you are not circumcised you won't have clean genitals after you urinate. If then you pray, your prayer won't be legal" (Moore, 2004). The Assalaam Foundation has held free mass circumcisions for males and females for almost 50 years, with 400 people participating in total. The circumcisions were timed to honor the Prophet's birthday and were growing in popularity each year.

The Center for Reproductive Health, on the contrary, does not recognize female genital cutting as a religious practice. It is viewed as a cultural practice. In a statement, it notes:

Communities that practice FGM maintain their customs and preserve their cultural identity by continuing the practice . . . While religious duty is commonly cited for the justification of FGM, it is important to note that FGM is a cultural, not religious, practice. In fact while FGM is practiced by Jews, Christians, Muslims, and members of other indigenous religions, in Africa, none of these religions require it. (Center for Reproductive Rights, 2004)

Clearly, there is controversy over the role of religion in the practice of female genital cutting around the world. To understand this relationship, one must begin by examining what it meant to ancient cultures.

ANCIENT AND INDIGENOUS CLAIMS

As indicated earlier, the origins of female genital cutting date back thousands of years. It has been argued that the practice predates God's covenant with Abraham to circumcise his people, thus predating both the Bible and the Quran because it dates back 4,000–5,000 years (Elchalala, et al., 1997: 643–651; Bastow, 1999). While this assertion does not necessarily negate the religious claims, it is difficult to pin the practice on one specific religion. In my previous work, I trace the themes of natural androgeneity, bisexuality, and hermaphroditism to ancient and indigenous claims about the origin of female genital cutting. According to these claims, special characteristics of the gods, which are part of human souls, are also manifest in the bisexuality of individuals and are possessed at birth. This belief is traced to Egyptian Pharaonic mythology, which claims that human beings, who are naturally created as androgynous, must be circumcised in order to perfect their femininity or masculinity (Shalam, 1982: 271). Genital cutting is believed to be rooted in the mythical idea that the foreskin represents the feminine part of the male and the clitoris the masculine part of the female. The removal of extra tissue through genital cutting was believed to help define one's sexuality. This notion of natural androgeneity, intrinsic bisexuality, and physical hermaphroditism that were part of the Egyptian Pharaonic belief in the hermaphroditic nature of their deities is similar, in some ways, to those found in some indigenous communities. It was believed that if one was uncircumcised, his or her inherent bisexual natures would compete during sexual intercourse to disrupt coitus and the reproductive process. Furthermore, it was believed that by circumcising both girls and boys, human beings could and should prevent this bisexual nature, an extraordinary characteristic appropriate only for the gods (Abu-Saleh, 2001: 223–224; Ahmadu, 2000: 295–296). According to Egyptian Pharaonic belief,

> Just as certain gods are believed to be bisexual, so every person is believed to be endowed with the masculine and feminine "souls". These souls reveal their respective physiological characteristics in and through the procreative organs. Thus, the feminine soul of the man is in the prepuce, whereas the masculine soul of the woman is situated in the clitoris. This means that as the young boy grows up and is finally admitted into the masculine society, he has to shed his feminine properties. This is accomplished by the removal of the prepuce, the feminine portion of his original sexual state. The same is true with a young girl, who upon entering the feminine society is delivered from her masculine properties by having her clitoris or her clitoris and her labia excised. Only thus circumcised can the girl claim to be fully a woman and thus capable of the sexual life. (Shalam, 1982: 271)

In most indigenous communities of Africa, a similar explanation of the origin of female genital cutting exists. The Dogon and Bambara of Mali, West Africa, for example, believe that female genital cutting is used to distinguish the sex of a child. They argue that when a child is born, it has two souls, which are inhabited by an evil spirit or power—*wanzo*—that prevents fertility. To destroy the power of *wanzo*, the prepuce and the clitoris must be cut off (Griaule, 1965: 21). The myth clearly narrated in this community describes how the Supreme Being—*Amma*—created the earth from clay, and had intercourse with her.

The earth, which is often viewed as the feminine aspect in the universe, is described in feminine terms. Its sexual organ, the vulva, is represented by an anthill. This act, often described in this Dogon myth as the first breach of the order of the universe, is considered to have caused all the troubles in the world. Below is the myth as described by Marcel Griaule thus:

> The God Amma . . . took a lump of clay, squeezed it in his hand and flung it from him, as he had done with stars. The clay spread and fell on the north, which is the top, and from there stretched out to the south, the bottom, of the world, although the whole movement was horizontal. The earth lies flat. . . . It extends east and west with separate members like a fetus in the womb. . . . This body, lying flat, face upwards . . . is feminine. Its sexual organ is an anthill, and its clitoris a termite hill. Amma, being lonely and desirous of intercourse with this creature, approached it. . . . At God's approach the termite hill rose up, barring the passage and displaying its masculinity. It was as strong as the organ of the stranger, and intercourse could not take place. But God is all-powerful. He cut down the termite hill, and had intercourse with excised earth . . . from this defective union there was born, instead of the intended twins, a single being Thos aureus or jackal, a symbol of difficulties of God. (Griaule, 1970: 17)

To the Dogon, therefore, god is the origin of human troubles. According to this myth, the clitoris obstructed any sexual union because it housed the jealous male aspect of the female earth, which resisted the Supreme Being's sexual advances (Griaule, 1965: 17).

Consequently, God had further intercourse with his wife—the earth—without further mishaps. Water, the divine seed, entered the womb of the earth, and a normal reproductive cycle led to the birth of the Nummo twins, two beings that were half human and half serpents. These spirit beings were homogenous products of the blending of God and divine essence like himself. They were created from God's seed—water—the substance of life force. While in heaven, the Nummo twins brought garments from heavenly plants as garments to cover the earth's nakedness. These garments, placed over their mother's genitalia, were filled by water and speech, which symbolize Nummo's presence. The jackal, the deluded and deceitful son of God, desired to possess speech, and therefore laid hands on his mother's skirt, in which language was embodied. This act is often interpreted as an incestuous action on the part of the jackal. The earth resisted by burying herself in her own womb—in the anthill, disguised as an ant. Since the hole the earth made was not deep enough, the Jackal found her and was able to have intercourse with his mother. This action initiated the struggle between men and women, which often ends in the victory of the male.

Realizing the havoc that the Jackal was causing, the Nummo's spirit sought to balance things. As we have seen, according to this myth, all human beings are created as androgynous beings with both male and female souls—a status similar to that of the gods. When the spirits realized that each human being was endowed with two souls of different sex, or two principles corresponding to two distinct persons, they understood that humans are not capable of supporting both beings. To ensure proper balance, each person would have to transform himself or herself into the sex for which he or she appeared to be best fitted. The Nummo therefore circumcised the man to remove the femininity from his prepuce, symbolized by a lizard-like animal called *nay*. The removal of the woman's masculinity was achieved by detaching her clitoris, which was symbolized by the scorpion. Possessing a dual soul is dangerous, the Dogon believe, and the only remedy is circumcision. Through excision, they believe, the Nummo comes down to earth to enter the anthill, thus replacing the masculine element in the male and the feminine element in the female. This way, the Nummo pair can proceed to work with Amma in the original regeneration of life (Griaule, 1970: 16–29).

Hence, as boys grow up, they are expected to shed their female souls by removing the prepuce, a necessary condition for admission into masculine society and adulthood. Meanwhile, girls are expected to shed their male souls by removing part or all of the entire clitoris and the labia in order to be admitted into feminine society, and hence womanhood. It is therefore necessary that circumcision of both the girls and the boys is performed to perfect the femininity and the masculinity of the girl and the boy. The Dogon are said to be of Egyptian descent. They lived in Libya for some time before their migration to Mali, West Africa. In most African communities, it is believed that prayer must be offered during the genital-cutting ritual to stabilize the soul of the initiates and to help release the unwanted masculine or feminine spiritual force that will hinder the initiates from fulfilling the gender and sexual roles expected of them. Through genital cutting, the masculine or feminine self is reborn. It is in this sense that most Africans who practice female genital cutting view it as a decree of the gods or ancestors. It is assumed that those who are circumcised attract blessings that include fertility, good health, and general welfare. A woman whose genitals are not cut is likely to be promiscuous, in addition to encountering misfortunes arising from curses and the wrath of her ancestors and gods. Misfortunes associated with failure to undergo genital cutting are believed to include infertility, still births, the death of siblings or a spouse, incurable diseases, insanity, and even death (Wangila, 2007).

The persistence of the Dogon/Bambara myth in modern African communities is clearly illustrated in the speech of Ngonya, the leader of a revival movement known as the Thaai Fraternity of Kenya. He explains:

> Our organization is called Thaai Fraternity of Kenya bent on salvaging our sinking boat or ship of our African traditional religion through reviving the lost values of our forefathers. I am not propagating anything but I am saying what our forefathers were instructed by the almighty, the creator, so in our society, we do not have mutilation. What we have and we still advocate for it is female clitoridectomy. This is very simple biologically for those who know that a man and a woman have got both organs. So, I Ngonya, before I was circumcised I had both organs. I had two organs in me and time had to come when the two organs were supposed to be separated. For the woman, the female organ is that thing they keep fighting for—the clitoris. And for the man, what represents the woman in the man is the foreskin, So you see, because of the wisdom of the almighty the creator, the foreskin had to be taken off and that other thing hanging had to be taken off, so that now we can meet free people together. (Longinotto, 2002)

These myths remain persistent in Africa and even in diasporic communities. According to Laurenti Magesa, female genital cutting is deliberately intended to be painful. The girls are expected to be stoic and courageous—qualities that are celebrated in indigenous communities. It is argued that if boys and girls do not display courage and bravery, "the clan's life force withers and dies" (Magesa, 1997: 18). Bravery was necessary to defend a community for men and procreation for women. The ritual also taught self-denial and the reality of suffering. Identity formation, which is also significant in the values associated with this ritual, is believed to be part of initiation. The blood that is shed serves as a binding force, uniting initiates with ancestors. As initiates mingle and share blood through initiation knife, herbs, and meals, brotherly and sisterly love is established between initiates. Reintegration of initiates into society signifies their physical and moral maturity and the approval of their new status by the clan's ancestors.

JUDEO-CHRISTIAN INFLUENCE

Although female genital cutting is not mentioned in the Hebrew Bible, there is evidence that it was practiced among some Jews. Studies indicate that around 1,000 tribes of Eastern Jews practiced female genital cutting to reduce sexual sensitivity. Strabo, a Greek philosopher of the first century BCE, mentions female genital cutting as a practice of Creophagi Jews when he says, "The males have their sexual glands mutilated and the women are excised in the Jewish fashion" (Kessler, 2012: 50). He continues, "One of the customs most zealously observed among the Egyptians is this, that they rear every child that is born, and circumcise the males and excise the females, as is also customary among the Jews who are also Egyptian in origin, as I have already stated in my account of them (UNHCR: 3–4).

Strabo also remarks that the successors of Moses practiced "circumcision and excision." In another passage, he explains how "the Creophagi (lit.: "meat eaters") of Ethiopia . . . are mutilated in their sexual organs and the women are excised in the Jewish manner" (Remondino, 1891: 28–30). Strabo was referring to the Falasha Jews of Ethiopia, who are said to have practiced female genital cutting in Jerusalem during King Solomon's time. Those of their descendants who are presently found in Ethiopia continue to perform excision on their women, casting doubt on claims that African cultural traditions are the source of the practice among this group.

Female genital cutting was also performed among the Jews in Egypt before Christ. These Coptic Jews maintained the practice even after their conversion to Christianity and then to Islam. In the 6th century, Aetius of Amida, the Byzantium court physician, wrote that reasons for the removal of the clitoris include the fact that it grows, it is "unseemly and shameful," and women can become aroused when their garments rub on it (Abu-Sahlieh, 83). In 1959, a Jewish physician, W. G. Rathmann, wrote that Jews and Western physicians practiced female genital cutting in the United States—a claim that was vehemently refuted by the Jews in America (Rathmann, 1959). It has been reported that some contemporary Jews have instituted a ceremony for baby girls parallel to the ceremony surrounding male circumcision. The purpose is to correct the perceived inequality between men and women represented by male circumcision. In the ceremony, the girl is admitted to Abraham's alliance with a Hebrew name. God changed the name of Abraham's wife from Sarai to Sarah and Abram to Abraham. Some scholars have argued that if circumcision was a sign of the covenant, the circumcision of Sarah would be included in the decree. Some have argued that the circumcision of Hagar by Sarah would not have happened if the practice wasn't common among the Jews. As recently as 2004, female genital cutting was reported amongst the Israeli Negev Bedouins. However, the practice is said to be declining among this groups (Asali et al., 1995).

Although Christianity has been described as the most vocal religion opposing female genital cutting, this practice is also found among Christians. Female genital cutting has also been legitimized in some Christian teachings, as I have shown in my earlier work (Wangila, 2007). A common narrative cited to justify female genital cutting is that of Abraham's circumcision, recorded in the book of Genesis 1: 1–14. This narrative, which featured prominently in responses to the question, "Why perform female circumcision?" has baffled some Christians, mainly because it is about male circumcision. Christians who cite this narrative believe that God could not have sanctioned male circumcision without sanctioning a similar procedure for females. Like male circumcision, they believe, female genital cutting plays the role of sealing the covenant between the individual and God (Abu-Sahlieh, 2001: 19). As one of my informants argued, "Since Abraham was circumcised as a sign of his faith in God, we also should emulate him if we want to be righteous before God the way he was" (Interview, 2005).[3]

Some Christians have used the Virgin Mary's narrative to justify female genital cutting (Matt. 1: 23ff; Luke 1: 27). The Virgin Mary, the model of a true faithful woman of God, is believed to have been cut in order to confirm her virginity. In most genital cutting communities, it is believed that no girl's virginity can be ascertained without undergoing the genital cutting ritual. As Abu-Sahlieh explains, the term "Virgin Mary" means "an unmarried woman who is initiated, and therefore circumcised" (2001: 219). Mary is believed to have maintained her virginity only by virtue of the fact that she was circumcised (Abu-Sahlieh, 2001: 219). Therefore, some Christian women believe that they should emulate Mary by undergoing the initiation rite that enables a woman to maintain her virginity. This rite includes examination to confirm that a woman's virginity is intact, as well as genital cutting. This, they believe, is the only way to demonstrate chastity and faith in their God as Mary did.

ISLAMIC INFLUENCE

Although female genital cutting is not mentioned in the Quran, Islam is widely associated with this practice. During my research, most of my respondents attributed female genital cutting to Islam. Yet, within the

Muslim community, there are also those who oppose the practice. It is important to understand that female genital cutting was a common practice in some Middle Eastern countries even before Islam. It was found in Arab countries such as Egypt, Sudan, Yemen, and even in Arabia, where Muhammad lived prior to Islam (Abu-Sahlieh, 2001: 176–177). Female genital cutting is said to have been prevalent in Arabia during the time of Muhammad. The Victorian author, Richard Burton, has described female genital cutting as an ancient custom amongst the Arabs. He explains how the operation was performed on girls at puberty in Egypt several centuries before Strabo. He cites Sheikh al-Nawazir, who claimed that the practice was universal in Egypt and Hijaz. It is argued that during the battle of Uhud, one of the battles which the early community of Muslims waged in defense of Islam, Hamza, the uncle to Prophet Muhammad proclaimed when he saw the army of a Quraysh chief, "Come on, you son of a she-circumciser" (Burton, 1855). This statement is interpreted to mean that female genital cutting was a common practice in Arabia before Islam. After the Gulf War, for instance, Palestinians are said to have referred to the practice when denouncing Iraqi refugees who fled to the city, describing them as those who "eat their pigs and cut their women," an insult intended to associate the practice with religious heresy and fanaticism. Today, female genital cutting is said to be practiced to some extent in Oman, South Yemen, Libya, Algeria, Lebanon, Iraq, and Palestine.

In Middle Eastern cultures, female genital cutting is referred to as *tathir* or *tahara*, an Arabic word for purification. Muslims who relate female genital cutting to purity often consider it *Khitan al sunna or al-sunna*, which means "compliant with the tradition of Muhammad." They view the practice as a way to rid women of "dirty surpluses that if left would hide the demon" (Abu-Salieh, 2001: 11, 143). Among the Arabs, mythical stories associated with this practice occur neither in the Bible nor in the Quran. Burton further explains how Egyptians and Hijazi Arabs reference the popular narrative about Sarah, Abraham's wife, and Hagar. This is among other narratives found in the hadith, a record of sayings and actions of the Prophet. These narratives provide evidence for the prevalence of female genital cutting during the time of Prophet Muhammad. The hadith records numerous instances in which the prophet discussed the issue of genital cutting.

For instance, a narrative frequently cited references the advice that Prophet Muhammad gave to Um-Habibah/Um-Atiyyah in a conversation on the subject. This woman who was famously known as an exciser of female slaves was one of the women who had migrated with the Prophet to escape persecution. In this conversation, he is said to have asked her whether she continued her profession of circumcising *jawari*. Um-habibah is said to have responded, "Yes . . . unless it is forbidden and you order me to stop doing it." The Prophet Muhammad is said to have replied, "Yes, it is allowed. Come close so I can teach you. If you cut, do not overdo it, because it brings radiance to the face and it is more pleasant for the husband" (Abu-Sahlieh, 2001: 112–113). Advocates of female genital cutting believe that the Prophet sanctioned the practice in this conversation; otherwise, he would have disapproved of it then. Other assumptions are drawn from the reference that Muhammad's wife Aisha makes to the practice in response to the question whether or not a man should clean himself after intercourse even if he does not ejaculate. Aisha is said to have responded to this question saying, "If the two circumcisions meet or touch each other, it is necessary to wash" (Abu-Sahlieh, 2001: 112).

According to this narrative, also recorded in Judeo-Christian history (Gen. 16: 1–16), female genital cutting began with Hagar, the mother of all Muslims. Sarah, who was apparently jealous of Hagar—Abraham's Egyptian slave girl and concubine—sought to diminish Abraham's apparent love for her by cutting her clitoris while she was asleep. Sarah's jealousy was caused by her inability to give Abraham a child for fertility reasons. Realizing that her husband did not have an heir, she offered him their slave, Hagar, as a wife so he could beget an heir to his property—a common tradition at the time (Abu-Shalieh, 2001: 219). Hagar conceived a child and gave birth to Ishmael, Abraham's first-born son, through whom Muslims claim descent to Abraham. Out of jealousy, Sarah vowed to cut three of Hagar's body parts. Fearing that she would cut her nose and two ears, Abraham ordered Sarah to pierce Hagar's ears and to circumcise her. Sarah decided to cut Hagar's clitoris while she was asleep in order to diminish Abraham's love for her. Realizing what they had done, God then ordered both Abraham and Sarah to cut themselves as well. So began the practice of both male and female circumcision. Muslims who justify female genital cutting believe that both male and female genital cutting are Islamic injunctions in memory of Abraham and Hagar (Thiam, 1986). The other version of this narrative explains how Abraham told Sarah to circumcise Hagar "so that female circumcision becomes a tradition amongst women" (Ibn-Abd-al-Hakam, 1922: 11–12; Abu-Sahlieh, 1999: 151). As Abu-Sahlieh explains, this story serves to relate female circumcision to the foremother of Muslims, Hagar, just as male circumcision relates to the forefather, Abraham. The narrative is frequently referenced by some Muslims to justify the practice. For instance, Abu-Uthman Umar Ibn-Bahr Al-Jahiz is quoted as saying, "Male and female circumcision have been practiced by Arabs since the time of Abraham and Hagar until today" (Al-Jahiz, 1996: 27). Suleyman Al-Jamal has also referenced this narrative, saying, "Abraham was the first circumcised man and Hagar the mother of Ismael, was the first circumcised woman" (Al-Jamal, n.d: 174; Al-Amili, 1982: 168).

Abu-Sahlieh has also explained how classical Sunnite and Shiite Muslims frequently reference this story as the origin of female genital cutting. He explains how Al-Jawziyyah Shams-al Din Ibn-Qayyim referenced the story, saying, "After the circumcision of Hagar, this practice became sunnah among women" (Ibn-Qayyim, 1987: 166).

Although this story is not found in the Quran, it is commonly told in most Muslim communities, including African communities, and is used by some to sanction female genital cutting. Awa Thiam narrates:

> Long before the time of Mahout, there was a prophet named Ibrahim (Abraham) who was married to his cousin Sarata (Sara). He went up to the land of Gerar, where reigned King Abimelech, who delighted in taking to himself all men's wives who are remarkable for their beauty. Now it happened that Sarata was unusually fair. And the king did not hesitate to try to take her from her husband. A supernatural power prevented him from taking advantage of her, which so astonished him that he set her free. And he restored her back to her husband and made her the gift of a handmaid named Hadiara (Hagar).
>   Sarata and her husband lived together for a long time but Sarata bore Ibrahim no child. And eventually, Ibrahim took Hadiara to wife; some say it was Sarata who said to her husband that he should take her handmaid to wife since she herself could not bear any children. And so Sarata and Hadiara became co-wives to Ibrahima and Hadiara bore him a son and his name was Ismaila (Ishmael) and Sarata also bore a son to Ibrahima and he was called Ishaga (Isaac). In the course of time, the relationship between the two women deteriorated. And so it came to pass that one day Sarata excised Hadiara. Some say that she only pierced her ears while others maintain she did indeed excise her. (Thiam, 1986: 59)

Because this story is not found in the Quran, some like Abu-Sahlieh have argued that it probably is one of the many Hebrew legends in circulation at the time that ended up filtering into Islamic books. This, as he validly argues, can be interpreted to suggest that Jews at the time of Muhammad practiced female genital cutting and that this practice is one of the many influences of Jews on Arabs.

Other advocates of female genital cutting have based their arguments on fatwas, opinions of Muslim religious leaders, which are respected as authoritative in Muslim communities. The fatwa that is often cited by Shiite Muslims is that of Ali, the fourth caliph (successor) of Prophet Muhammad. Ali is said to have sanctioned female genital cutting by declaring it a "meritorious act." He is said to have maintained that "a man's circumcision is indispensable," but to this comment he added, "What thing is better than a meritorious act?" (Abu-Sahlieh, 2001) Advocates of female genital cutting believe that this statement left no choice for women. An honorable woman is expected to get cut. Another popular fatwa on this issue was issued in 1981 by Sheikh Mahmoud Shaltout, a former Sheikh of Al Azhar University in Cairo, a famous Islamic university. Sheikh Shaltout urged Muslims not to give up female genital cutting, explaining that the Prophet favored it. He argued that lessons of the Prophet should not be abandoned in favor of the teachings of infallible beings such as doctors. Shaltout believes that parents have the responsibility to ensure that their daughters are circumcised and that those who avoid it are violating the prophet's definition of their duty.

Although advocates of female genital cutting have turned to Islam to justify the practice, opponents of the practice do not recognize a link between the practice and Islam because it is unknown in some Muslim countries. This claim was first raised in 1943 by a Muslim scholar, Dr. Usamah, in a text published in the magazine *Al-Risalah*. As observed by Abu-Sahlieh, Usamah dismisses arguments about cleanliness, chastity, and aesthetics associated with this practice and describes female genital cutting as a "crime against a girl's body that no one has the right to commit" (Abu-Sahlieh, 2001: 262). Narratives used to justify female genital cutting are dismissed as misinterpretations and corruptions of Islamic teachings, since the words "female genital cutting" are not mentioned in the Quran (Abu-Sahlieh, 2001: 113). Citing the health risks of this practice, opponents describe female genital cutting as ungodly. They do not see how God would command an action that is harmful, painful, and as physically and psychologically damaging as female genital cutting.

They also dismiss the claim that the prophet endorsed female genital cutting, arguing that Prophet Muhammad would not have sanctioned the practice if he did not circumcise his own daughters. According to Sheik-Abd-al-Rahman Al-Najjar, "Muhammad had four girls and there is no mention in his biography—the *hadith*—that he circumcised them" (Abu-Sahlieh, 2001: 109). The odds that this would have been excluded from the hadith are very slim. Regarding his conversations with Uh Habibah Um Atiya, in which he advises minimal cutting if cutting is done, opponents of the practice have argued that the Prophet's actions should be viewed in the context of his situation. Female genital cutting was prevalent in the community in which he lived, and he realized that he could not suddenly stop a practice that was so entrenched without causing uproar. By allowing the practice but suggesting that it be done in a very minimal way, as he did during this conversation, he initiated a significant step toward ending the practice.

Critics who embrace a universalist approach to morality believe that female genital cutting is a violation of women's basic rights to good health, sexuality, and choice. These critics see it as a cultural practice that was prevalent in pre-Islamic Arabia that should be considered ungodly because it damages a healthy organ of an innocent woman. God, they argue, would not command an action that is as harmful, painful, physically and psychologically damaging as female genital cutting. The practice was continued by some Muslims to reinforce sexual control and chastity in women and to ensure that wives give birth only to children sired by their husbands (Hassan, 1990: 118). This assertion is validated in Sura 4: 34, which proclaims the following in Abdullah Yusuf Ali's translation:

> Men are the protectors and maintainers of women, because Allah has given the one more (strength) than the other, and because they support them from their means. Therefore the righteous women are devoutly obedient, and guard in (the husband's) absence what Allah would have them guard. As to those women on whose part ye fear disloyalty and ill-conduct, admonish them (first), (Next), refuse to share their beds, (And last) beat them (lightly); but if they return to obedience, seek not against them Means (of annoyance): For Allah is Most High, great (above you all). (Sura 4: 34)

According to Robinson, references to the hadith are neither credible nor authentic. She argues further:

> God apparently created the clitoris for the sole purpose of generating pleasure. It has no other purpose. There is no instruction in the Qur'an or in the writings of the Prophet Muhammad which require that the clitoris be surgically modified. Thus God must approve of its presence. And so, it should not be removed or reduced in size or function. The Qur'an promotes the concept of a husband and wife giving each other pleasure during sexual intercourse. For example: "It is lawful for you to go into your wives during the night preceding the (day's) fast: they are as a garment for you and you are as a garment for them." (2: 187) ". . . and He has put love and mercy between you" (30: 21). (Robinson, 2001)

It is clear that conflicting opinions exist amongst Muslims regarding the position of Islam on female genital cutting. Even though there is no specific Quran verse that addresses female genital cutting in Islam, scholars like Janice Boddy have established a link between purity teachings and female genital cutting. According to Boddy, genital cutting prepares a woman's body for womanhood by completing and purifying "a child's natural sexual identity" which is viewed as incomplete without cutting (Boddy, 1989: 58). It is a way to ensure the maintenance and renewal of virginity. This act helps remove vestiges of maleness that enables *aql* (reason) to triumph over *nafsi* (emotion). Infibulation is necessary to enclose the "vaginal meatus and her womb" in order to make it "impervious and virtually impenetrable and ostensibly fertile," Boddy explains (1989: 74). Women whose genitals are left intact are said to bring irreparable shame to their family through misbehavior (Boddy, 1989: 53). In these Arab communities, infibulation was common, and the honor of the family was closely linked to the chastity of their women, as ascertained by the size of the virginal opening. The smaller the infibulated opening, the higher the honor and bride price for the girl's family. It should be remembered, however, that Islam is not the only religion with conflicting positions on this practice. In fact, conflicting opinions are indicators of the thin line between culture and religion. As modern values exert themselves, cultural as well as religious norms are bound to be negotiated.

NEGOTIATING VALUES IN MODERN SOCIETY

Conflicting opinions on female genital cutting among Jewish, Christian, and Muslim communities explain why some maintain the practice while others oppose it. The ambiguous link between female genital cutting and religious duty is a matter of inference and interpretations of ambiguous scriptural verses. It is for this reason that some have categorically denied any association of female genital cutting with religion. For instance, B. A. Robinson writes, female genital cutting "was, and remains a cultural practice, not a religious practice," a sentiment reiterated by Anika Rahman and Nahid Toubia, who also write, "It is important to note that FC/FGM is a cultural, not a religious practice" (Robinson, 2001; Rahman and Toubia, 2006: 6). Some scholars have argued that because the practice predates Christianity or Islam, it should not be associated with these religions.

To dismiss female genital cutting as a cultural practice that has nothing to do with religion because it not mentioned in the Bible or the Quran, however, is to ignore the strong relationship between religion and culture. Although most scriptures do not actually endorse a specific practice, most religions and scriptural teachings draw from the cultural norms that existed in cultural contexts from which they emerged. Although attempts to distinguish between culturally and religiously legitimate practices are often embedded in a desire to highlight the universal principles of social justice embedded in modern monotheistic religions, it is important to recognize that religion is more than just scripture. Speaking on the role of religion in social construction, sociologist Peter Berger has argued that just as religion is a world constructor, the world, in turn, constructs religion. In other words, culture influences religion in the same way religion influences culture. The relationship between the two is that of legitimation. The effective role of religion lies in its grounding of social realities in the "sacred *realissimum* which is beyond the contingencies of human meanings and human activity" and in the "infusion of this reality with meanings given to the social." This legitimizing process grants social reality the semblance of ultimate security and permanence. Referencing something beyond human society—a supernatural being, God, divinities, or ancestors—infuses any given religious community with fear, awe, and reverence. The result is an unwavering obedience among religious adherents, who perceive religiously sanctioned practices as absolute and unchangeable.

It is also important to recognize that scripture is not the only document with authoritative influence on social behavior. For instance, to argue that culture has nothing to do with religion is to ignore the authority that non-scriptural religious documents such as the hadith possess. It is to ignore the importance of the *Talmud* and *Halakha* to the Jewish community or of the hadith or *sunna* or *Shariah* to the Muslim community. The Talmud and the *Shariah* are codes that regulate all aspects of life and are widely accepted by their respective religious communities of Jews and Muslims. Although some critics have questioned the validity of hadith collections, dismissing them as a mere record of Arabic culture, some Muslims revere these documents as sacred (Fazlur, 1968).

Culture and religion operate interdependently. Sociologist Dorothy Smith argues that religion participates in ruling relations by reinforcing, regulating, organizing, governing, and limiting people's behavior in society (1999: 50, 77–78). In most developed countries such as the United States, immigrant women are confronted daily with the dilemma of negotiating religious values about sexuality in a world where universal and cultural values may offer other options. Recognizing the interplay between religious and cultural values is the first step toward addressing their dilemma. Because female genital cutting is considered both a cultural tradition and an injunction made by ancestors, God, *sunna*, or fatwa, it is difficult to challenge such convictions. As long as cultural norms find legitimacy in religious values, they are normalized, internalized, and legitimized. It is important, therefore, not to underestimate the role of religion in social behavior. Whether this role is implicit or explicit, its influence on social behavior is significant. Religious leaders opposed to the practice could utilize religious values to undermine the practice.

Although religion is a significant factor in the persistence of female genital cutting in developed countries such as the United States and the United Kingdom, the tenacity of this practice in a modern society raises significant theoretical questions. First, as an indigenous cultural practice, female genital cutting poses a significant challenge to evolutionist and secularization assumptions that traditional values are rural, agrarian, pre-scientific, and resistant to change and innovation. According to these assumptions, the practice is destined to decline as scientific and secular ideas become dominant.[4] Contrary to the reductionist understanding of social phenomena, social units are bound to adapt. Social change is the result of social critique—a process that determines which traditions should be retained and which should be discarded or abandoned. As I indicate in my other works, as the result of this social critique, subsequent generations will discard certain values and traditions that are no longer needed or accepted (Wangila, 2007: 10). Often, those who insist on maintaining certain norms or cultural practices tend to brand these norms and practices as traditional. What is often overlooked is that tradition is a set of values passed down and modified over generations. While enduring elements are inherited from the past, others are discarded along the way (Gyekye, 1997: 218–219). Culture, then, is actually a human creation, and human beings are social agents who participate in its production.

Regardless of who produces culture, however, individual humans respond to culture differently. Sociologist Margaret Archer observes that the response of humans to culture often depends on how it affects them. They can either reinforce a cultural system, or they can resist its influence upon them, especially when it is perceived to inhibit their well-being (Archer, 1988: 77–78, 143). If social reality is a human construction, as Berger asserts it is, there is bound to be resistance to certain aspects of culture (1969: 32–33). As rational beings, humans will modify previous cultural norms that they come to consider irrelevant to human flourishing. Continual cultural appraisal, then, is a significant part of the process of social change. Whether any given cultural value is accepted, maintained, rejected, or abandoned often depends on prevailing norms and other rational tests of a value's utility within the current social context. Once they are accepted, these values are refined, and the adaptation process continues.

Contributing to social change is cultural criticism, a healthy exercise that people undertake for various reasons. If a cultural value is considered to impede the progress of a given society, it can be labeled dysfunctional, and therefore irrelevant. Second, if a cultural practice contradicts the ethos of a new set of cultural values embraced by a new generation, it can be critiqued and rejected. Third, if a cultural practice is deemed morally unacceptable, it can be abandoned. Fourth, if a cultural value contradicts other more prized parts of the tradition, its influence can be minimized. Fifth, if a cultural practice becomes irrelevant because the metaphysical foundation on which it is based is found implausible, it can be left behind. According to philosopher Alasdair Macintyre, such cultural practices are discarded because they are dead. In other words, they have ceased to be part of a living tradition that maintains its relevance in contemporary society (MacIntyre, 2007: 222). Although female genital cutting has shown its vitality and ability to transform, adapt, and assimilate in the face of social change, the process of cultural criticism has informed its adaptation process. As Grassie explains, the tenacity of any practice that is associated with religion is embedded in religion by virtue of its memetic success, a variable that enables it to persist (2007: 15). A religious practice is like a *meme gene* that adapts but never disappears. They acquire new values in the new social context as defined by contemporary values. Religion as a social phenomenon is no exception. Describing the tenacity of African rituals generally, Christine Ayorinde has argued that the vitality of African religions lies in their unique tendency to predict, explain, and control events, a characteristic that modern culture and Western religions have attempted unsuccessfully to replace (2004: 8).

Central to the persistence of a cultural practice, therefore, are questions of meaning—questions that are fundamental to religious beliefs. Religious practices tend to persist when they continue to express meaning about an ultimate reality, a reality that cannot be dismissed on the basis of scientific evidence. As James C. Livingston has aptly observed, as long as they have lived, humans have been religious, responding to existential questions that make their environment meaningful (1998: 3–30).

Is it possible that modern societies have failed to address sociocultural needs that have led to the persistence of female genital cutting? Is it possible that certain needs are so essential to certain individuals' identity and meaning that they must be met regardless of where and when they live? Is it possible that those who are defying laws against female genital cutting in Western countries such as the United States perceive themselves as meeting obligations that transcend legal and even societal expectations? I ask these questions because in my research, I have encountered respondents who believe that the modern promiscuous lifestyle is responsible for the resurgence and persistence of female genital cutting. The display of images showing women in revealing clothing in the mass media is perceived to indicate prevalent promiscuity and immorality, and the need to tame such behavior using female genital cutting. With such an attitude, and the legitimating role of religion, is it possible to combat the practice of female genital cutting? This question forms the gist of discussion in the following chapters.

NOTES

1. Details are elaborated in *Female Circumcision: The Interplay of Religion, Culture and Gender in Kenya* (2007).
2. Data was collected over a period of six years. See the tables for analysis.
3. This interview was held in New Jersey in June 2005.
4. This predisposition associated with classical anthropologists and sociologists, such as Herbert Spencer (1820–1903), Edward B. Taylor (1871) and James B. Frazer (1854–1941), Karl Marx (1818–1883), Durkheim (1857–1917), and Max Weber (1864–1920) was fueled by a Eurocentric mindset, which viewed non-Western norms as inferior.

6

◆❖◆

Policies on Female
Genital Cutting

Due to health and moral concerns associated with female genital cutting, most countries around the world have instituted intervention policies, which include the establishment of legal stipulations as well as the provision of health and awareness outreach programs. While efforts to curb the practice have been realized in local, statewide, and international communities, there remain significant challenges. This chapter outlines existing policies in industrialized countries with the objective of highlighting the strengths and weaknesses of these policies in protecting the girls who live with the risk of female genital cutting. Of those interviewed, 54 percent expressed ignorance of their countries' policy position on female genital cutting. While ignorance is a significant factor in attitudes and the persistence of the practice in industrialized countries, further analysis reveal issues of health awareness and the human rights implication of the practice, including political problems, in enforcing existing policies.

Research indicates that most countries' solution to female genital cutting is the establishment of bills and statutes to criminalize the practice. Criminalization is viewed as a necessary step to declare the practice illegal in order to discourage its practice. Legal enforcement as a strategy is viewed as a necessary step to communicate to various communities that female genital cutting will not be tolerated. The assumption here is that legal interventions will provide protection and support to women and children who wish to resist the practice within their communities.

Pat Schroeder, the former Democratic Congresswoman and a longtime champion of women's rights sponsored the bill to outlaw female genital cutting in the United States. She argued that legislating against female genital cutting would deter the practice. Schroeder explained her confidence in the efficacy of the law thus—"I think it's been a very strong statement," she says. "If you want to live here—we don't do this" (Tuhus-Dubrow, 2007). A law professor at Duke University, Doriane Coleman, is in favor of this position. She argues, "It ought to send a message that this is impermissible behavior" (Tuhus-Dubrow, 2007).

Criminalization of female genital cutting can be effective if well executed. In Scandinavian countries, for instance, evidence exists to illustrate that strict prohibition of female genital cutting can work even among Somali immigrants who are notorious for this practice. As Essen and Johnsdotter observe, studies have shown that most Somali women who live in Scandinavian countries have abandoned the practice. In these countries, prohibitions against female genital cutting involve the risk of custodial loss of one's children. The main motivation is the internal conversation based on existing laws as well as demystification of the practice. The fear of Swedish social authorities and an awareness of the risk of losing custody of the children reinforce their change of attitude (Essen and Johnsdotter, 2004: 612). Countries that have passed laws criminalizing female genital cutting include Australia, Belgium, Canada, Denmark, New Zealand, Norway, Spain, Sweden, the United Kingdom, and the United States.

It should be remembered that various countries' positions on female genital cutting are informed by the position of the United Nation (UN) and the World Health Organization (WHO) on the practice. As indicated earlier, the WHO led in speaking against female genital cutting repeatedly since the 1970s. Calls for the criminalization of the practice were based on the 1948 principles stipulated in the Universal Declaration on Human Rights. The human rights principles provided a solid foundation for classifying female genital cutting as a human rights violation. At the Platform for Action of the Fourth World Conference on Women (Beijing 1995), governments were instructed to eradicate female genital cutting. According to paragraph 232 of the Platform, governments were to:

> Prohibit female genital mutilation wherever it exists and give vigorous support to efforts among non-governmental and community organizations and religious institutions to eliminate such practices.

Soon, these efforts were duplicated at local levels, including the Council of Europe (CoE) Parliamentary Assembly Resolution 1247 of 2001;

European Union (EU) Parliament Resolution on FGM of 2001; CEDAW article 2(f); Declaration on the Elimination of Violence against Women article 2(a); CRC article 24, paragraph 3; African Charter on the Rights and the Welfare of the Child article 21, paragraph 1(a) and (b); Protocol to the African Charter on Human Rights and Peoples' Rights on the Rights of Women in Africa article 5; and Platform for Action of the Fourth World Conference on Women (Beijing 1995) paragraph 232(h). Consequently, countries that are members of WHO and the UN are required to adhere to stipulations by adopting a number of strategies to intervene against the practice.

In Africa, where this practice is prevalent, the African Charter on Human Rights and People's Rights on the Rights of Women in Africa crafted a stipulation in Article 5, which categorizes female genital cutting as a harmful practice that should be eradicated. The Statute reads:

> States Party shall prohibit and condemn all forms of harmful practices which negatively affect the human rights of women and which are contrary to recognized international standards. States Parties shall take all necessary legislative and other measures to eliminate such practices, including:

(a) Creation of public awareness in all sectors of society regarding harmful practices through information, formal, and informal education and outreach programmes;

(b) Prohibition, through legislative measures backed by sanctions, of all forms of female genital mutilation, scarification, medicalization and para-medicalization of female genital mutilation and all other practices in order to eradicate them;

(c) Provision of necessary support to victims of harmful practices through basic services such as health services, legal and judicial support, emotional and psychological counseling as well as vocational training to make them self-supporting;

(d) Protection of women who are at risk of being subjected to harmful practices or all other forms of violence, abuse and intolerance.

THE UNITED STATES

In the United States, the public was unaware of the practice of female genital cutting for a long time. It was not until the practice was covered in the media in 1996 during the asylum case of Fauziya Kassindja that the public's interest was aroused (Kassindja and Bashir, 1998). The outrage against the practice led to action. The United States adopted multiple strategy in effort to combat female genital cutting. First, it defined the practice as a federal criminal offence unless necessary to protect a young person's health. Second, it sought to impose economic sanctions on nations that did not attempt to eliminate the practice among its citizens (Boyle, 2002). Third, it sought to educate illegal immigrants on the subject.

Legislation criminalizing FGC was first introduced in 1993 during the first session of the 103rd Congress by Representative Pat Schroeder (D-CO) as part of the Women's Health Equity Act. It did not pass until 1996, after Senator Harry Reid (D-NV) offered it as an amendment to the Senate version of immigration reform legislation. In 1995, a federal bill was passed to prohibit female genital cutting. This bill provides for prison of up to five years for anyone who "circumcises, excises or infibulates the whole or any part of the labia majora or labia minora or clitoris of another person who has not attained the age of 18 years." Section 2 (116) title 18 amendments of the bill reads as follows:

Female genital mutilation:

(a) Except as provided in subsection (b), whoever knowingly circumcises, excises, or infibulates the whole or any part of the labia majora or labia minora or clitoris of another person who has not attained the age of 18 years shall be fined under this title or imprisoned not more than 5 years, or both.

(b) a surgical operation is not a violation of this section if the operation is:

(1) necessary to the health of the person on whom it is performed, and is performed by a person licensed in the place of its performance as a medical practitioner; or

(2) performed on a person in labor or who has just given birth and is performed for medical purposes connected with that labor or birth by a person licensed in the place it is performed as a medical practitioner, midwife, or person in training to become such a practitioner of midwife.

(c) in applying subsection (b)(1), no account shall be taken of the effect on the person on whom the operation is to be performed if any belief on the part of that or any other person that the operation is required as a matter of custom or ritual.

(d)   whoever knowingly denies to any person medical care or services or otherwise discriminates against any person in the provision of medical care or services, because:

   (1)   that person has undergone female circumcision, excision, or infibulation; or
   (2)   that person has requested that female circumcision, excision, or infibulation be performed on any person; shall be fined under this title or imprisoned not more than one year, or both.

Later, Congress mandated the Department of Health and Human Services (HHS) to identify communities that practice female genital cutting in the United States and educate immigrants about the harm of genital cutting. The HHS was to design and carry out outreach activities to educate individuals in these communities on the physical and psychological health effects of genital cutting (520(b) (2)). These outreach activities were to be implemented "in collaboration with representatives of ethnic groups practicing mutilation and with representatives of organizations with expertise in preventing such practice" ((520(b) (2)). The HHS was also instructed to educate medical professionals about treating genitally cut women. On April 26, 1996, it passed a legislation requiring that the Secretary of the HHS conducts a study on female genital cutting in the United States and initiates instructional outreach on the practice to relevant communities. Specifically, HHS was to "compile data on the number of females living in the United States who have been subjected to female genital cutting either in the United States or in their own countries of origin, and to document a specific number of girls under the age of 18 who have undergone female genital cutting" (520(c).

The HHS was also asked to develop and disseminate recommendations for the education of students of schools of medicine and osteopathic medicine regarding female genital cutting and complications arising from the practice (520(b) (3)). At the request of the HHS, the Center for Disease Control and Prevention (CDC) undertook a study to determine the prevalence of female genital cutting in the United States. Using census data, the CDC estimated that 168,000 girls and women living in the United States had been exposed to or were at risk of genital cutting (Jones, 1997: 372). The HHS Office of Women's Health (OWH) organized a series of community meetings in Washington D.C., and other parts of the country[1] and funded the Research, Action, and Information Network for the Bodily Integrity of Women (RAINBO), a nonprofit organization to develop training materials on the subject. These materials, which included a technical manual for health care providers, were to be distributed widely to health professional schools and organizations. The law provides also that The Secretary of Health and Human Services shall carry out the following activities:

(1) compile data on the number of females living in the United States who have been subjected to female genital mutilation (whether in the United States or in their countries of origin), including a specification of the number of girls under the age of 18 who have been subjected to such mutilation.

(2) identify communities in the United States that practice female genital mutilation, and design and carry out outreach activities to educate individuals in the communities on the physical and psychological effects of such practice. Such outreach activities shall be designed and implemented in collaboration with representatives of the ethnic groups practicing such mutilation and with representatives of organizations with expertise in preventing such practice.

(3) develop recommendations for the education of students of schools of medicine and osteopathic medicine regarding female genital mutilation and complications arising from such mutilation. Such recommendations shall be disseminated to such schools.

On March 29, 1997, a law went into effect criminalizing female genital cutting, with culprits facing a penalty of $250,000 while organizations such as hospitals faced a penalty of $500,000. In spite of this, the first charges under the law were made in late 2003, when a California couple was arrested in an FBI sting operation allegedly after having agreed to perform a female genital cutting procedure to two fictitious girls (Costello, 2004).

As part of the Illegal Immigration Reform and Immigrant Responsibility Act of 1996, Congress instructed the Immigration and Naturalization Services (INS) in cooperation with the Department of State to make available information on the practice for all immigrants who are issued with immigrant or nonimmigrant visas, prior to or at the time of entry in the United States as per Illegal Immigration Reform and Immigrant Responsibility Act of 1996, Pub. L. 104–208, 1996. This information was to communicate the severe physical and psychological harm that female genital cutting could cause to one's health. According to the act, it was to be ensured that the information on the subject was compiled and presented in a manner that was limited to the practice itself and respectful to the cultural values of the societies in which such practice existed (Pub. L.104–208, at 644(a) (1)). In addition, each immigrant was to be informed about the potential legal consequences of: (a) performing female genital cutting in the United States, (b) allowing a child under his or her care to be subjected to female genital cutting (Pub. L. 104–208, at 644(a) (2)). The INS produced and distributed information on female genital cutting in six languages, namely French, Arabic, Somali, Swahili, Amharic; and Portuguese and distributed the material to overseas embassies in designated countries by April 2000 (CRC, 2004: 12).

For example, section 116 of the Illegal Immigration Reform and Immigrant Responsibility Act of 1996 reads:

(a) Except as provided in subsection (b), whoever knowingly circumcises, excises, or infibulates the whole or any part of the labia majora or labia manora or clitoris of another person who has not attained the age of 18 years shall be fined under this title or imprisoned, not more than 5 years, or both.

(b) A surgical operation is not a violation of this section if the operation is:

(1) necessary to the health of the person on whom it is performed, and is performed by a licensed person in the place of its performance as a medical practitioner, or

(2) performed on a person in labor or who has just given birth and is performed for medical purposes connected with that labor or birth by a person licensed in the place it is performed as a medical practitioner, midwife or a person in training to become such a practitioner or midwife. (Rahman and Toubia, 2001: 237)

Efforts to prevent genital cutting in the United States were duplicated at the state level beginning 1994. Sixteen states, including Minnesota, Rhode Island, Tennessee, California, Colorado, Delaware, Maryland, Missouri, New York, Oregon, West Virginia, and Nevada criminalized female genital cutting. Minnesota, Rhode Island, and Tennessee prohibited female genital cutting on adult women as well as females under the age of 18. California, Colorado, Delaware, Maryland, Missouri, New York, Oregon, and West Virginia addressed female genital cutting by declaring the conduct of a parent or guardian who permits or allows female genital cutting on her or his daughter as a criminal. They called for culturally sensitive education and outreach to relevant communities.

In Nevada, a person may be prosecuted for the removal of a child from the state for the purpose of performing female genital cutting. In California, for instance, the California Prohibition of Female Genital Mutilation Act (the California FGM Law) was passed in 1996 and became effective in January 1997. According to this law, the State Health Services, in consultation with the State Department of Social Services and appropriate federal agencies, was required to commence "appropriate education, preventive, and outreach activities" for the purpose of informing members of, in particular, new immigrant population, of the "health risks and emotional trauma inflicted by" female genital cutting and informing these populations and the medical community, of the prohibition of the practice (West, 1996).[2]

In Colorado, the Criminal Code was amended to classify female genital cutting as a form of child abuse on May 24, 1999.[3] This legislation defined a child as a person under the age of 16. According to this code, a "parent, guardian, or other person legally responsible for a female child or charged with the care or custody of a female child" commits child abuse if he or she "allows" the procedure to be performed on the child (401(1) (b) (I)). This practice was not to be defended as a custom, ritual, or standard practice; neither was the consent of the minor, her parent, or legal guardian to be considered as a defense to a charge under this law. Culprits were to be punished by a minimum of four years imprisonment (Colorado Rev. Stat. tit 18, art1, &105). Colorado has expressed its commitment to preventing female genital cutting by creating a fund to support education and outreach activities (Center for Reproductive Rights, 2004).

In Massachusetts, a Judiciary Committee of the Legislation held a public hearing on the Massachusetts State Prohibition of Genital Mutilation Act in March 2010. According to the bill, it was a criminal offense to cut any part of the genitals of a minor except when medically necessary. Eighteen people spoke in favor of the bill, and an additional 500 people submitted supporting materials to the legislature. Three people testified against the bill.

Today, U.S representatives of the World Bank and similar financial institutions are required to oppose loans to countries where female genital cutting is prevalent and in which the practice is not criminalized. In April 26, 2010, the United States passed the Girls Protection Act (H.R 5137), a bipartisan Federal legislation that would make it illegal to transport a minor girl living in the United States outside the country for the purpose of female genital cutting.

EUROPE

In Europe, female genital cutting was declared a human rights violation in accordance with the European Union Parliament resolution on Female Genital Mutilation of 2001; the Council of Europe under Resolution 1247 specifically urges governments:

    i. to introduce specific legislation prohibiting genital mutilation and declaring genital mutilation to be a violation of human rights and bodily integrity.

ii. to take steps to inform all people about the legislation banning the practice before they enter Council of Europe member states;

iii. to adopt more flexible measures for granting the right to asylum to mothers and their children who fear being subjected to such practices;

iv. to prosecute the perpetrators and their accomplices, including family members and health personnel, on criminal charges of violence leading to mutilation, including cases where such mutilation is committed abroad.[4]

The report asserts that female genital cutting in Europe cannot be justified on the grounds of cultural relativism (Miller, 2004). Based on this resolution, the European Commission was instructed to develop a strategy to eliminate the practice in the European Union (Miller, 2004: 5).[5]

UNITED KINGDOM

The United Kingdom is a country with a high number of immigrants, with most immigrants from countries such as Eritrea, Ethiopia, Somalia, and Yemen having arrived in the country about 40 years ago. Many of them live in London. However, female genital cutting as an issue is reported mainly in those who live in Manchester, Liverpool, Cardiff, and Sheffield (Dirie, 2005: 76). In Britain, health officials have observed that girls living in this country have been cut in operations organized by family members. It is estimated that about 86,000 women have been exposed to genital cutting (Powell, 2002; Leye, 2008), with about 7,000 girls under 17 at risk.[6]

Yet, the United Kingdom is the first European country to introduce a specific criminal law prohibiting female genital cutting. Although there is no constitution or bill of rights in the United Kingdom about female genital cutting, the 1985 Prohibition of Female Circumcision Act made it a criminal offence for any person to perform this procedure and for other persons to aid, abet, counsel, or procure the performance of these acts. Anyone guilty of this offense is liable to a fine or to imprisonment for a period not exceeding five years or to both. This was reinforced by the Human Rights Act of 1998, which became effective in October 2000. The act incorporates the European Convention on Human Rights into domestic law ensuring the equality of men and women, the right to liberty and security of each person, the right to respect private and family life, and freedom of religion. The 2003 Female Genital Mutilation Act repealed, re-enacted, and strengthened the provisions of the 1985 Act by increasing the maximum penalty for female genital cutting from 5 to 14 years imprisonment. Other changes of the act include the introduction of the applicability of the principle of extraterritoriality; the prohibition of the practice extends outside the United Kingdom territory as well. The name of the act was changed from Female Circumcision Act to Female Genital Mutilation Act. The Female Genital Mutilation Act of 2003 states in part as follows:

Article 1: Offence of Female Genital Mutilation

(1) A person is guilty of an offence if he excises, infibulates or otherwise mutilates the whole or any part of a girl's labia majora, labia minora or clitoris.

(5) For the purpose of determining whether an operation is necessary for the mental health of a girl it is immaterial whether she or any other person believes that the operation is required as a matter of custom or ritual.

Article 2: Offence of Assisting a Girl to Mutilate Her Own Genitalia

A person is guilty of an offence if he aids, abets, counsels or procures a girl to excise, infibulate or otherwise mutilate the whole or any part of her own labia majora, labia minora or clitoris.

Article 5: Penalties for Offences

A person guilty of an offence under this act is liable

(a) On conviction on indictment, to imprisonment for a term not exceeding 14 years or a fine (or both),

(b) On summary conviction, to imprisonment for a term not exceeding six months or a fine not exceeding the statutory maximum (or both).

Article 6: Definitions

(1) Girl includes woman.

(2) A United Kingdom national is an individual who is

(a) A British citizen, a British overseas territories citizen, a British National (Overseas) or a British Overseas citizen,

(b) A person who under the British Nationality Act 1981 (c. 61) is a British subject, or

(c) A British protected person within the meaning of that Act.

(3) A permanent United Kingdom resident is an individual who is settled in the United Kingdom (within the meaning of the Immigration Act 1971 (c. 77)).

This act was enforced in March 2004. Although the United Kingdom does not have a written constitution as in the case of France and other industrialized countries, it has laws that protect children's rights (BMA, 2004: 3). According to a special child protection law; the Children Act of 1989, Part 5 protects children from abuse. While citizens are not required to report knowledge or suspicion of abuse, any professional who identifies a child at risk of suffering harm is obliged to report the information to the social services to ensure that the child is protected. This requirement is recorded in the policy document *Working Together to Safeguard Children*, issued by the Department of Health, and endorsed by professional guidelines. Article 8 of the Child Act of 1989 prohibits travel to another country with a child in order to perform female genital cutting. This policy may include the removal of the child from the family or suspension of the parental authority in order to protect the child.

The United Kingdom also recognizes female genital cutting as a reason to grant asylum. The Immigration Appellate Authority states that social, cultural, and religious behavioral requirements, traditions, and norms may consider gender-related harm to be an acceptable practice (Immigration Appellate Authority, 2000). In fact, there are successful asylum claims in the United Kingdom based on the threat of female genital cutting. Article 3 of the European Convention on Human Rights protects the right not to be subjected to torture, inhuman, or degrading treatment (BMA, 2004: 5; Powell, 2004). Quite often, however, new immigrant asylum seekers and refugees are unaware of the legal prohibition of female genital cutting in the United Kingdom and about the possibility of seeking asylum on the basis of the practice.

Like most industrialized countries, the United Kingdom's policies on female genital cutting leave loopholes that have been exploited to maintain the practice. It is important to note that although Article 1 of the Female Genital Mutilation Act prohibits all forms of female genital cutting, the United Kingdom, like other industrialized countries, is not clear in its law especially where re-infibulation is concerned. This practice is not mentioned in the Female Genital Mutilation Act of 2003. Also not mentioned is the piercing and tattooing practices. Although the WHO is clear in its classification of piercing and tattooing as a form of female genital cutting (type 4), and therefore, prohibits them, the United Kingdom as well as other countries chose to ignore this fact in its laws. While this may appear to be minor forms of genital cutting, they are prohibited because they signal a possible loophole to be exploited to maintain female genital cutting. It is therefore important to have clear language about these practices and to provide specific guidelines to ensure that all types of genital modifications, whether cultural or modernized, are prohibited.

Related to non-clarity of re-infibulations and piercing and tattooing is the practice of cosmetic genital surgery—a common phenomenon in industrialized countries that includes vaginal tightening, lifting of the labia, and trimming of the labia minora. This surgery, often performed for nontherapeutic and aesthetic reasons, is similar in some sense to the results, and sometimes consequences, of female genital cutting. If the United Kingdom does not address this issue in the same way it addresses female genital cutting, the problem of double standard emerges—a factor that is significant in the persistence of female genital cutting in industrialized countries. The other issue of concern in the United Kingdom's policy has to do with the perceived voluntariness claimed often to preserve family and community. This is an issue since voluntariness has a lot of gray areas to be addressed. Unless voluntariness is clearly defined and addressed to ensure that only informed consent qualifies as voluntariness, many have taken this as a loophole to exploit to maintain female genital cutting.

Also, the Female Genital Mutilation Act of 2003 does not consider it an offence if an approved individual performs a surgical operation on a girl which is necessary for her physical or mental health. It is unclear what is meant by mental health. Similarly, although the law of extraterritoriality applies to United Kingdom nationals or permanent residents as per article 3 and article 4 of this 2003 Act, non-British children are not protected. Newly arriving legal immigrants are not protected either because they often take several years before they can acquire the status of national or permanent resident. With such loopholes, it not surprising that in spite of the increase of the practice in the United Kingdom, prosecutions have not been brought against anyone as of 1998. The lone case reported in 1993 was that of a physician who was charged with contracting to perform female genital cutting. The case was dismissed due to lack of evidence.

FRANCE

France is described as one of the most offensive countries where criminalization and enforcement of laws against female genital cutting is concerned It is the first country in the world to sentence a female genital cutting practitioner. It is estimated that between 40,000 to 65,000 girls and women from female genital cutting countries live in France. Between 13,000 to 27,000 have been subjected to the practice while 4,500 live with the risk (Poldermans, 2006: 32–37; Leye, 2006, 2004). In the 1980s, the practice was outlawed following efforts by Linda Weil-Curiel, a lawyer for the Commission for the Abolition of Female Genital Mutilation. "I have participated in some forty cases in the Paris region," Weil-Curiel explains, "All cases have led to prison sentences, suspended or not, for around a hundred parents. Two excisors have been sent to jail," she adds (Bangre, 2008). The Commission for the Abolition of Female Genital Mutilation is an organization founded by Awa Thiam, an author renowned for denouncing the practice in her famous book, *La Parole aux Negresses* (1978). Her work helped the French authorities recognize this procedure as a health issue. In spite of this progress, France continues to face the challenge of curbing female genital cutting. As Habibou Bangre explains, the 2004 report from the French national Institute for Demographics reported that 53,000 women living in France had been exposed to some form of female genital cutting (Bangre 2008). In 2007, another prevalence study estimated the figure at 61,000 (European Institute for gender Equality).[7]

Although there is no specific law outlawing female genital cutting, France has relied on existing criminal legislation to prosecute both practitioners of the practice and parents who procure the services for their daughters. The French Constitution article 3 guarantees equality of women and men, and especially to the protection of a child's health. Within the French legal system, the practice was declared as an act of violence, making it an offence that could be tried according to existing French law. French law calls for prison sentences of up to 20 years for parents who subject their daughters to female genital cutting as well as those who perform the procedure. France prosecutes even when the practice is performed abroad. As a result, some activists have argued that the practice is not as common as it was in the 1980s. Bangre attributes this success to awareness campaigns, deterrent laws, and a growing understanding of the many negative health implications of the practices (Bangre, 2008; BBC News, 1999).

In 1983, the French High Court recognized that female genital cutting cases could be prosecuted under Article 312 of the Penal Code often comparable to Article 222 of the current Penal Code. According to this Article, acts of violence toward children that result in mutilation shall be tried in the highest criminal court (*Court d'assisses*). Thus, female genital cutting is criminalized under Penal Code articles 222–7, 222–8, and 229–9. The articles read:

Article 222–7 reads:

Acts of violence resulting in unintentional death are punishable by 15 years' imprisonment.

Article 222–8:

The offence defined in Article 222–7 shall be punishable by 20 years' imprisonment when committed:

1. on a minor under the age of 15;
2. On a person whose particular vulnerability, due to age, illness, disability, a physical or mental handicap or a state of pregnancy, is obvious or known to the author;
3. on a legitimate or natural ascendant or on the adoptive father or mother;
10. with the threat or use of a weapon. The punishment incurred shall be increased to 30 years' imprisonment when the offence defined in Article 222–7 is committed on a minor under the age of 15 by a legitimate, natural or adoptive ascendant or by any other person with authority over the minor.

The first two paragraphs of Article 132–23 relating to the term of imprisonment shall be applicable to the offences covered by this article.

Article 222–9:

Acts of violence resulting in mutilation or permanent disability shall be punishable to ten years' imprisonment and a fine of 150,000 euros.

Article 222–10:

The offence defined in Article 222–9 shall be punishable by 15 years' imprisonment when committed:

1. on a minor under the age of 15;
10. With the threat or use of a weapon, the punishment incurred shall be increased to 20 years' imprisonment when the offence defined in Article 222–9 is committed on a minor under the age of 15 by a legitimate, natural or adoptive ascendant or by any other person with authority over the minor (IPU).

Because of these stringent measures, which ensure enactment of laws is followed by enforcement, France has prosecuted 26 female genital cutting cases successfully under existing laws from 1978 to 2003, with 25 resulting in convictions. These convictions and the imprisonment of persons performing the procedure as well as the parents of girls subjected to the practice have proven effective in efforts to intervene against the practice in this country. The French experience has been used to illustrate the fact that one does not need a special statute in order to prosecute female genital cutting offenders. It is also a demonstration of how a strong prosecution policy does not necessarily reduce the number of procedures performed.

The first case of female genital cutting was prosecuted in 1983, leading to the imprisonment of a woman who performed the procedure on her daughter. In 1991, another case resulted in a five-year prison sentence. In 1995, a 23-year-old victim told a judge that the woman of Malian origin had performed female genital cutting on her and her sisters when they were children. In February 1999, a Paris Court sentenced a Mali woman who had been practicing female genital cutting for 15 years in France. She was sentenced to eight years for cutting 48 girls between the ages of one month and 10 years. Twenty seven mothers and fathers who solicited her services received suspended sentences from three to five years. In February 2004, a French court sentenced a Mali mother who lived in Paris for compliance in female genital cutting procedures for her daughter (Webster, 2004: 25).

According to Bangre (2008), French's attention was drawn to this issue in the 1970s after small girls bled to death after circumcisions. The government ordered for investigations in areas that were predominant with African immigrants to determine whether or not girls had been cut. Findings determined that over 500 girls had already been cut. The project enabled the French courts to convict several parents who consented to performing the practice on their daughters. These efforts helped to reduce the numbers of new cases dramatically.

France, like other countries, has faced the challenge of vacation female genital cutting. Bangre explains how Fatou, a 24-year-old French student she interviewed thought she had protection from her mother until she encountered her relatives in Senegal. She explains, "During the holidays in Senegal, when I was 11, members of my family discovered that I had not undergone it. They waited for my mother to leave and then they organized my mutilation" (Bangre, 2008). To discourage the transportation of girls to their countries of origin for the procedure, France enforces the extraterritoriality principle. Further, French medical staff members were asked to instruct immigrant parents that their daughters will be examined especially after they visit their countries of origin. France allows the sentencing of culprits even if the procedure is performed abroad. Unfortunately, because these check-ups were performed only on girls up to the age of six, allowing some parents evade the law by postponing the cut until it could not be detected, this step helped to increase awareness of the problem in the community. It is for this reason that some have argued for the need for legislation that not only helps to reduce the excision of babies and toddlers, but ensures the protection of adolescents as well, especially during their visits to their countries of origin or before a forced marriage (Webster, 2004). France's latest National Action Plan on Violence against women 2011–2013 deals specifically with female genital cutting. In the plan, a detailed set of guidelines on how to deal with female genital cutting is presented, including a budget for each measure against the practice (European Institute for Gender Equality).

AUSTRALIA

In Australia, criminal laws covering female genital cutting have been in force in six of the eight states since 1994–1997. The states include Australian Capital Territory, Northern Territory, New South Wales, South Australia, Tasmania, and Victoria. Although the Constitution does not include the Bill of Rights, it acknowledges rights and liberties in judicial and legislative efforts. It also considers female genital cutting a human rights issue. During 1995–2000, a national education program on female genital cutting was directed at various community health and welfare professionals. It should be noted that Australia was significantly involved in the drafting process of the Universal Declaration of Human Rights (1948), the Convention on the Elimination against Women (CEDAW) (1979), the Convention on the Rights of the Child (1989), the Declaration on Violence against Women (1993), and the Declaration and Platform for Action of the Fourth World Conference on Women (1995). It is therefore not surprising that Australia has included in its Constitution the Criminal Code articles 323A and 323B, which are designed to prohibit female genital cutting. The articles read as follows:

Article 323A

   (1)   Any person who performs female genital mutilation on another person is guilty of a crime. Maximum penalty is 14 years imprisonment.

   (2)   It is not a defense that the other person, or if the other person is a child, a parent or guardian of the other person consented to mutilation

   (3)   In this section—

"Female genital mutilation" means—

   (a)   Clitoridectomy; or

   (b)   Excision of any other part of the female genitalia

   (c)   Or a procedure to narrow or close the vaginal opening; or

   (d)   Any other mutilation of the female genitalia; but does not include—

(e) A sexual reassignment procedure; or

(f) A medical procedure for a genuine therapeutic purpose.

The removal of a child from the state for female genital cutting is covered under article 323B, which reads:

Article 323B

(1) Any person who takes a child from the state, or arranges for a child to be taken from the . . . Maximum penalty—14 years imprisonment.

(2) In the absence of proof to the contrary, it is to be presumed that a person took a child, or it is to be presumed that a person took, or arranged for a child to be taken, from the State with the intention of having female genital mutilation performed on the child if it is proved.

  (a) the person took the child, or arranged for the child to be taken, from the state; and

  (b) female genital mutilation was performed on the child while outside the state.

(3) In this section—

"Child" means a person under 18 years.

The Constitution explains clearly what is meant by "medical procedure for a genuine therapeutic purpose" and "Sexual reassignment procedure." A medical procedure for a genuine therapeutic purpose refers to the procedure directed only at curing or alleviating a physiological disability or physical abnormality. However, a sexual reassignment procedure refers to a procedure intended to give a person the genital appearance of a particular sex, whether male or female. Female genital cutting is also prohibited under other laws such as the Common Law, Community Welfare Act, the Children's Services Act of 1986, and the Family Law Act (Skaine, 65). These laws prohibit the practice within the jurisdiction as well as the removal of the child to another jurisdiction for the performance of the procedure. Generally, punishment ranges from 7 to 15 years imprisonment and consent is no defense.

The first flaw in the Australian legal system is that laws do not require mandatory reporting of female genital cutting. This makes it difficult for health professionals to check and even report children who are at risk. The second problem relates to the enforcement of existing laws. As of 1998–1999, there was no information available on enforcement. In 1993, a case of child abuse was brought before the Magistrate Court in Melbourne. The case involved a father of two girls who had been infibulated.

This was the first case involving female genital cutting. Unfortunately, little is known about the outcome.

AUSTRIA

The World Conference on Human Rights that was held in Vienna, Austria on June 25, 1993 to condemn violence against women made female genital cutting a significant issue in Austria. It is estimated that 8,197 women from a country that practice female genital cutting live in Austria (Polderman, 2006). The 1998 visit by Waris Dirie, an activist against female genital cutting, publicized the practice. Even then, it was not until the newsmagazine *Profil* published an undercover research in 2001, revealing that Austrian doctors exercised female genital cutting, that public debate on the issue ensued. In that same year, a law was designed to prohibit female genital cutting. The law emphasized the serious consequences of female genital cutting, particularly the fact that damage from the procedure was irreversible. The law also prohibited all forms of female genital cutting even where consent was involved.

The Austrian law against female genital cutting falls under articles 83–87 of the Austrian Penal Code. This law categorizes the practice as a form of serious bodily injury, the loss of essential parts of the body, permanent and incurable corporal lesions, and or permanent loss of functional capacity and as an offence that causes death. Articles 83–90, which address the practice, read as follows:

Article 83: Bodily Injury

1. Whoever inflicts a bodily injury or an impairment of one's health upon another person is punished with imprisonment up to one year or with a fine of up to 360 day's rates.
2. Likewise is punished who insults another person bodily and thereby negligently inflicts a bodily injury or an impairment of one's health upon the insulted person.

Article 84: Serious Bodily Injury

1. If the offence has caused impairment to the injured person's health lasting more than 24 days, or if the injury or impairment to one's health is serious in itself the offender is punished with imprisonment up to three years . . .

Article 85: Bodily Injury with Serious, Lasting Consequences

If the offence has caused . . .

2. a considerable mutilation or a striking deformation or
3. a serious suffering, lingering illness or professional inability forever or for a long period of time, the offender is punished with imprisonment of six months to five years.

In case of death, article 86 is invoked.

Article 86: Bodily Injury Resulting in Death

If the offence has caused the death of the injured person, the offender is punished with imprisonment of one to ten years.

Article 90 of the criminal law addresses injury by consent. It states:

1. Bodily injury or endangering one's bodily safety is not illegal, if the injured or endangered person has consented to it and the injury or endangering as such does not violate good morals.

The article, in paragraph 3, is also clear that it is not "possible to consent to a mutilation or other injury of the genitals that may cause a lasting impairment of the sexual sensitivity."

According to this article therefore, female genital cutting cannot be performed under any circumstances. The article which is part of the Austrian Penal Code (*Strafgesetzbuch*) became effective in 2002 (Dirie, 2005: 23).

Austrian laws are also flawed in the sense that they are nonspecific and unclear with regards to re-infibulation, cosmetic genital surgery, as well as categorization of genital piercing and tattooing. In February 2006, the Austrian cabinet passed legislation to change the statute of limitation for female genital cutting as a criminal offence. The statute of limitation—the time frame within which a person can press criminal charges—begins to run when one attains the age of 18. The main objective was to give a girl or woman enough time to deal with the consequences of the procedure before they can pursue criminal charges. It is argued that this increases the chances of girls to press charges.[8] This legislation went into effect on July 1, 2006.

Austria, as a member of the European Union, can also invoke laws that govern the Union, including the European Convention for the Protection of Human Rights and Fundamental Freedoms (ECHR), which are ranked the same as the country's constitution. In Austria also, child protection laws exist. The Austrian Civil Code (*Allgemeines Burgerliches Gesetzbuch*) states in article 146 that parents must guarantee the physical well-being and health of their children.[9] Article 176 of the Austrian

Civil Code grants a judge the authority to withdraw custody of a child if their wellbeing or health is endangered. Article 1325 allows one to claim damages for bodily harm. In Austria, as in most European countries, female genital cutting may be considered for asylum. The first asylum case was held in March 2002, when the Independent Federal Asylum Senate granted asylum to a woman from Cameroon to prevent her from undergoing infibulation in her country. In Austria also, the extraterritoriality regulations apply. However, they are determined by the principle of double criminality. In other words, in order for one to be held liable for criminal offences related to female genital cutting, the act has to be a criminal offence in both the country of nationality or residence and the country where the crime was committed (Leye, 2004: 19). Although Austria has enacted the extraterritoriality regulations, the principle of double criminality provides a loophole that may inhibit the enforcement of this law. Some parents have easily exploited this loophole to perform the procedure to unsuspecting girls in countries where the law is not on the books or is lax. It is therefore not surprising that Austria, like most industrialized countries, has not prosecuted any case of female genital cutting in spite of the criminalization of practice within the country's policy since the year 2002.

THE NETHERLANDS

Due to its history of tolerance and trade, the Netherlands has attracted a lot of immigrants, including those from countries that practice female genital cutting. According to National Office of Statistics, the number of women from one of the 29 countries where female genital cutting is practiced rose from 51,000 in 2005 to 64,000 in 2011 (European Institute of Gender Equality).[10] Marja Exterkate, estimates the figure at 70,000 in 2012 (Exterkate, 2013). The majority of immigrants live in large cities such as Amsterdam, the Hague, Rotterdam, Utrecht, and Tilburg. It is estimated that between 29,000 and 39,000 in the Netherlands have been cut, with 14,000 living with the risk (Exterkate, 2013; Poldermans, 2005/2006: 18–24; Dirie, 2005: 77–85). Public attention was drawn to the severe health and social consequences of female genital cutting in the 1990s. Because most come from Egypt, Eritrea, Somalia, and Sudan, the most common type of female genital cutting in the Netherlands is infibulation— the most serious of the types of this procedure.

In the Netherlands, female genital cutting is illegal. It is prohibited under general criminal law articles 300–304 of the Dutch Penal Code, where it is categorized as a form of abuse. In the Netherlands, the survivor of female genital cutting is allowed to press charges regarding female genital cutting after she turns 18, just as in other cases of sexual abuse. This measure is supposed to increase the chance of victims pressing charges as the girl or woman who has been subjected to female genital cutting is given time to deal with the psychological consequences of the practice and to think seriously about the consequences before pressing criminal charges.

A Dutch national or permanent resident of the Netherlands can be held liable if the practice of female genital cutting occurs outside the Netherlands territory. The law of extraterritoriality—double criminality may also apply outside the territory of the Netherlands if the individual in question is a Dutch national or a permanent resident of the Netherlands. This principle is only applicable if: (1) the individual involved is a national or permanent resident and (2) the act in question is a criminal offence in both the country of nationality or residence and the country where the crime was carried out. Also, if preparation of the acts occurred while in the Netherlands, he or she can be held liable (Kwaak et al., 2003: 53; Poldermans, 2005/2006).

The Netherlands also has laws about child protection. The Dutch Civil Code (*Algemeen Burgerlijk Wetboek*) provides in Book 1, article 254, paragraph 1, the possibility of the judge to give temporary custody of the child to a special child custody institution. Article 261 provides for the possibility to remove the child from her parental home for a longer period of time, if necessary. Other laws applicable to female genital cutting are found in the Dutch Constitution. The Constitution guarantees equality between men and women and prohibits gender discrimination. Article 11 of the Constitution provides the right to physical and mental integrity. The right to health is provided for in article 22. Article 10 of the Constitution also provides the right to respect individuals' life. The Netherlands has a special medical law— *Wet Berfoepen in de Indivuduele Gezondheidszorg*—which holds anyone in the medical profession liable for executing, and or providing assistance to the practice of female genital cutting, or damaging his or her body.[11] In addition, article 436, paragraph 2 of the Penal Code punishes persons crossing the reasonable/moral boundaries of their profession with a fine.

Recognizing that the practice has cultural underpinnings, the Netherlands provides for possible alternatives to female genital cuttings. Like the United States and Australia, symbolic cutting was proposed as an alternative to female genital cutting in 1992. However, the practice was later prohibited under articles 300–304 of the Dutch Penal Code which qualified it as a form of abuse (Poldermans, 2006: 18–24). The articles read:

Article 300

1. Physical abuse is punishable by a term of imprisonment of not more than two years or a fine of the fourth category.
2   Where serious bodily harm ensues as a result of the act, the offender is liable to a term of imprisonment of not more than four years or a fine of the fourth category.
3. Where death ensues as a result of the act, the offender is liable to a term of imprisonment of not more than six years or a fine of the fourth category.
4. Intentionally injuring a person's health is equivalent to physical abuse . . .

Article 301

1. Premeditated physical abuse is punishable by a term of imprisonment of not more than three years or a fine of the fourth category.
2. Where serious bodily harm ensues as a result of the act, the offender is liable to a term of imprisonment of not more than six years or a fine of the fourth category.
3. Where death ensues as a result of the act, the offender is liable to a term of imprisonment of not more than nine years or a fine of the fifth category.

Article 302

1. A person . . . guilty of aggravated physical abuse is liable to a term of imprisonment of no more than eight years or a fine of the fifth category.
2. Where death ensues . . . the offender is liable to a term of imprisonment of not more than ten years or a fine of the fifth category.

The terms of imprisonment prescribed in articles 300–303 may be increased by one-third in cases where the offender commits the serious offence against his mother, his legal father, his spouse, or his child. Despite the fact that female genital cutting has been declared a criminal offence in the Netherlands since 1992, not a single case has been prosecuted. This fact was surprising even to the Dutch Parliament itself in 2004, when they learned how France was effectively addressing this issue. The Council of Health was instructed to develop a more effective strategy in comparison to that of France. As Poldermans explains, this recommendation was disregarded by Mr. Hoogervost, then Minister of Health and Wellbeing and Sports, who argued that it was unnecessary to change current criminal provisions as it would not result in a more effective criminal policy (Poldermsn, 2005: 22–23). Instead, the council established a special commission; the Commission Combating Female Genital Mutilation *(Commissie Bestrijding Vrouwelijke Genitale Verminking)*, which only suggested that female genital cutting be "addressed as an aggravated form of abuse with an increased penalty for this form of abuse" (Poldermans, 2005: 22–23).

CANADA

In Canada, it is estimated that there are 70,000 immigrants and refugees from Somalia and 10,000 from Nigeria (Omayme, 1995). The Canadian Charter of Rights and Freedoms guarantees the equality of men and women, and the right to life, liberty, and security for all is guaranteed. In 1994, after the recognition of female genital cutting as a violation of human rights, the then Ministry of the Solicitor General and Correctional Services issued a memorandum to all chiefs of police and the Commission of the Ontario Provincial Police, explaining that the practice was a criminal offence. He also informed them of the investigative and charging procedures related to female genital cutting. This was followed by a memorandum from the Ministry of the Attorney General to all Crown Attorneys on how to prosecute charges related to female genital cutting.

On May 26, 1997, the federal government amended the Canadian Criminal Code to prohibit female genital cutting under Section 268. Under this section, the procedure is considered an aggravated assault that is punishable by imprisonment for a term not exceeding 14 years. Consent is no defense. The stipulation reads: -

(1&2)   Every one commits an aggravated assault who wounds, maims, disfigures or endangers the life of the complainant . . . is guilty of an indictable offence and liable to imprisonment for a term not exceeding fourteen years.

(3)   For greater certainty, in this section, "wounds" or "maims" includes to excise, infibulate or mutilate, in whole or in part, the labia majora, labia minora or clitoris of a person, except where:

(a)   a surgical procedure is performed, by a person duly qualified by provincial law to practice medicine, for the benefit of the physical health of the person or for the purpose of that person having normal reproductive functions or normal sexual appearance or function; or

(b)   the person is at least eighteen years of age and there is no resulting bodily harm.

(4)   . . . no consent to the excision, infibulation or mutilation, in whole or in part, of the labia majora, labia minora or clitoris of a person is valid, except in the cases described in paragraphs (3) (a) and (b)."

The Criminal Code in Section 273.3 ensures that children who are ordinarily resident in Canada (citizens or landed migrants are protected children) are not removed from the country and subjected to female genital cutting in another country. The Code reads:

(1)   No person shall do anything for the purpose of removing from Canada a person who is ordinarily resident in Canada and who is under the age of eighteen years, with the intention that an act be committed outside Canada that if it were committed in Canada would be an offence against section 155 or 159, subsection 160(2) or section 170, 171, 267, 268, 269, 271, 272 or 273 in respect of that person.

Culprits are liable for punishment for a term not exceeding five years (Criminal Code, R.S.C. 1985). In addition to legal penalties, medical associations in most Canadian provinces have passed prohibitions against performing this procedure. As of 1999, no instances of arrest have been recorded.

JAPAN

Although no case of female genital cutting has been reported in Japan and no laws exist outlawing this practice, female genital cutting is considered an offense under the Japan Penal Code (Act No. 45 of 1907). According to the Code:

Article 204: Bodily Injury

A person who causes another to suffer bodily injury shall be punished with imprisonment with forced labor for not more than 15 years or a fine of not more than 500,000 yen.

Article 205: Bodily Injury Resulting in Death

A person who causes another to suffer bodily injury resulting in death shall be punished with imprisonment with forced labor for a fixed term of no less than 3 years.

Article 206: Instigating Bodily Injury

A person who at the scene of the crime prescribed for in the two preceding Articles instigates the offender in committing the crime shall, even though the person does not cause another to suffer bodily injury in person, be punished with imprisonment with forced labour for not more than one year or a fine of not more than 100, 00 yen or a petty fine."

Unfortunately, there is no judicial precedent which has ruled whether parental consent makes female genital cutting on the young nonpunishable.

GERMANY

Although there are no specific laws against female genital cutting per se in Germany, the practice is considered a serious and grave bodily harm that is criminal. It is estimated that between 30,000 and 50,000 minor girls live with the risk in Germany (Diesie: Wiener Program for Francengesundheit).[12] The German Constitution guarantees the equality of all people. It recognizes the right to life and to physical integrity and provides the freedom of a person as inviolable. In 1996 and 1997, the German Medical Association condemned the participation of a physician in any form of female genital cutting. In 1999, the Minister of Justice stated the need for the police and prosecutors to investigate and familiarize themselves with female genital cutting. The German Penal Code, Section 223 on bodily injury reads:

Whoever physically maltreats or harms the health of another person, shall be punished with imprisonment for not more than five years or a fine . . .

Section 224: Dangerous Bodily Injury

(1) Whoever commits bodily harm . . . 2. by means of a weapon or other dangerous tool; 3. by means of a sneak attack; 4. jointly with another participant; or 5. by means of a treatment dangerous to life, shall be punishable with imprisonment from six months to ten years, in less serious cases with imprisonment from three months to five years.

. . .

(3) Imprisonment for not less than one year shall be imposed if the perpetrator by the act places the ward in danger of 1. death or serious health damage; or 2. a substantial impairment of his physical or emotional imprisonment.

(4) In less serious cases under subsection 2. imprisonment from three months to five years shall be imposed, in less serious cases under subsection 3. imprisonment from six months to five years.

Section 226: Serious Bodily Injury

(1) If the bodily injury has, as a result, that the injured person . . . 2. loses or permanently can no longer use an important bodily member; 3 is permanently disfigured in a substantial way or becomes infirm, paralyzed, mentally ill or disabled, then the punishment shall be imprisonment for one year to ten years . . .

Section 227: Bodily Injury Resulting in Death

(1) If the perpetrator causes the death of the injured person through the infliction of bodily injury (Sections 223 to 226), then the punishment shall be imprisonment for not less than three years.

In Section 228, the document addresses the issue of consent. It says:

Whoever commits bodily injury with the consent of the injured person only acts unlawfully if the act is, despite the consent, contrary to good moral (IPU).

NEW ZEALAND

Although there are no statistics on female genital cutting in New Zealand, female genital cutting is criminal. New Zealand has actively supported international efforts to eliminate traditional practices such as female genital cutting which affect the health of women and girls. First, it co-sponsored the biennial resolution on "Traditional or customary practices affecting the health of women and girls" in the Third Committee of the UN General Assembly as well as the resolution on the "Elimination of violence against women" at the Commission on Human Rights. Second, New Zealand is among the first countries to ratify the CEDAW and its Optional Protocol as well as the UN Convention on the Rights of the Child, which seeks to protect and promote the rights of women and children. The Constitution protects individual rights and freedoms. The Bill of Rights guarantees equality of men and women, the right to life, security of persons, and rights of minority.

In 1995, an amendment was made to the Crimes Amendment Act of New Zealand, making female genital cutting a crime. It became effective on January 1, 1996. Culprits were liable to imprisonment of up to 7 years.

By 1998, there was no record of criminal investigation of the practice based on the law. The New Zealand government established a National Female Genital Cutting education program to prevent the practice through community education, support, and health promotion. Guidelines have been established by this program and the New Zealand College of Obstetricians and Gynecologists for women who have undergone the procedure. New Zealand also has child protection laws. Under Public Act 204A and 204B, female genital cutting is criminal. Public Act 204A reads:

Everyone is liable to imprisonment for a term not exceeding 7 years who performs, or causes to be performed, on any other person, any act involving female genital mutilation.

(3) Nothing in subsection (2) of this section applies in respect of (a) Any medical or surgical procedure (including a sexual reassignment procedure) that is performed on any person (i) For the benefit of that person's physical or mental health; and (ii) By a medical practitioner; (b) Any medical or surgical procedure that is performed on any person (i) While that person is in labor or immediately after that person gives birth; and (ii) For the benefit of that person's health or the health of the child; and (iii) By a medical practitioner or a registered midwife or a trainee health professional, or by any other person in any case where the case is urgent and no medical practitioner or registered midwife or trainee health professional is available . . .

Public Act 204B reads:

Everyone is liable to imprisonment for a term not exceeding 7 years who, with intent that there be done, outside New Zealand, to or in relation to any child under the age of 17 years (being a child who is a New Zealand citizen or is ordinarily resident in New Zealand), any act which, if done in New Zealand, would be an offence against section 204A of this Act, (a) Causes that child to be sent or taken out of New Zealand; or (b) Makes any arrangements for the purposes of causing that child to sent or taken out of New Zealand.

(2) Everyone is liable to imprisonment for a term not exceeding 7 years who, in New Zealand, aids, incites, counsels, or procures

the doing, outside New Zealand, in relation to any person who is a New Zealand citizen or is ordinarily resident in New Zealand, of any act which, if done in New Zealand, would be an offence against section 204A of this Act, whether or not the act is in fact done.

(3) Everyone is liable to imprisonment for a term not exceeding 7 years who, in New Zealand, incites, counsels, procures, or induces any person who is a New Zealand citizen or is ordinarily resident in New Zealand.

It is therefore a crime to aid, permit, or perform female genital cutting outside New Zealand since this practice is an offence in New Zealand according to section 204A of the Public Act. Consent is no defense.

NORWAY

The experience of Kadra's and the Gambian woman and imams awakened the government to the reality of female genital cutting in this country. The realization that girls born in Norway lived with the risk of female genital cutting, and that sometimes parents used school vacation days in July and August to perform the practice led to a stern response by the government. First, an emergency strategy was created to protect girls from exposure to this procedure. The girls under the age of 18 were to be denied passports and the right to travel outside the country when there is clear suspicion that a girl may be at risk. All girls or at least girls of high risk backgrounds were to undergo mandatory check-ups of their genitals regularly. It was argued that this would prevent the parents from cutting their daughters for fear of being discovered. Although these measures were to inconvenience girls and families who had no intention to engage in female genital cutting, the government saw this as the only possible way to protect the girls. Critics resisted them, claiming that they were drastic and in violation of the rights of the children. By singling out girls of cultures that traditionally embrace female genital cutting, the law encouraged discrimination, stigmatization, and humiliation of these girls and communities that embraced the practice.

The Norwegian Constitution provides that the state should respect and ensure human rights. In 1995, Norway enacted a law specifically criminalizing female genital cutting. Act No. 74 of December 15, 1995 prohibits female genital cutting. It reads:

Any person who wilfully performs a procedure on a woman's genital organs that injures or permanently changes the genital organs will be penalized for female genital mutilation. The penalty is a term of imprisonment of up to 3 years, or up to 6 years if the procedure results in illness or occupational disability lasting for more than 2 weeks, or if an incurable deformity, defect or injury is caused, and up to 8 years if the procedure results in death or substantial injury to the woman's body or health. A person who aids and abets another in the practice of female genital mutilation may be penalized in the same way.

Penalties as mentioned in the first paragraph will be imposed for reconstruction of female genital mutilation.

Consent does not provide exemptions from criminal liability. (The Norwegian ministry of Health and Social Affairs, 2002)

According to the law, any person who violates this prohibition may be punished by fines or imprisonment of up to three, six, or eight years, depending on how severe the consequences of the procedure are. The girl or woman herself cannot be penalized. The act penalizes anyone who intentionally "damages" or "permanently changes" a woman's genital organs. If the procedure has resulted in "illness or occupational disability lasting more than two weeks" or "an incurable defect, fault or injury," the penalty is a term of imprisonment of up to six years. If the procedure results in "death or substantial injury to the woman's body or health," a term of imprisonment of up to eight years may be imposed (IPU).

Consent does not exempt somebody from punishment. A person who aids or abets another in the practice of female genital cutting may be penalized in the same way as the person who actually carries out the procedure. Since the act applies in Norway and abroad, any person who has carried out or was aided in the carrying out of the procedure and who is a Norwegian national or is resident in Norway is not exempt from punishment even if the procedure itself is carried outside the country's boundaries (IPU).

In 1998, no prosecutions had been brought against the practice so far. At the instruction of the Norwegian Parliament, the government formulated a Plan of Action to combat female genital mutilation in October 2000. This Plan was to: (i) Draw attention to and achieve better cooperation with organizations and individuals working to combat genital cutting of girls within the relevant communities in Norway, (ii) Ensure that female genital cutting was prohibited by law in Norway, (iii) Initiate preventive measures both in the health service and in schools, and (iv) Strengthen the international cooperation on these issues. The Ministry of Children and Family Affairs responded by issuing the Governmental Action Plan against Female Genital Mutilation. Norway also has child protection laws. Although the Health Department provides funding for education and outreach programs, there is no a medical ethics provision or guidelines for medical professionals.

POLAND

While there are no reports of female genital cutting in Poland, the practice is considered criminal under article 156 of the Penal Code. The article reads:

1. Whoever causes grievous bodily harm in a form which: 1) deprives a human being of sight, hearing, speech or the ability to procreate, or 2) inflicts on another a serious crippling injury, an incurable or prolonged illness, an illness actually dangerous to life, a permanent mental illness, a permanent total or substantial incapacity to work in an occupation, or a permanent serious bodily disfigurement or deformation shall be subject to the penalty of the deprivation of liberty for a term of between 1 and 10 years.
2. If the perpetrator acts unintentionally he shall be subject to the penalty of deprivation of liberty for up to 3 years.
3. If the consequence of an act specified in § 1 is the death of a human being, the perpetrator shall be subject to the penalty of the deprivation of liberty for a term of between 2 and 12 years. (IPU)

SWEDEN

In Sweden, it is estimated that female genital cutting has been criminalized since 1982. The Act Prohibiting the Genital Mutilation of Women (1982) has been amended twice. Section 1 states:

An operation may not be carried out on the outer female sexual organs with a view to mutilating them or bringing about some other permanent change in them ("circumcision"), regardless of whether consent has been given for the operation or not.

Section 2 states that:

Anyone committing a breach of Section 1 is to be sentenced to a term of imprisonment of not more than four years. If the offence has caused danger to life, serious illness, or has involved conduct of an unusually ruthless character in some other respect, it shall be regarded as grave. For a grave offence the sentence is a term of imprisonment of not less than two years and not more than ten years. A sentence for liability pursuant to Chapter 23 of the Penal Code is to be passed on anyone found guilty of attempting, preparing or conspiring to commit the above offence, or of failing to report it. (Act 1998: 407)

SWITZERLAND

Although Switzerland has a law against female genital cutting, the IPU has no official information on the subject and the existence of a specific legislation. Yet, it is estimated that 7,000 women and girls have undergone genital cutting or live with the risk of being genitally cut in Switzerland (Leye, 2008: 46–47). A change in the Swiss Penal Code on this practice went into effect on July 1, 2012. The objective of the law was to prevent Switzerland-based families from cutting their daughters in Switzerland or abroad. Under the new legislation, anyone who performs genital cutting on a child is held responsible and punished. The degree of cutting determines the severity of the sentence, which involves up to 10 years in prison or substantial fines. This law came after the UNICEF Switzerland collected 20,000 signatures calling for stronger measures against female genital cutting.

Responding to this development, Katrin Piazza, Spokeswoman for the Swiss National Committee of the United Nations Children's Fund had this to say, "The new article is a clear and unmistakable signal that Switzerland does not tolerate this violation of human rights, FGM is a violation of human rights and a severe violation of children's rights, which explicitly guarantees the right of physical integrity" (Vogel-Misicka, 2012). Andrea Candrian, vice head of the Federal Justice Office's International Criminal Law Unit had this to say: "Thanks to the new provision in our criminal law, mutilation of female genitals can be prosecuted and punished by a Swiss judge, even in cases where the offence has taken place abroad and when not punishable under the country's law." In addition, she observes, "Persons who have assisted in such a crime or contributed in another way can be prosecuted as well. For example—if a girl's family has organized a mutilation—then not only the circumciser but also the family members involved can be prosecuted."

The first prosecution of female genital cutting was reported on July 10, 2012. A 54-year-old Somali woman resident of Bern Switzerland for 20 years was charged in the Fribong Cantanal Court for forcing female genital cutting. She received 240 hours of community service (Vogel-Misicka, 2012). Regarding the efficacy of the law on eradicating this practice, Candrian notes, "Measures and information campaigns with regards to prevention among immigrants might be even more important and more useful tool in the fight against mutilation" (Vogel-Misicka, 2012). Piazza observes, "Legislation alone isn't enough: there's always the risk that circumcision is simply practiced underground. When an entire community share a harmful social practice, it is almost impossible for an individual to defy it—even if he or she is aware of its danger" (Vogel-Misicka, 2012).

BELGIUM

In Belgium, where it is estimated that 12,415 immigrants exist, excluding asylum seekers and illegal immigrants, female genital cutting is explicitly forbidden under article 409 of the Belgian Penal Code. According to statistics, about 2,745 women have been exposed to the procedure, with about 534 girls under the age of 16 living with the risk (Leye, 2008). It is not only a criminal offence to perform female genital cutting, it is also criminal to participate in and to facilitate the performance of the practice. According to the Code:

1. Anyone who performs, facilitates or promotes any form of mutilation of the genitalia on a person of the female sex, with or without her consent, will be punished by a term of imprisonment of three to five years. Attempted mutilation will be punished by a term of imprisonment of eight days to one year.
2. If the mutilation is undertaken on a minor or in pursuit of profit, the punishment is confinement of five to ten years.
3. If the mutilation has caused an apparently incurable illness or a lasting incapacity for work, the punishment is confinement of five to ten years.
4. If the mutilation results in death, even though there was no intent to kill, the punishment is confinement of ten to fifteen years.
5. If the mutilation is . . . undertaken on a minor or a person who, by reason of their physical or mental state, are not in a position to provide for themselves, by their father, mother or another blood relation in the ascending line, or by any other person who has authority over the minor or the legally disqualified person, or by a person who occasionally or usually lives with the victim, then the minimum punishment . . . is doubled in the case of a term of imprisonment and increased by two years in the case of confinement.

A survey carried out in 2004 on the implementation of this law revealed that no case of female genital cutting had been prosecuted in Belgium. Girls at risk of female genital cutting had not been reported neither to the police nor to social services, and no cases had been brought to court (Leye et al., 2004; Leye et al., 2008: 182–190). Some have argued that this is because, in Belgium, female genital cutting is not an issue of public debate (Daniels et al., 2000). Therefore, it receives very little coverage. There are guidelines on the clinical management of delivery of infibulated women, including discouraging re-infibulation of these women since 2000 (Daniels et al., 2000).

To conclude this chapter, it is important to state that while it is apparent that some industrialized countries have initiated and enacted laws, policies, or found a way to intervene against female genital cutting using the existing legal system, a lot more is needed to protect the rights of children and women in these countries. Some countries such as Italy, Luxemberg, Andora, Bouvet Island, Bulgaria, Cyprus, Czech Republic, Denmark, Estonia, Faroe Islands, Finland, Gibraltar, Greece, Hungary, Iceland, Latria, Lithuania, Malta, Portugal, Romania, Slovakia, Slovania, and Spain lack specific legislation to prevent, combat, or sanction against female genital cutting. Due to space constraints, detailed examination of these countries is not possible. It is, however, important that all countries, industrialized or not, work at instituting laws about female genital cutting and to ensure that these are as specific as can be in order for enforcement to be carried out.[13] It can be argued, however, that the challenge to protect children and women at risk of this practice lies in the effectiveness of these policies.

Studies indicate how difficult it is to enforce laws on a deep-rooted cultural practice such as female genital cutting. As Celia Dugger explains, it is difficult to ascertain whether the rite was performed when the wound has healed. Francouer (1999) has also explained how some immigrants have resorted to taking their daughters out of the country for the rite to evade the law. Enactment of policies and laws without serious commitment by governments and its officials can be counterproductive. Ellen Gruenbaum has particularly taken issue with governments that criminalize female genital cutting out of external pressure because this signals non-commitment (2001: 205). Other statistics indicate that female genital-cutting intervention programs that have relied on outside authorities or financial incentives have been unsuccessful. When policies and ensuing laws are not specific, and unenforced, the community will not take them seriously.

Statistics also indicate that sympathetic doctors have failed to report incidences of genital cutting for fear of breaking up tight-knit families, as discussed earlier. It is important to note that allowing any form of genital cutting is to increase loopholes to be exploited by some. Alongside this is the question of double standards. As indicated earlier, the existence of laws against female genital cutting without the condemnation of similar practices such as male circumcision and medical genital modification surgeries as practiced in most industrialized countries have led to claims of double standard and discrimination. When laws communicate the idea that some cultural beliefs and traditions are tolerated while others are not, they become difficult to promote effectively; thus, the challenge of double standards. Cultural relativists have critiqued laws that single out female genital cutting as immoral, while overlooking other forms of genital alterations found in these countries. Coleman's defense of the practice evokes similar sentiments when she argues that the procedure is less severe than the circumcision of boys. She insists that hospitals must either perform such a procedure on girls, if requested, or stop circumcising boys. She believes that the procedure should be allowed under the Equal Protection Clause (Adhikari and Salahi, 2010). Similar sentiments are expressed by my respondents who argued that female genital cutting was being singled out for demonization. It is for this reason that the proposal by the AAP and RANZCOG to allow the pinprick or nick form of genital cutting was made. While it is erroneous to compare female genital cutting to male circumcision, given the difference in health and moral implications, as discussed earlier, it is important that the law seeks to protect all individuals without bias.

Cultural insensitivity: Statistics also indicate that often, coercion has led to clandestine performance of the practice. It is therefore important that legal measures be supplemented by community-based initiatives, the task in the next chapter. While the importance of criminalization policies must be viewed as a way to empower activists to be more effective, effectiveness of these laws can only be achieved by use of a cultural sensitive approach. Although demeaning and retributive aspects of the law may ensure the documentation of the practice and that it is not tolerated in the country, it takes a culturally sensitive approach to engage the community at the level of appreciating the values behind the practice and to promote a change in attitude.

NOTES

1. Office of Women's Health, Development of Health and Human Services, OWH: Programs and Health activities, Reproductive Health, http:www.4women.gov.owh/prog/reprod.htm.
2. *Cal. Health and Safety* Code § 124170 (West: 1996).
3. 1999 Colo. Legis. Serv. Ch. 216, §§ 2, 4 (99–96) (West).
4. Council of Europe, P.A. Resolution 1247, paragraph 11, 2001.
5. European Union, E.P. Resolution 2001/2035 (INI), paragraph 7.

6. Department of Health CMO Update 37, February 2004 is available at DH website: www.dh.gov.uk.
7. These data were retrieved from the European Institute for Gender Equality (EIGE) website: eige.europa.eu.
8. *Anderung des Strafrechts bei Genitalverstummerlung und Zwangsheirat, in* "Die Presse," February 23, 2006. See also *Osterreichische Platform gegen weibliche Genitalverstummelung, Rechtsinformationsblatt zum Informationsabend uber FGM fur ArzInnen und Hebammen*, 28 June 2006.
9. Australian Civil Code, articles 146–146d (Obsorge).
10. The source can be accessed at www.eige.europa.eu.
11. *Wet Berfoepen in de Indivuduele Gezondheidszorg.*
12. Diesie, n.d., "Female Genital Mutilation," *Wiener Program Fur Franengesundheit*, www.diesie.at/English/FGM.
13. This information and that of other countries not discussed above can be reviewed on the IPU website: http://www.ipu.org/wmn-e/fgm-prov.htm.

7

❖

Community-Based Intervention

Although efforts to provide intervention programs against female genital cutting in industrialized countries have been met by challenges related to policy enactment and enforcement, it is apparent that most industrialized countries such as the United States have taken significant measures to protect the rights of children and women. While most have initiated legal and educational measures to eradicate female genital cutting, the increase and persistence of the practice in these countries is indicative of loopholes and flaws in existing intervention programs. As illustrated earlier, existing policies and legal measures are flawed in ways that perpetuate the practice. Social resistance to legal policies is another significant flaw in the criminalization policies. In this chapter, I explore ways to promote effective intervention programs in industrialized countries. I argue that in addition to establishing clear and enforceable legal policies, it is important to pursue community-based initiatives that are broad enough and yet specific in order to capture various aspects that lead to the persistence of the practice of female genital cutting.

In order to effect behavior change, however, it is important that intervention programs link their goals of targeting attitude change to realities in the communities involved. When a question about eradication of female genital cutting was posed in a survey of 113 respondents, 89 percent of those interviewed were of the opinion that female genital cutting should be eradicated. Eleven percent preferred that the practice be left alone as a cultural right. These responses are similar in some fashion to those held in the United Kingdom. In a survey by a famous organization based in the United Kingdom, the Foundation for Women's Health, Research and Development (FORWARD), based in London, 85 percent were of the opinion that the practice should be eradicated while 16 percent wanted it to be left alone (Dorkenoo, 2007).

According to the World Health Organization (WHO) and Appropriate Technology in Heath (PATH), effective female genital cutting intervention programs must be broad in the sense of targeting both men and women in an effort to convince them to abandon the practice. This goal can be achieved by the following: (1) The establishment of strong and capable institutional programs at national, regional, and local levels; (2) supporting these programs by strong policies, laws, and resources; (3) ensuring that female genital cutting is institutionalized as an issue, to be addressed by national reproductive health and development programs; (4) ensuring effective coordination between governments and nonprofit organizations in addressing female genital cutting; (5) ensuring that health providers are trained in order to effectively recognize wounds and complications associated with female genital cutting; and (6) promoting effective advocacy that fosters positive policy enactment and legal measures against female genital cutting. All these aspects are community-based initiatives that, if properly executed, can effect behavior change.

COMMUNITY-BASED INITIATIVES

Central to community-based initiatives are not only the education and the awareness component they provide, these initiatives are also embedded in grassroots action. Grassroots action is geared toward stimulating the agency that is necessary for change to take place. While they are described as the most successful initiatives toward combating a culture-based social practice such as female genital cutting, they must be supplemented by legal policies. In recognition of the role of community-based initiatives in behavior change, WHO/UNICEF/UNFPA produced the following statement:

> Culture is not static but it is in constant flux, adapting and reforming. People will change their behavior when they understand the hazards and indignity of harmful practices and when they realize that it is possible to give up harmful practices without giving up meaningful aspects of their cultures. (WHO/UNICEF/UNFPA, 1996)

Community-based initiatives that have been successful have utilized the cultural sensitivity approach. Cultural sensitivity to the values and other social variables that inform attitudes toward the practice is a significant component to consider and appreciate even as behavior change is encouraged. Community-based initiatives that have failed have been critiqued for using patronizing and demeaning language in reference to the practice. They utilize approaches that are confrontational. Confrontational strategies include those that blame either men or women for perpetuating the practice. Patronizing and demeaning language is often associated with the Western connotation that has viewed female genital cutting as an uncivilized barbaric practice that is performed by unloving parents toward their daughters. For instance, the general tendency among some advocates to categorize female genital cutting as genital mutilation is not indicative of cultural ignorance of why the practice is performed; it communicates that the practitioner is demeaning and insensitive—an erroneous assumption about those who embrace the practice. Strategies such as these undermine the identity and agency of men and women in communities that practice female genital cutting or neglect cultural values within which the practice is embedded. Female genital cutting is like any other cultural practice embraced for socialization process. It is viewed as a rite of passage that is necessary for the girls to transition into marriageable status. For this reason, it was traditionally performed for the good of the girl and the community. It is important that this fact is recognized and appreciated if at all efforts to change perspectives in these communities are to be effected.

Adopting a nonjudgmental approach is preferred because it facilitates dialogue that is necessary for promoting a safe and confident environment for sharing views and expressing opinions. Thus, community members are encouraged to become active agents who control their own development rather than passive recipients of information. Through dialogue, deep-seated feelings about female genital cutting are likely to be voiced and collaboration on how to end the practice is initiated. This approach, applied in Guinea by a German Agency for Technical Cooperation (GTZ), was described to be "their most effective intervention" (UNICEF, 26). Through dialogue, both women and men shared their views and ambivalences about the practice in a respectful and nonjudgmental setting. Thus, a new discourse is introduced as behavioral options are presented to the community. As Crossett explains, it is important that advocates recognize that women involved love their daughters and that they fear that their daughters will be ostracized unless they are cut.

ALTERNATIVE RITES OF PASSAGE

In communities where the practice is associated with the coming-of-age ceremonies, some have suggested the need to develop alternative rites of passage in order to maintain necessary cultural values without necessarily cutting girls' genitals. Rites of passage that often involve socialization in the societal values of one's heritage and the celebration of these values through traditional dances, singing, feasting, and gift-giving hold a deeper meaning for the communities concerned than the act of genital cutting. Where introduced, alternative rituals have been a success. They are illustrations to the community of the positive sociocultural aspects of how their culture and how these can be retained without enduring harmful practices By celebrating the coming-of-age rituals through alternative rituals, a community publicly declares that female genital cutting is not necessary to coming of age.

The Ntaanira na Mugambo Case

One example of alternative rituals offered through community-based initiatives is known as "*Ntaanira na Mugambo,*" a Kenyan Kikuyu community phrase that translates literally as "circumcision through words." This program first employed in Kenya by the Program for Appropriate Technology in Health (PATH) is considered successful because it involved family and community members (PATH/WHO, 1999: 8). It offers girls in genital-cutting communities an alternative way to be initiated into adulthood. Initiates attend a week-long program of counseling, training, and instruction about womanhood. They learn about anatomy and physiology, sexual and reproductive health, hygiene, gender issues, respect for adults, and the importance of self-esteem (Stanlie, 2002: 104–105). On the last day, a ceremony is performed in the presence of the entire community to signal the girls' passage into womanhood. In six years of operation, the project has prevented more than 1,000 genital cuttings (Shell-Duncan and Hernlund, 2000: 37). By encouraging the observance of rituals associated with female genital cutting, it acknowledges the cultural value associated with this practice.

Girls in the program have reported how training helped their self-esteem and confidence that was necessary to resist community pressure to engage in female genital cutting. Also, initiates are helped to form support groups that strengthen their new role in the community culture. Women in an alternative program such as PATH are enabled to negotiate community support. By providing these women with basic education against female genital cutting, they are enabled to participate in informed dialogue that will foster participation in the decision-making process. By asking community members to pledge not to engage in female genital cutting activities and their sons not to insist on marrying cut women, such a program counters social coercion that is central to the sustenance of this practice.

While successful to some extent because of their sensitivity to cultural mores, alternative rituals approach has been critiqued by some as having limited impact on the promotion of social justice. It has been argued that it fails to address the underlying patriarchal social values that are associated with female genital cutting and human rights. Critics prefer that the norms that motivate female genital cutting should be discouraged as well. In immigrant communities, alternative rites can be encouraged as part of cultural appreciation and celebration of events. Appreciation of positive cultural values through multicultural appreciation of diversity and difference is a way to open dialog to discuss this issue in immigrant communities. Appreciation of cultural values related to puberty rites is important, but this does not necessarily have to include the performance of practices that have been established as harmful.

LOCALIZED INITIATIVES

Community initiatives recognize that dialogue within a female genital-cutting community is important and that it must be led by the community itself. Thus, it is important that initiatives are also localized in order to promote such dialogue and to capture vital community components to the intervention process. Localized initiative will not only engage local activists who are thoroughly versed in the historical, political, and social context of local communities; educators and key figures in the intervention programs are drawn from the communities themselves (Stanlie, 2005: 259–262). As observed by Erin Crossett, localized advocacy helps engage the community in intervention process, thus enabling them to define their own social needs and solutions. By involving the community at all levels, all are encouraged to work together to achieve initiatives to transform attitudes toward female genital cutting.

Most community-based localized programs are mostly based on the individual and social change or empowerment model, which recognize the reality of social change, and cultural appraisal in social reality (Parker, 1996). The underlying assumption is that if a community is empowered about its social reality, problem solving becomes a participatory endeavor. This means, community members are not only informed about their personal, social, economic, and political situations, they also become initiators of action to improve their situations (Israel, 1994). An empowered community is often enabled to control, own their situation, and seek solutions that they deem fit (Werner et al., 1997). In the case of female genital cutting, therefore, such a community would involve everyone, including men and women, leaders, advocates, practitioners, and survivors of the practice since all in the community should be given an opportunity to participate in behavioral change efforts. It is important that social transformation is addressed at all levels in order for cultural appraisal to take place, which will, in turn, initiate a change in behavior. The success of this strategy is reported in communities such as Senegal, where a localized advocacy initiative led to collective pledges against female genital cutting, with over 5,000 villages across the country abandoning this deep rooted practice (Crossett, 1995).

The Bagayoko Case

Ms. Miriam Bagayoko's experience is another illustration of how attitude change must happen at the village level. In her article, "Mutilating Africa's Daughters: Laws Unenforced, Practices Unchanged" (2004), Tina Rosenberg introduces us to Bagayoko, a powerful and respected person in Bamako, the capital of Mali. Today, she is shunned and criticized by many of her neighbors. This mother of three girls and three boys used to perform female genital cutting in a country where more than 90 percent of the girls are subjected to the practice. She explains, "It is a trade I had learned from my aunt at the age of 25" (Rosenberg, 2004). At the age of 14, Mariam was subjected to female genital cutting herself, when a group of women took her alongside other teenage girls to "a dark hut, pinned them down, grabbed a knife and cut off parts of their genitals" (Voa News, 2009). A group of women who were in charge of genital cutting told her and the group of other girls that their father would shoot her if she discussed the experience with anyone.

In 1988, Bagayoko began to receive frequent visits from Kadidia Sidibe, who is the director of a Bamako women's group that is against female genital cutting. Although she resisted their visits and messages for seven years, she yielded after seeing photographs of girls who had undergone the procedure and experienced serious medical problems. These photographs finally persuaded her to stop performing the practice. She was mostly concerned with the fatal childbirth effects for both the mother and the baby. Bagayoko recounts how she had witnessed many women suffering from gynecological problems and how these were explained away. She explains, "People say it's because of bad spirits. It's not attributed to the circumcision." Her conversion however came too late for her two daughters, who had already been subjected to female genital cutting. Today, she is the leader of a group of former circumcisers who speak out against female genital cutting to women. The group also trains teenagers to speak out against the practice in schools. She explains, "I have laid down the knife and have now converted into a merchant, selling fabrics and soap. I will no longer perform FGM. I now will encourage others to do the same" (IRIN News, 2013).

When Bagayoko speaks to women in an attempt to persuade them not to have their daughters undergo the procedure, she is frequently told that she is betraying their culture for purposes of profit, rendering girls and women unmarriageable, subsequently forcing them into a life of poverty. While on a trip to Nairobi, Bagayoko met with eight women from several countries who used to perform female genital cutting who are now advocates against the practice. Equality Now, a New York-based group that finances African women's organizations that work to stop female genital cutting, organized the meeting.

Currently, there are several groups in Mali that are actively working to stop the practice from occurring. One such group is Sini Sanuman. Recently, the group convinced one of the country's most important Muslim leaders to join the fight against female genital cutting. This is considered a huge victory in the effort to change attitudes toward the practice. Due to Sanuman's efforts in Mali, over 14,000 people have signed a pledge to stop female genital cutting. Ms. Bagayoko is concerned, however, about the social pressure associated with this practice. "I know many families that have decided not to circumcise their daughters," says Ms. Bagayoko. "But they can't talk about it openly lest their daughters be shunned."

EMPOWERMENT INITIATIVE

Community-based initiatives are also successful if they are characterized by an empowerment initiative. Most community-based initiatives have included the educational component into their programs for this reason. Education is very critical to community awareness and behavioral change. Amina Salum Ali, the African Union Ambassador to the United States, has also argued that the most effective way to end female genital cutting is through education, information, and advocacy. This is the only way to raise public awareness about health consequences associated with the practice and to bring about changes in attitudes within these communities. Raising awareness about negative consequences is critical not only because it changes people's attitudes toward the practice of female genital cutting; it gives them an opportunity to make informed choices.

Effective education must be specific to issues related to the subject of concern. A Nigerian feminist, Ifi Amadiume, has advised that effective education must define its content clearly by tailoring it toward specific objectives. In the case of female genital cutting, it is important that reproductive health is addressed as a subject of empowerment. While it is important to target health risks of female genital cutting, in raising public awareness, overemphasis on these risks outside the social context ignores the underlying motivations for the persistence of the practice. In most cases, such strategies have led to the recent trend in the increase of calls for the medicalization and symbolic interventions approach. The assumption is that if the girls are cut by trained professionals, health risks will be minimized. According to a study carried out by the population reference bureau (PRB), educational strategies that have adopted a health risks or harmful traditional practice approach have often led to medicalization of this practice (PRB, 2001). While it is important to speak about the health risks associated with female genital cutting, it is more effective if the message is empowering as well.

Empowering education should address the components of empowerment, related to social justice issues such as human dignity and the freedom of choice (Freire, 1970; 1985). A social justice empowerment intervention initiative aims at educating the community through conscientization. Concerns about educated people who practice female genital cutting fail to recognize the fact that these individuals never received conscientizing education on the issue. The Brazilian scholar, Paulo Freire, explains how conscientization process works. It is like a painful birth because it involves an excruciating moment, a rebirth, an awakening to the realization that one has to abandon convictions once held because of the new principles that have to be embraced (Freire, 1985). The need to promote education that conscientize is therefore crucial.

A significant component to the empowerment initiative is the holistic human rights approach. According to RAINBO, an NGO group that has been involved in female genital-cutting intervention programs, a review of the methods used to sensitize communities to abandon the practice reveals that the human rights approach is especially effective in empowering girls and women to change attitudes and behavior. This is because the approach empowers the individual by cultivating agency that enables them to make informed choices. Through this approach, positive cultural values in the community are harnessed as everyone is encouraged to talk about their perceived values in light of human rights and individual responsibilities. Equipped with knowledge and responsibilities, community agency is enabled through individual agency, which leads to informed decisions on this issue. Individuals and the community at large are given the opportunity to explore the relationship between cultural values, and basic rights and entitlement of girls and women as beloved members of their family.

Most successful community-based initiatives introduce a paradigm shift in their strategy. Because a woman's marriageability is central to the persistence of female genital cutting, it must be addressed as a significant factor. Marriage preconditions need to be redefined. Most parents submit their daughters to genital cutting because they perceive it to be in the child's best interests. While some may be aware of the potential serious physical and psychological implications of the practice, there is the perception that the benefits to be gained from the procedure outweigh the risks involved. Finding ways to resolve these tensions for both parents and their daughters is crucial to the eradication process. It is important that societies shift their philosophy on marriage and expectations as part of the social change process. Parents should also be educated about cultural dynamism and how social values change over time. They should help these parents to understand that what they call tradition is essentially a package that has changed over time through review processes. Engaging cultural appraisal as a necessary component to the social process of abandoning irrelevant cultural values as healthy and relevant ones are embraced is significant to the empowerment initiative. As parents are sensitized to the fact that their daughters will not feel ostracized if everyone in the village pledges to not cut them or require men to marry cut girls, it will foster dialog.

Community-based approaches that have proven to be successful include those established in Senegal (Tostan), Ghana (Navrongo), and Ethiopia (IntraHealth and Care). In spite of some challenges they have encountered, they serve as models of emulation. A review of one is in order.

The Tostan of Senegal

In Senegal, for instance, the Tostan Community Empowerment Program (CEP), developed 30 years ago has been described as the most widespread community-based initiative because it is effective for social change (Tostan, 1999; 2012). The success of the program was realized in Malicoumba, a village in West Senegal, when women from this village who participated in the Tostan's Community Empowerment Program declared their commitment to abandon female genital cutting. One of these women was Maimouna Traore, who served as the coordinator of the Community Management Committee (CMC) and Chair of the Advisory Committee of Women of Malicoumba Bambara. On July 31, 1997, over 15 years ago, they declared before the media their intention to abandon female genital cutting and to work toward eradication of the practice in their country. Although they initially met with criticism, they were able to defend their decision using knowledge of human rights they had acquired in attending the Tostan Program. Soon, national dialog on the subject was ignited. This was followed by Abdou Diouf, then President of Senegal, supporting their declarations publicly in Congress meetings. Fifteen years later, 5,000 communities in Senegal abandoned female genital cutting (Tostan, 2012).

Implemented in local communities over a 30-month period, this program is not only holistic in its approach; it is also based on the concept
of organized diffusion discussed earlier. It is based on the philosophy that
"ideas, perspectives and discussions shared by participants are likely to
spread throughout the community and surrounding areas. By engaging
social networks, such as local Tostan supervisors and facilitators, with
local experts to adapt education about female genital cutting to the cultural needs of the community, it empowers the community to take initiatives in identifying problems and solutions to their own situations. The
program is also educational and based on human rights values, specifically
advocating women's right to good health.

The Tostan approach credited for this success was later incorporated
in Senegal's National Action Plan for Female Genital Cutting Abandonment 2010–2015. In her speech on the success of education in effecting
social behavior, Traore noted:

> Today, we are more in harmony with our traditions and culture. We
> are Bambara more than ever. We strengthened our positive tradi-
> tions and abandoned those that are harmful to our well-being. We
> changed because we are now more responsible and caring and proud
> of what unites us. (Melching, 2012)

Since it is embedded in values that emphasize respect, participation,
and sustainability, the Tostan program has been effective. Currently,
CEP is being implemented in about 230 communities in ten regions in
Senegal.[1]

TARGETED INITIATIVES

Although empowerment initiatives are significant in providing intervention education, this education must also be targeted at the right group.
It can be difficult to change attitudes toward a cultural practice such as
female genital cutting if attempts are not made to educate women and
men on the health risks associated with the practice. Through education,
the community is not only sensitized to possible consequences of the practice, dialog on the issue is initiated at all levels. It is therefore important
that empowering education is offered at various levels and to all—as in
schools, families, religious congregations, and other community forums. It
must also be offered to both skilled and unskilled worker at all levels. For
instance, gender-tailored education is necessary to address gender needs
associated with female genital cutting. Because female genital cutting has
always been associated with gender marginalization, it is important that

education about the value of women in society is offered to all in the community. Since it has been argued in some cases that women succumb to this practice because they are dependent economically on men who insist on this practice, discussion about the need to educate women for economic independence is necessary if the community is to equip them with tools to end the practice.

Targeted initiatives are central to the success of community-based initiatives since specific audience in the community is targeted. While targeted initiatives are significant to community-based initiatives, they must also be strategic. They must be formulated in relation to intervention goals. It is important to identify the relevant audience and messages specific to a target group as relates to the process of attitude change. For example women, men, opinion leaders, religious leaders, and traditional midwives can be identified as a significant variable audience for whom a specific message is designed in order to effect attitude change. Statistics indicate that daughters of mothers who are more highly educated are less likely to be cut than those of mothers with little or no education, even though this is not always a guarantee (UNICEF, 2008). This is because the more aware they are about consequences associated with female genital cutting, the less likely they are to "have their daughters cut" (Amadiume, 2000).

The case of Israel Bedounin is a good illustration of this fact. In a recent study by researchers at Ben-Gurion University of the Negev (BGU) in Beer-Sheva, the once-prevalent cultural practice of female genital cutting among Israel's Bedouin population in the Negev region had virtually disappeared (Halila S and Belmaker, 2009). This study was a follow-up of the 1995 study of this Bedouin community by Professor Belmaker, who had described how a large number of women in these communities had planned to continue to practice female genital cutting as a cultural requirement and vowed to perform the practice on their daughters.

When BGU researchers led by Halila S and Belmaker re-surveyed this heterogeneous community 15 years later, they found that none of the women investigated had been exposed to female genital cutting. Through physical gynecological examination and oral questionnaires, no case of scarring of any kind previously reported was found on 132 women studied. Commenting on the findings, Belmaker observes, "it is of great interest to define processes or situations that can lead to a reduction in the incidence of this phenomenon in cultures where it is practiced." She adds, "FGM is a culturally entrenched procedure and unless a prohibition of the practice is accompanied by educational efforts, the effectiveness of legal action is low . . . Direct eradication by making the custom illegal has limited success. As in several other areas, such as childhood immunization and literacy, in the elimination of female genital surgery, Israel's Arab population is among the leading populations in the Middle East" (Halila, 2009). Although the success is attributed to empowering education, Israel Bedouins' social structural improvements over the 15 years of progress have contributed to behavior change. Better health care, school attendance, level of education, and literacy are described as significant factors in behavior change. Today, about 180,000 Bedouins live in Southern Israel (Halila, 2009: 70–73).

Following the targeted initiative approach, some educational programs have targeted excisers. This is because a large majority of girls and women are cut by a traditional practitioner, a category generally given to all local excisers and specialists, including birth attendants that are willing to do this. The assumption here is that if the supply of excisers is restricted and eliminated, the issue of female genital cutting will be resolved as a void in the services of cutters will be created, reducing the practice. The main aim of the programs is to educate these excisers and to provide them with opportunities for alternative sources of income. Thus, the program is designed to help them stop turning to female genital cutting as a means of livelihood. It usually combines education on the harmful effects of female genital cutting with the development of new skills, and provisions of loans or other incentives for the excisers to find an alternative source of income. Through this education initiative, excisers are not only educated about the health concerns associated with female genital cutting, they are also provided alternative sources of income. In some cases, this training is followed by a private or public ceremony, which involves excisers denouncing their practice and symbolically surrendering their instruments or making an oath on the scripture to stop their activities. In Tanzania, where advocacy efforts were embraced, excisers laid down their tools and underwent income generation programs.

It has been argued that men should be targeted as a group because they are important in terms of socialized demands that women who are cut are ineligible for marriage. Approaches that ignore the role of men where cultural practices are concerned have often failed because men play a significant role in the persistence of female genital cutting. In Burkina Faso, for instance, studies indicate how immense a father's decision is to the practice of female genital cutting (PRB, 2001: 23).

The youth as target group are important because society depends on them to pass on cultural values from one generation to the next. The youth as a significant social group can be effective in influencing their peers and parents in order to change the social convention that creates the demand for the practice. A good example of the role of youth in this issue was recently displayed in the United Kingdom. The youth concern in this country led to the first successful national conference on FGM held on July 14, 2012 at the University of Bristol. The conference was aimed at educating health practitioners, education and legal professionals on the devastating impact of female genital cutting and how to prevent it. The conference also discussed the political indifference to the issue due to claims of political correctness. It was argued that some politicians are afraid of being called racist for condemning this practice. This attitude continues to interfere with the fundamental responsibility to ensure child protection in the United Kingdom. Such efforts are significant in intervention process (Desertflower, 2012).

It is important that community leaders are targeted as a social group that is significant to attitude and behavior change. As significant members of the community, their opinion on this issue is relevant to that of the community at large. Enabling community leaders to discuss female genital cutting encourages them to publicly decry the practice. According to this theory, when people are exposed to new ideas, they are likely to adopt the idea that has received favorable evaluations, especially from respected members of the community (Kegele, 1996). Since community leaders are authoritative and respected members in female genital-cutting communities, their opinion is likely to influence attitudes toward female genital cutting (Wangila, 2007). The role of religion in social transformation is often embedded in the diffusion of innovation and empowerment theories (Roger, 1983). A sociologist, Christian Smith, describes religious authority as the "transcendent motivation." Religion possesses an inherent ability that grants it the sacred authority to sanction social behavior (Smith, 1996: 9). Because female genital cutting is a cultural practice that finds justification in religious norms, it makes sense that religious values are used to demystify such legitimation. The notion that female genital cutting is required by a God or other divine beings is intended to elevate the practice beyond the rational discourse. Knowing that most religions teach the need for one to sacrifice oneself for God, or religious cause, religious values associated with genital cutting are often accepted by some as a way to demonstrate their commitment to God or their ancestors (Wangila, 2007). Where faith is concerned, empirical evidence may not matter.

RELIGIOUS LEADERS

Involving religious leaders as a target group is particularly important. In using the pulpit, religious leaders have an opportunity to express their opinions on matters that are likely to influence attitudes and behavioral change. Because their opinions are often accepted as sacrosanct, they are often not challenged. It is within this framework that the role of religious leaders in social transformation is acknowledged. As agents of social change, therefore, religious leaders have the responsibility of promoting social welfare of their congregants. This responsibility rests in their ability to demystify long-held, religiously sanctioned myths that undermine the rights of women.

Religious leaders have the task of starting this initiative in order to encourage social justice within their communities. It is important, however, that these leaders are empowered and trained through seminars and workshops to acquire skills of how to demystify harmful cultural practices. Through such forums, they will learn how to conceptualize effective religious-based intervention programs that are specific to female genital cutting in their own communities. For instance, they will learn to disentangle more transcendent human values of social justice from culturally-defined behavior that undermine the humanity of others. They will also learn how to promote individual agency and social involvement at all levels. The experience of Isnino Shuriye serves as an isolated case that helps to illustrate this argument.

The Case of Isnino Shuriye

The experience of Isnino Shuriye, an elderly mother of eight, a Muslim woman from the small village of Ijara, Garissa in Northeastern Kenya illustrates the significant role of religious leaders in empowering community members toward a change of behavior. As a trained exciser of girls in her community, Shuriye believed in her practice as a "good thing mandated by her God." This was a practice her mother had performed before. She recalls how she would hold girls down while they underwent female genital cutting when her mother was a practitioner. In an interview by Mark Lacey of the *New York Times*, Shuriye remembers how proud she was to be an exciser. She recollects performing the procedure on all three of her daughters with a knife. Each time she made the cut, she would sew the wound together as soon as she saw the blood begin to flow. She sewed her daughters' vaginas almost entirely closed. "I was full of pride," she recalled. "I felt like I was doing the right thing in the eyes of God. I was preparing them for marriage by sealing their vaginas." Shuriye would excise the clitoris and cut off the labia of seven-year-old girls, sew them up, leaving a small opening for menstrual flow and urine. Ms. Shuriye did not use any form of anesthesia, and would bind the girl's legs together for several weeks so that scar tissue would be able to form.

One day, an activist grassroot group, which works with Somalis, known as members of Womankind Kenya, founded by Sophia Abdi Noor, visited her home to convince her to abandon her practice. She sent them away from her property, claiming that she did not wish to interact with people who did not agree with her way of life. She believed they were there to plant Western ideologies in her mind. Persistence by members of Womankind paid off. Sophia Abdi explains, "It was difficult to change her mind . . . We knew she was respected, and we wanted her on our side." It was this group's hope that converting Shuriye would influence other excisers like her, and in fact, other women to abandon the practice. They hoped to convince her that cutting girls' genitals was not only a violation of their rights; Islam does not condone the practice. When the women's activist group realized that they could not convince her to abandon the practice on their own, they invited liberal Muslim clerics to accompany them. As a Muslim, Shuriye could not turn an Imam away. She was soon convinced that genital cutting was not only harmful; it was not dictated by or consistent with the Quran. The clerics also told Shuriye to tell her victims that she is sorry, and offer them camels. Although Shuriye did not have any camels to give to her victims, she begged to be forgiven by the women she cut. "I now feel like I've committed a sin against God," she said. It is worth noting that when Shuriye was informed about genital cutting not being an Islamic practice, she was shocked beyond words. She expresses her shock by abandoning the practice she once valued. Her reaction is indicative of the authority of religion in social behavior.

Due to conscientization, Shuriye turned from being an exciser to an active opponent of female genital cutting. She made house calls on other girls to convince them to abandon the practice. She has persuaded 12 other excisers to denounce their practice. After her transformation, she recounts with remorse her brutal acts that she believed were divinely sanctioned (Lacey, *New York Times*, June 8, 2008). It is because of experiences such as this that I argue for the need to integrate faith-based communities in efforts toward protecting girls and women who live with the risk of female genital cutting. Religion is a crucial element to the persistence of female genital cutting. It is, therefore, important that as the reality of this practice in the United States is acknowledged, attempts to promote cultural diversity must recognize challenges related to cultural ambiguity that those who seek to end the practice by enforcing rules and caring for those who live with the risk and consequences are confronted with.

While group targeting is important, it is important to be cognizant of challenges of targeting just one group. For instance, in the case of targeting excisers, it has been argued that that the assumption that restricting the supply of excisers will resolve the issue of female genital cutting ignores the reasons for the demand for the practice. Often, the approach is a failure where parents seek out other excisers. In addition, most excisers hold a very low social status. While they are a factor in this community initiative, reducing their number is inconsequential if other group initiatives are not targeted as well. While effective community-based education must focus on reducing demand for female genital cutting, it must recognize and address other variables in play as well (PRB, 2001: 17). It is, however, important that targeted initiatives are explored when administering community-based approaches. As Crossett explains, local education targets local solutions (Crossett, 2012).

FAITH-BASED INITIATIVES

Due to the fact that female genital cutting is associated with religious values, it is important that faith-based initiatives are integrated in intervention programs. One such strategy that has been successful is the need to persuade religious leaders to dispel the ubiquitous, incorrect belief that Islam requires girls and women to undergo female genital cutting. In reviewing the United States' efforts at educating immigrants, it was noteworthy to see instances where Muslim clerics were included in intervention efforts. Recognition of this role is a significant step toward strategizing against female genital cutting. When religious institutions serve as activist agents of their communities, they become moral articulators of social justice. When they acknowledge how religion has been used to undermine the rights of women, they become participants in the critical appraisal of their culture—a necessary step in undermining harmful cultural practices such as female genital cutting. It should be remembered, however, that although religious social institutions can be instrumental to social transformation, the success of any intervention program hinges on the cooperation of all individuals involved. It is therefore important that the reality of female genital cutting in the United States is acknowledged in the entire community.

DEMYSTIFICATION MODEL

Although religion is implicated in the persistence of female genital cutting, some see it as a source of empowerment and liberation from the practice. Those who have argued for the possibility of religious reform cite fundamental virtues embedded in these religions. Reformers have argued that every religion contains unbiased truths; truths that affirm basic human rights and values. Since religion embodies values of morality, justice, human rights, and the general good of humanity, these values can be the basis of demystifying demeaning cultural practices. By rendering all cultural and religious practices that undermine the rights of women as inadequate and irreligious, religion can becomes an instrument for negotiating human rights and social justice.

In Islam, for instance, Muslim scholars such a Leila Ahmed, Riffat Hassan, and Denise Carmody have argued for human rights values in Islamic teachings of social justice and respect of human worth. Writing on Islam and the status of Muslim women, Ahmed explains how the egalitarian message of Islam has been suffocated by cultural values and practices of communities that shaped this religion (1992: 41–64). She argues for the need to distinguish the original message of Islam found in the Quran from culturally conditioned teachings recorded in other Islamic sources such as *hadith*, and the shariah. Similarly, Riffat Hassan has argued that human rights are consistent with Islamic values (Hassan, 1991).To these scholars, reform of Islam is possible through rereading and reconstruction of the past in order to highlight teachings of the Prophet Muhammad about social justice.

Social reform in Islam, they argue, is accounted for in the teachings of the Quran. Abduh explains how reform (*islah*) and revival (*tajdid*) find their rationale not only in Islam but also in the tradition of the Prophet (Abduh, 2002: 45–51). To these Muslims, therefore, social reform is an act of social liberation that includes the liberation of women from demeaning cultural practices. Ammah and Engineer cite Prophet Muhammad's teachings and actions as liberating for women. His prohibition of the practice of infanticide that was prevalent in Arabia is indicative of his concern for the plight of women (Ammah, 1997: 75–76; Engineer, 1992: 21). They argue that the role of Islam in social reforms dates back to the time of Prophet Muhammad. Islam began as a movement for social justice, equality, and brotherhood (Engineer, 1989: 3, 143). *Sura* 5: 8 instructs Muslims to "do justice, it is closest to piety." The Quran denounces *zulm* (oppression). *Sura* 5: 75 of the Quran is often cited to justify claims of social reform and justice:

> "And what reason" says the Qur'an, "have you not, to fight in the ways of Allah, and of the weak among the men and the women and the children, who say: Our lord, take us out of this town, whose people are oppressors, and grant us from thee a friend and grant us from thee a helper."

By controlling reckless polygamous marriages among Muslims, he confronted and deconstructed a social structure that was abusive to women, thus promoting a liberating message that affirmed their rights as humans. By advocated monogamy in *Sura* 4: 3 and 4: 129, he elevated the status of women to that of men. In the sight of God, a woman is completely free and deserving of respect. "She is equal to man for when God instructs humankind in the Quran to worship God, both men and women are addressed," says Ammah (1997: 75).

The Prophet Muhammad recognized the fact that cultural practices that divided the Arabs were responsible for social injustices that were prevalent during his lifetime. He condemned oppressive cultural practices such as infanticide, unregulated polygamy, unconditional divorces, and all forms of oppression in the name of Allah even though this behavior was considered the norm at his time. As a social reformer, the Prophet Muhammad confronted these cultural practices because they alienated Arabs from basic human values. Recognizing this fact, Ashagar Engineer has described Islam as a movement of social justice, equality, and brotherhood. As the rich were chastised of corruption, the poor and the oppressed, including slaves, were drawn to the Prophet (1989: 143–144). The Prophet's mission of social reform was aimed at purging social injustice from his community.

Scholars of social reform have also argued for the need to utilize empowering role models to promote social reform and social justice. Because role models are inspirational, they are likely to influence social change. For instance, in Islam, female inspirational role models include Khadija, Aisha, Fatima, Zubayd, and Rabia al Adawiyah of Basrah, Iraq, (Carmody, 1989: 197; Clarke, 2004: 196). Khadija's immense contribution to the development of Islam is described as significant. Her constant support of Prophet Muhammad is highlighted as a display of courage and the need to pursue the right cause. Aisha is praised for her leadership skills. She spent time reading the Quran, fasting, praying, and freeing slaves. Whenever she witnessed social injustice, she acted in defense of the weak. Her acts of charity and social justice for the enslaved are remembered and admired among most Muslims. When she feared for Islam, she went to war to protect it. Along with Umm Salama, Aisha is considered a great source of *hadith*. Her contributions to the compilation of the *hadith* are especially recognized. Fatima, the daughter of the Prophet, is recognized for her zeal and courage in defending Islam from corruption. Zubayd, the queen of Harun al Rashid is remembered by Muslims for showing "how piety could flourish in the midst of difficult surroundings" (Carmody, 1989: 197). Rabia al-Adawiya, also known as Rabia al Basra, is remembered for her zeal for mysticism, a spiritual endeavor restricted to men at her time. Her courage to pursue what she knew to be right for her is admired and is a source of inspiration for many women. These women serve as models because they stood for social justice. They challenged the status quo to promote good in their society.

As attempts to reform religions are made, it ought to be remembered that religion as a social phenomenon is dynamic and bound to change. Just as culture, religion can and should be reformed to conform to contemporary needs. As agents of social construction, humans are responsible for evaluating cultures and religions in order to adapt them to current situations. As sociologist Margaret Archer observes, the response of an individual to his or her own culture depends on the effects it has on humans and how humans affect it (1988: 143). Human needs and actions can reinforce a cultural system or resist its influence when it is perceived to be inhibitive to the common good. Even though culture acts on humans, it is important to remember that it is also a product of human agency (Archer, 1988: 77–78).

HERMENEUTICS AND REFORM

Demystification is possible within the framework of hermeneutics. Hermeneutics, the science of scriptural interpretation, is a tool of religious reform. If well utilized, it can help reconstruct the past in order to adapt it and make it relevant to present experience. A feminist theologian Elisabeth Shussler Fiorenza has articulated a feminist hermeneutics that is necessary in reforming religion in light of women's rights. According to Fiorenza, the first step in scriptural interpretation is to acknowledge that all scriptures are "historical prototype rather than a mythic archetype" (Fiorenza, 1984: 10). This means scriptures should be viewed as models of continuous revelation. The goal of revelation is to transform social experience. Fiorenza (1984) outlines four strategies of reform based on scriptural interpretation that can help with the reform process. The first stage, 'the hermeneutics of suspicion," refers to assumptions that a reformer brings to the interpretation process. He or she should proceed from the assumption that patriarchal religions possess androcentric scriptural texts. For instance, one must recognize the fact that the language of such a text is generic unless proven otherwise. To transform an androcentric perception in a religion, it is important to begin by translating and making the language gender-inclusive. Applying this approach to rituals, symbols, and other aspects of an androcentric religion is likely to isolate discriminating aspects that need reform.

The second stage of interpretation, "the hermeneutics of remembrance," involves the process of rereading and recollecting women's experience based on human rights values. Recollecting women's lives, stories, and struggles within the human rights framework will affirm these stories, experiences, and general contributions to human existence. Ultimately, demeaning cultural practices will be undermined as basic human rights values are elevated. The third stage of interpretation, "the hermeneutics of evaluation and proclamation," involves assessing the significance and power of a scriptural text before applying it to the community. This means one should avoid using a scriptural text that evokes cultural practices that are irrelevant to contemporary needs of the community or contrary to the basic human rights of women. In the fourth stage, "the hermeneutics of creative actualization," a reformer seeks to retell the scriptural story within the human rights framework. This means that a scriptural message that goes contrary to women's experience can be reconstructed and retold in order to affirm their experience (Fiorenza, 1984, Gross, 1996). Most Muslim feminists have advocated the use of feminist hermeneutics to affirm the agency of the woman within the egalitarian message of God as revealed by Prophet Muhammad. The feminist hermeneutics is a necessary tool for distinguishing what was revealed to the Prophet Muhammad from what he said and what was added over time. According to Ahmed, it is possible to distinguish the Prophet Muhammad's original message from androcentric cultural corruptions and reconstruction that Islam was exposed to over time. She is convinced that a critical evaluation and appraisal of this message will reveal the egalitarian message Allah intended for all Muslims. In this message, the rights of both men and women are upheld and respected. She explains how a critical evaluation of the practices sanctioned by Muhammad within the first Muslim society would reveal far more positive attitudes toward women.

Using feminist hermeneutics of remembrance, Muslim feminists have uncovered experiences of women they consider models for women in Islam today. As Carmody explains, hermeneutics of interpretation has enabled Muslims to uncover other role models for women in Islam such as Khadija, Aisha, Fatima, and Zubayd to serve as a source of inspiration for women's agency in the struggle against social injustice (1989: 197). The courage and motivation of women like Khadija, Amina, and Fatima to excel in cultural contexts where women were subordinated is inspirational to women who confront social injustices in contemporary society. In Islam, Hagar's narrative found in the *hadith* and in the Hebrew Bible's, Genesis, 16: 1–16, is particularly used to empower women. Hagar was a slave of Abraham and Sarah. When Abraham could not get a child, his wife Sarah asked him to sleep with Hagar as was the tradition at the time in order to beget him an heir. Out of jealousy, Sarah told Abraham to send her away. She was sent into the desert where out of desperation she wandered with her son Ismail in search of water and food. She survived because of her faith in God's grace. Hagar's story is empowering to women because it describes her struggle to overcome the obstacles and injustices she experienced as a slave and a woman. She did not give up hope for life even after she was sent away by her mistress Sarah. She confronted all odds against her with courage. Her faith in God enabled her to sail through the difficulties she faced in the midst of a culture that despised slave women. Her determination made her a heroine. These Muslim women leaders are not only respected as mothers of believers, they are recognized for their unique contribution to the development of Islam and their courage to fight social injustice.

To most feminists, therefore, sexist and cultural practices that undermine the rights of women can be reconstructed and reinterpreted in accordance with the Prophet Muhammad's egalitarian message, which is in tune with human rights and agency. This message should guide and trap the undermining cultural practices. It ought to be remembered that religions, like all social phenomena, are dynamic and susceptible to social change. As they transform, they represent an adaptation to new norms that often reflect a contemporary consciousness and general knowledge. In recognition of this fact, the Muslim scholar Muhammad Mashuq ibn Ally has advised that Muslims must continue to grapple with the task of rediscovering the relevance of Islam to present-day problems. As they formulate answers to challenges of the modern age, a renewal of Islamic thought is necessary in order to meet the modern ideational challenge. They should reach out to persons who are disposed to righteousness in order to live up to Islamic values embedded in Islamic *Jammah*. They should strive to bring about societal change through individual conversion and collective effort, in which the mosque, as the community base, becomes the focus and locus of activity. Considering that education is the spearhead of human development, a new cadre of leaders should be trained at intellectual, social, and cultural levels (Ally, 1992: 59–60). This should be considered as an effort by all religious organizations to serve justly the communities they embrace.

It is important to acknowledge the fact that some industrialized countries have established programs to ensure effective intervention against the practice. In the United States, for instance, the National Organization of Circumcision Information Resource Centers (NOCIRC), a networking organization has brought together social scientists and medical practitioners from all over the world to fight all forms of sexual mutilations. NOCIRC also founded the Female Genital Cutting Awareness and Education Project in August 1996 with the objective of creating a female genital cutting module that will provide information and training material to health care professionals. Such efforts should be encouraged. RAINBO has conducted research and worked on establishing grassroots programs in the United States on women's reproductive sexual health as well as on female genital mutilation, both locally and internationally.

Some overdue effort is being put forth to stop the practice of female genital cutting, but there is still a great deal of work that has to be done. Self-education as well as education of others is a way to act upon the convictions and principles that guide human rights. This is because, there are a great deal of individuals who are still unaware that female genital cutting exists, let alone the fact that it is still widely practiced. It is crucial that industrialized countries come up with effective ways to protect the rights of children and women as described above.

NOTE

1. www.tostan.org/country/senegal.

8

◆◆◆

Health Care Intervention

Medical care in the United States for women with female genital cutting is lagging and many women don't trust doctors who appear to frown on their condition, say advocates. (Raush, 2011)

Studies indicate that women who have been cut are more apprehensive about pregnancy-related health care services in industrialized countries. This is because of demoralizing, insensitive, and sometimes alienating reactions and comments about their health needs. Further, those who chose to undergo the practice are confronted with the challenge of performing it in underground circumstances, some which are very risky. This reality is indicative of how the influx of immigrants to industrialized countries poses a challenge to health care systems. This is in addition to language barriers and culturally insensitive services. Industrialized countries' health care providers are increasingly finding out that they are naively ignorant of some medical and cultural needs of a significant population in their communities. In this chapter, I explore ways to ensure that health intervention is part of female genital cutting intervention programs in industrialized countries.

I proceed here by acknowledging that female genital cutting is a reality in industrialized countries as in native countries. Recognizing this fact, I argue for the need to explore various approaches to this issue in order to fully address the needs of women who live with the risk and consequences of the procedure. In order to ensure women who are likely to choose to go through the procedure access a safe environment and those who live

with consequences of the practice access adequate services, it is important that health care facilities and guidelines are put in place to facilitate
these unique needs. I demonstrate the need for broadening medical services in industrialized countries in order to address female genital-cutting
cases. I also demonstrate ignorance and lack of adequate facilities in most
industrialized countries. I argue for (1) the medicalization of female genital cutting where this is desired by individuals with informed consent and
(2) the provision of special health care services, including reconstructive surgery to those in need of these services. With the realization that
the health needs of the immigrant communities are needs of industrialized countries, it is hoped that the medical profession can restructure to
address this challenge.

MEDICALIZATION OF FEMALE GENITAL CUTTING

In three out of four cases, it is observed that health issues associated with
female genital cutting can be serious, depending on the type of the procedure, instruments used to perform the procedure, and/or location of the
procedure. Consequently, immediate consequences such as severe pain,
urine retention, shock, hemorrhage may be contained or overcome. Long-
term consequences, such as, cysts, abscesses, Keloid, scarring, damage to
the urethra, dyspareunia, difficulties with child birth, and sexual dysfunction can be chronic and life-altering. Whenever a woman is at risk of
female genital cutting, she is confronted with challenges regarding where
and from whom to seek help. Often, she is disappointed, and sometimes,
this disappointment has cost lives. As Katherine Raush validly explains,
"Her chances of finding a knowledgeable physician . . . or talking about
her condition—aren't very good" (2011). In a country where this procedure is illegal, it is even more challenging to get help from a medical
professional. These challenges can be addressed with health care intervention. Addressing the needs of girls or women who desire safe procedures and after procedure care is crucial to intervention programs.

Calls for the medicalization of female genital cutting emerge out of
respect for multiculturalism and cultural right. While the goal is not to
encourage the practice, some have argued for that possibility. It is recognized that health risk can be minimized with the provision of sanitary conditions. As argued by Obiora, medicalizing female genital cutting
is not only sanitary, adverse health consequences for women and children will also be limited (Obiora, 1997: 309). Some have recommended
the need to modify the procedure to reduce health risks further. In the
United States, for instance, two cases are illustrative of efforts to medical-
ize and/or modify the practice in recognition of cultural sensitivity. The

first argument in favor of cultural sensitivity was brought up at a World Health Organization (WHO) meeting. A proposal was presented from the Harborview Medical Center of Seattle, Washington hospital, calling for cultural sensitivity to the Somali immigrants. In the proposal, it was suggested that doctors should be allowed to perform a symbolic form of female genital cutting known as *sunna* on the daughters of Somali immigrants because the Somalis threatened to have a traditional form of cutting performed on the girls if the hospital did not do something. Dr. Miller explains how her patients expressed confusion about how "Americans encourage the circumcision of their sons, but refuse a less invasive symbolic *sunna* for their daughters" (Coleman, 1998: 749). Below is a common response from expecting women during delivery.

> Obstetrician to Pregnant Woman: "If it's a boy, do you want him circumcised?" Pregnant Woman: "Yes, and also if it's a girl."
> The proposal was rejected by the WHO. (Coleman, 1998: 717)

In May 2010, a similar proposal was presented by the American Academy of Pediatrics (AAP) in a statement titled "Ritual Genital Cutting of Female Minors." In the statement, this organization of physicians called for a review of the Federal ban of all forms of female genital cutting in order to allow pediatricians to perform a ceremonial pinprick or nick on the clitoris of newborn girls from communities that embrace female genital cutting. Cultural sensitivity was also cited as the reason for the request (Chen, 2010; Belluck, 2010). In Australia, around the same time, the Royal Australian and New Zealand College of Obstetricians and Gynecologists (RANZCOG) was also reported to be considering the sanctioning of medically performed ritual nicks to satisfy the cultural needs for allowing genital cutting of girls in a bid to protect them from more severe forms (Matthews, 2011: 139; Tatnell, 2010). Although all these proposals were abandoned due to uproar from human rights activists, the practice persists.

Human rights activists have opposed the medicalization of female genital cutting because of a number of reasons. First, it is argued that doctors should not perform any form of female genital cutting as their profession requires them to not harm their patients, despite cultural beliefs and practices. Second, while girls or women would have the opportunity to undergo the practice in safe and hygienic conditions, medicalization is viewed as a step to endorsing the practice, thus undermining efforts to protect the rights of girls to reproductive rights. As has been argued by Nahid Toubia and reiterated by Aziza Kamil, "No action will entrench female genital mutilation more than legitimating it through the medical profession" (Toubia, 1995: 16; Anderson, 2005: 177). As Obiora observes, the term "mild circumcision" is ambiguous as it can encompass a wide range of operations and it does not preclude the risk of serious infection or injury (Obiora, 1997: 365–367).

It is argued in the book that the medicalization of female genital cutting should be viewed as a short-term solution to the current challenge and that it must be supplemented with community awareness programs to empower the community to abandon the practice. Medicalization of the practice should be based on the fact that female genital cutting is a real issue that persists in various communities. Since there are members of the community that are going to be exposed to this practice, they should be provided access to sanitary conditions to ensure that risks are minimized. It is important that procedures are in place to ensure that consent is first established and that those in emergency situations are catered for. Providing parents and doctors opportunities to provide safe forms of genital cutting is crucial, especially in cases where it is established that such practices are likely to be performed no matter what. This should not be construed as allowing the performance of female genital cutting. In my view, it is an acknowledgement of the reality that is at hand and addressing it as a necessary evil. It is a necessary evil because it is something that is currently happening and addressing it in this form is necessary even as it is hoped that the practice will be curbed in the future. It is to acknowledge that while the ultimate goal is to change attitudes toward the practice, in situations where a woman is likely to undergo the procedure, safety mechanisms should be put in place to minimize health risks. This is likely to save a life or to prevent dangerous underground procedures. Thus, medicalization should be the first necessary component to health interventions. It is my argument that while a short-term solution may be made available for girls and women in immigrant communities, ultimately, efforts should be concentrated on discouraging the practice through education.

Even with medicalization of the practice, it is particularly important that immigrant communities are targeted with health education geared toward empowering them about the health concerns. Health education should then be followed by the provision of facilities to make the procedure safe and to treat its consequences. Specifically, the health education should include two main components: a) Knowledge about female genital cutting, health consequences, and legal ramifications of the practice in industrialized countries. b) Awareness of health services that specifically deal with this issue. Although girls and women are agents or victims of this cultural procedure, it is important that they are empowered in order to promote action at the individual level and at the community level. It is particularly important that they are educated on how to ensure that the procedure will bring about minimal risk to their health.

AFTER-PROCEDURE CARE

Due to immediate and long-term health risks associated with female genital cutting, intervention programs should include immediate and prolonged care. Studies have shown the frequency of sexual problems in women who have been exposed to female genital cutting. They also show that these women consult gynecologists on sexual issues such as frigidity due to dyspareunia, injuries sustained during early intercourse, pelvic infections, orgasmic failures due to the amputation of the glans clitoridis, and coital difficulty and the inability to have vaginal intercourse at all (*apareunia*) because of stenosis of the vagina.

Statistics indicate that very few health services in industrialized countries are equipped to handle female genital cutting-related risks. Lack of specialized forms of care is particularly lacking. In the United Kingdom, for instance, Dr. Comfort Momoh of St, Thomas Hospital on London's South Bank, a recognized U.K. expert on female genital cutting explains how insufficient NHS clinics are for this growing problem. There are about 17 female genital-cutting specialist clinics in the United Kingdom. "I was in Glasgow recently," she says, "and they can't cope . . . We see women who are about to give birth. After they are cut, they are sewn up so tightly that the baby cannot get out when they go into labor. We have to cut them open," says Momoh (Robert, 2012). It is important to mention, however, that there are a few clinics that have recognized this dire need among immigrant communities and are doing something about it. Most of these clinics were established by doctors who have worked with immigrant communities.

In a general survey for this study regarding the adequacy of reproductive health care services for immigrants, 80 percent of respondents considered the services inadequate, mostly because of the ignorance of medical staff of needs related to female genital cutting. Respondents reported how they seek health care providers with specialists from their countries of origin or make arrangement to travel abroad for medical attention, except in cases of emergency. Pregnant respondents tend to request that a nurse or doctors from their community be present during delivery in order to assist with personal needs. They hoped that the doctors were trained in issues they confront daily so they are comfortable to have a discussion with them. Ignorance of female genital cutting, especially infibulation and de-fibulation process, is a serious concern in women who have been exposed to this type of procedure. Ignorance of this issue among health care professionals, such as doctors and nurses, ranges from not knowing anything about the practice at all, to not knowing how to respond when one encounters a patient with needs related to the procedure. If a health care provider cannot identify female genital cutting complications, including scars that often occur after the procedure, they are not able to help pregnant patients—a situation that can easily lead to death if not addressed promptly. Studies indicate how most professionals who are ignorant about the need to de-fibulate scar tissues from female genital cutting often recommend unnecessary cesarean section, that are often dreaded by some woman in these communities. If these professionals were to receive training in this technique, the scar would be successfully opened for the woman to deliver vaginally, thus preventing unnecessary complications that may arise with the cesarean section procedure. Research indicates that this ignorance is not specific to any one industrialized country.

In Belgium, for instance, a study among gynecologists in Flanders City uncovered a serious lack of knowledge about this issue. Of the 334 gynecologists interviewed, most had very little knowledge about female genital cutting. Others were unaware of the legal status of the practice. While 58 percent of those surveyed acknowledged having seen women or girls with genital cutting in their consultation, 53 percent admitted having consulted with them in the previous year. Some gynecologists had been asked to perform the practice or to refer to someone willing to do so. Although 45 percent were aware of the fact that the practice was illegal in Belgium, one third of the 334 interviewed actually discouraged their female patients from exposing their daughters to this practice. Most cited the need to respect these women's culture, while others feared to be labeled racist. Most (61%) expressed a desire for special medical training on matters related to female genital cutting as well as guidelines, including legislative policies on the matter in Belgium (Leye et al., 2008).

Ignorance is due to lack of training. Training of health worker is a priority in the global strategy to end the practice. It is important that health workers are trained to address this issue and to sensitize their communities about the health consequences associated with the practice. Knowledge about clinical management of women who have been exposed to the practice is not only paramount, health care worker, especially gynecologists need to be informed about female genital cutting, its consequences, and the legal status of the practice. It is also important, therefore, that gynecologists are empowered to be more assertive in dissuading women from performing female genital cutting on their daughters. This ignorance is compounded with lack of guidelines on this issue.

CULTURAL SENSITIVITY AS A MEDICAL STRATEGY

From the above, it is apparent that the health care component is fundamental to the intervention and care of girls and women who have been exposed to female genital cutting. It is important that as we diversify, industrialized countries should also evolve by diversifying their health care services in order to provide culturally competent services to all. Cultural competency entails cultural sensitivity such as ensuring that patients receive services targeted to their needs. While a nurse/physician may consider female genital cutting to be abhorrent, it is essential that the topic is approached in a culturally sensitive and nonjudgmental manner in order to establish trust. This is only possible if they are aware of the practice, its health implications, and the cultural context and values that inform their situation. When dealing with women who have been cut, therefore, it is imperative that health care providers demonstrate sensitivity to their condition and situation since sensitivity is crucial during discussions of the history and physical exam of the patient. Since judgmental attitudes often backfire when dealing with patients from communities that experience stereotypes such as those that embrace female genital cutting, health care providers must ensure that they are extra sensitive in the way they deal with these women. For instance, because, as Nawal Nour rightly observes, some women who have been cut do not consider themselves mutilated, it is offensive to reference their condition as a form of mutilation while examining them (Harvey, 2002; Mehren, 2004). Knowledge and understanding of diverse cultures is an important aspect of high quality health care.

In cultures where female genital cutting is practiced, it is also important to reassure them about respect of the values they hold. When a physician encounters a patient with genital cutting it is important that this is acknowledged and recognized if a trusting relationship is to be established between the patient and the nurse or doctor. To establish trust, therefore, a physician/nurse should ask her patients familiarity questions such as: (1) Have you ever had a female exam? (2) In some cultures, some women undergo a ritual procedure known as circumcision. Is this a practice in your community? (3) Are there special things done in your culture during female examinations that I need to know? Because it is culturally acceptable for husbands to answer questions and make decisions for their wives, it is important to clear this with the patient. Where a patient requires language interpretation, it is important that service is provided and a question in this regard is included in the questions asked. To promote trust, physicians must encourage patients to seek health services such as prenatal care, where necessary, or to correct the damage they have by referring them to existing services. Nurses and doctors should be provided with the necessary information so they can assist patients to identify the best options to correct infibulations and facilitate healthy functioning.

MODEL FOR SPECIALIZED HEALTH CARE

Two good examples of culturally sensitive clinics in the United States are the African Women's Healthcare founded by Dr. Nawal Nour in Boston and the Refugee Women's Health Clinic founded by Crista Johnson in Arizona state. These clinics can serve as models of improvement of specialized care for immigrant and other women with issues related to female genital cutting and other reproductive issues.

The African Women's Health Center

The African Women's Health Center (AWHC), which is located at the Brigham and Women's Hospital, affiliated with a Harvard Affiliated Hospital, was established with the mission of providing specialized health services for refugee and immigrant women who have undergone female genital cutting. It provides access, understanding, and community to women who have long-term complications from this tradition and who seek reproductive health care. Dr. Nawal Nour, MD, MPH, who established the center and now serves as the director of the center recognized the unique needs of immigrant women. Nour, who is the daughter of a Sudanese father and an American mother, grew up in the Sudan, where her father held the position of minister of agriculture, and Egypt, where her father was a diplomat. She was educated at the American School in London and Brown University in the United States.

Dr. Nour founded her clinic in the department of obstetrics and gynecology at Brigham and Women's Hospital in Boston, in order to cater for the needs of African women who have been cut. The clinic, one of the few specialized ones in the United States, and one of just two in industrialized countries, offers all the services found at any ob-gyn practice in a major teaching hospital. Although Nour was not cut herself, she is aware and sensitive to experiences of those who come to her clinic, the humiliations that they have to experience when they visit doctors who are unaware of their condition. It is because of her sensitivity that when she arrived at Brigham as chief of resident in 1995, she quickly gained popularity among the African immigrants in her community.

In an interview on her specialty, she explains that she tries to provide medical care for her patients in a manner that prevents the need for acute emergency care. "We talk a lot in this country about access to health care," Nour says, and often what is meant by that is transportation issues, lack of money, or the inability to find quality primary care. She continues, "When a cut woman shows up in an emergency room with a bladder infection or ready to deliver a baby . . . an inexperienced provider can make her feel like a freak. For instance, in a teaching hospital, the doctor may bring in a roomful of medical students, residents, and nurses to observe a patient's genitals. Think about it, . . . you have a woman so modest that she only wants a female provider; she's lying there in stirrups and all these other people are brought in."

As a doctor, Nour is primarily concerned with educating fellow health care professionals about the medical complications of genital cutting. According to her, knowledge on female genital cutting is very important. She insists that gynecologists and obstetricians should familiarize themselves with images of these procedures in order to be able to identify them on a patient. She explains how some unsuspecting doctors are likely to miss the least invasive form of the procedure that involves the removal of the clitoris when examining a patient. She emphasizes this point in her presentations. She makes sure that doctors see these images to internalize medical complications associated with the practice so that they can know what to expect in case they encounter a patient who is genitally cut. She explains how immigrants' reproductive challenges related to female genital cutting are further complicated by language and cultural barriers. A doctor's shock in reaction to her situation further demeans their challenges. She is however cognizant of the fact that the majority of doctors in the United States are extremely unlikely to work with women who have been cut, especially in the extreme manner of the women that she works with in her practice, where nearly 100 percent of woman have been genitally cut.

Nour's overwhelmingly primary concern is maternal mortality. She feels that doctors frequently and incorrectly assume that a woman who has been infibulated can only give birth via cesarean section. Nour prefers instead to surgically reopen the vagina of her patients when it is possible. This procedure, which Nour says is fairly basic, is called de-infibulation, and allows Nour to restore, as much as is possible, the normal anatomy of women. She has performed numerous de-infibulations on women who are dealing with chronic infections, who are planning to get married, and on others who are going to give birth to children.

Central to her approach is cultural sensitivity. To serve effectively in such a clinic, one has to develop a sense of cultural respect. In order to appeal to African women, Nour has had to adjust her cultural inclinations. She is described as a cultural chameleon because, as Harvey explains, she dresses as any American doctor on Mondays through Thursdays.

She often wears knee-length skirts and flats under her white coat. However, on Fridays, when the clinic for African women is open, she wears longer, more modest skirts and boots in order to avoid embarrassing the spouses of her Muslim patients. During presentations to natives of female genital-cutting communities, she ensures that she dresses appropriately and speaks in her native language as in the case when she gave a presentation in Sudan in Arabic wearing long sleeves and a long skirt. This way, she demands respect from her community as she is viewed as a successful Sudanese woman who has done well in the United States (Harvey, 2002).

Layla Guled, her assistant observed that the women who patronize the clinic wanted a doctor who was an African woman. For a community that does not trust doctors, Nour was like a miracle for them because she knew how to interact with them in a culturally sensitive manner. She spends time with her patients. Instead of rushing directly into pelvic exams, she asks patients about their families and daily lives. When it comes time for the pap smear, she explains what the procedure is like, and gives them the option of speaking to their husbands about it if they choose to do so. Nour is sensitive to the cultural implications of each decision that her patients have to make. Somali woman, for example, cannot make the decision to receive the procedure for herself. Rather, she needs to consult with a family member, as it is not culturally acceptable to make a decision such as this for herself unless she is very Americanized. Nour's approach of involving husbands in their wives' treatment is a cultural tactic just as it is a strategy intended to ensure that these men are aware of the pain their wives endure. This cultural strategy is what attracts most of her patients to her.

Nour is a feminist who finds the practice troubling and is very critical of it. However, she is equally critical of Westerners who are not sensitive toward the cultures that practice female genital cutting. For instance, she is critical of the Western categorization of the practice as mutilation. She explains that many of her patients do not feel that they have been mutilated, and furthermore, do not perceive themselves to be victims. They find it difficult to comprehend the Western fascination with their genitals, and they are tired of having to discuss it. They want to be treated and viewed as healthy. Nour is concerned that overzealous feminists and activists are forcing women who have been cut to rightfully become overprotective of their cultural practices, and to defend a procedure that threatens their daughters. She thinks it is important to be sensitive and bipartisan in her usage of these terminologies, and believes that fear is the motivating factor behind genital cutting. "They do it to make their daughters marriageable," she argues. In cultures that value a woman's chastity so highly, circumcision guarantees that a girl will remain a virgin. According to Nour, there are derogatory Arabic words that are used to describe women and girls who have not undergone female genital cutting. These words describe uncut women as dirty, smelly, unclean, and even filthy. One of her strategies to discourage the practice is to have Muslims who practice female genital cutting speak to those who do not. Nour observed a breakthrough confrontation at a workshop that she led for Somali and Kurdish Iraqi refugees and immigrants. At one point, she invited the Kurds who did not practice female genital cutting to have a challenge talk with the Somalis: "We don't circumcise our daughters. We're Muslims! Where does it say that in the Koran?" she explains. The women were able to educate one another because of this dialogue (Harvey, 2000; Mehren, 2004). At the individual level, she works at empowering these women to abandon the practice. This is because she encounters patients regularly who believe that cutting their daughters will make them into good Muslims. She sees it as her responsibility to inform them that the practice is not only illegal in the United States but is also un-Islamic. Nour explains that only one *hadith*, or saying traditionally attributed to Muhammad, recommends female genital cutting, and it is disputed.

Nour has ensured that interpretation is a significant component of specialized health care services because some immigrants face the challenge of communication. This unique need ensures that communication is not only effective, but the patient is also made to feel at home in her own language. Dr. Nour's assistant is Layla Guled, a Somali interpreter whose experience is not different from that of most immigrants they serve at the clinic. Layla, who was cut at the age of six, says she was fortunate because her family lived in the city. Unlike most girls, she was anesthetized for the procedure; even though she recounts the great deal of pain she experienced afterward, and has suffered ever since. "Girls from the countryside aren't so lucky," she explains to Harvey during the interview (2002). They "are often circumcised at home, their genitals are cut or scraped away with unsanitary knives, razors, or shards of glass and the remaining flesh stitched with household needles or even thorns," she adds (Harvey, 2002).

Layla joined the BWH African Women's Health Center when it opened in 1999 and spends every Wednesday interpreting for 6 to 15 female patients from Somalia in the center's clinic. As the only full-time Somali interpreter at BWH, Layla explains how language and cultural barrier is a huge challenge. As an insider and an interpreter, she helps bridge this cultural barrier. Her hospitality has enabled her to create a bond with her patients. "This clinic could not work without Layla," says Dr. Nour. "Our patients love her." Layla enjoys her work at the BWH. She is paged to help with interpretations in other areas of the hospital (Harvey, 2002).

In addition to running the clinic and operating on patients, Nour travels nationally and globally, lecturing and running workshops to educate refugee workers, asylum officers, and medical professionals about female genital cutting. Because of her work, she is currently one of the most influential people on the subject. In 2004, she was awarded the MacArthur "genius" award in recognition of her work with survivors of female genital cutting (Mehren, 2004).

The Refugee Women's Health Clinic

The Refugee Women's Health Clinic, located in Arizona, which also takes on a cultural sensitive approach to health care, was opened by Crista Johnson, an obstetrician-gynecologist and director of the clinic since 2008. It was established in order to provide comprehensive care largely to Africans, Asians, and the Middle Eastern refugee community in Maricopa County of Arizona state. Thus far, the clinic has served nearly 2,000 women from 19 countries. The clinic recognizes the fact that refugee women from non-English speaking countries faced numerous obstacles when it comes to accessing obstetrics and gynecological services in the United States. Some of obstacles identified include fear and anxiety about unfamiliar medical practices, cultural barriers, language and illiteracy, HIV/AIDS, and female genital cutting. According to Johnson, the cultural sensitive approach that the clinic adopts is very important because "Trust is a major issue amongst immigrant women especially refugees." She explains how most of her clients resist cesarean section when their fetus is in distress for cultural reasons. She explains how most of them fear a long recovery time that will keep them from caring for their family. Others worry that surgery will prevent them from having more children while some see surgery of any kind as a sign of impending death. To her, engaging in open dialogue without judging women who are affected by this procedure is central to effective health care. Building trust takes time and often may require multiple visits and good continuity of care (Raush, 2011). Apart from working with agencies that provide basic needs to these communities, such as diapers, car seats, and food stamps for mothers in order to access women who are in need of these services, the clinic provides translators, counseling, education, and transportation to the facility.

RECONSTRUCTIVE SURGERY

The most important thing is to have female genital mutilation stopped, because what we will get after the operation may look like original clitoris but

it will never be the same. . . . And the trauma of female genital cutting
will always stay with us forever, no matter what we do.

—Diaryatou Bah

Many girls and women who have undergone female genital cutting have
resigned themselves to their situation. This is because most industrialized
hospitals do not offer specialized services such as reconstructive surgery.
As Dr. Momoh explains, reconstructive surgery is not even offered in the
NHS clinics in the United Kingdom. It is important that intervention
efforts provide these women options of surgical reconstruction. Surgical
reconstruction is a procedure intended to reverse the effects of female
genital cutting for survivors. The surgical techniques developed utilize
the internal part of the clitoris to ablate scar tissue, and reconstruction of
the labia thus compensate for clitoral excision. The surgery exposes what
remains of the clitoris and uses the remaining tissues to reconstruct the
labia that may have been cut away. The painful scar tissue is also cleared.
The procedure is believed to give back certain sensations to the genitalia.
According to Bowers, the surgery is possible and may improve sensation
in the area as well as cosmetic benefits. She explains:

> The restoration (of sexual pleasure) is possible because the entire
> clitoris is sensory, not just the amputated portion. Sensation is
> robbed (through FGM) because the amputated portion retracts back
> and then gets covered by scar tissue. The clitoris is foreshortened by
> FGM but it isn't removed—not even a majority of it. The restora-
> tion surgery exposes the clitoral stump. Then, with plastic surgery
> techniques, we are able to bring the exposed portion to the sur-
> face, suture it there and even create new labia minora in many cases
> by utilizing the available surrounding skin. The exposed sensory
> portion, free of overlying skin and scar tissue, is then there to func-
> tion . . . Sexuality should be considered one of the basic human
> senses . . . imagine if we took our children and poked their eyes out
> in childhood or their sense of hearing or even smell? It would be an
> outrage and we all should feel no less outraged about this process of
> FGM and how important it is to do what we can to return that sense.
> (Clitoraid.org)

This procedure, which is viewed as hope for a better future for genitally
cut women, was developed and is offered by a few gynecologists such as
Dr. Pierre Foldes, Dr. Sebastian Madzou, Dr. Maci Bowers, Dr. Harold J.
Henning, Dr. John Reid, Dr. Larry Ashley, and Dr. Betty Dodson, among
others. These specialists argue that all individuals should access the best

form of health care in order to live a fulfilling life. While they own their individual clinics, their research motivated the founding of Clitoraid, a private nonprofit organization, where they consult. Located in Las Vegas, Nevada, Clitoraid's main goal is to empower women who have been cut to seek redress to their situation and to sponsor those who need help to perform the procedure in order to rebuild their clitoris. The mission of Clitoraid is to provide women who have been exposed to female genital cutting an opportunity for the physical restoration and rehabilitation of what they lost. Clitoraid hopes to build a "Pleasure hospital" in Burkina Faso, West Africa, in order to offer free medical services to women who seek this option. In addition to reconstructive surgery, the organization also trains doctors to assist in this procedure. Since 2006, Clitoraid has expanded services to other parts of the United States and France. Worthy of mention is the work of Pierre Foldes and Marci Bowers, among others.

Pierre Foldes

Foldes, a French urologist who owns a clinic on the outskirts of Paris, was inspired by modern science of the penis-lengthening procedures to develop his reconstructive surgery procedure. Using this procedure, he has performed over 2,500 operations. During an interview with Habibou Bangre of *The Root* in 2008, Foldes explains how the procedure works. "This operation is reversing a criminal act that was not desired by these women." Commenting on the experience of one of his patients, an "anaesthetized woman from Guinea Bissau," he says, "It will take only half hour . . . I restore the clitoris and labia, which were sliced off when she was six years old . . . this will help the woman enjoy normal sex and the delivery of a baby," he explains (Bangre, 2008; Robert, 2012).

According to Dr. Foldes, there is hope and possibilities for these girls and women to live a fulfilled life. Post-operation education and counseling is an essential part to clitoral repair surgery. He maintains that post-op women need help in understanding how to find pleasure through stimulation of their reconstructed organ. They also need help adjusting psychologically to the reality of their new physicality, since they have been conditioned since childhood to feel guilty and ashamed about their sexual needs. Foldes' patients pay nothing for this operation. The state picks up the costs. He has also operated on about 50 patients from the United Kingdom. Although he has faced challenges for promoting this surgery, he remains devoted to his work. He explains how he has been threatened several times for performing these surgical reconstructions.

Dr. Foldes is assisted by his student, Dr. Sebastian Madzou, a Congo-born obstetrician who has already performed over 50 surgeries on women in Burkina Faso and trained 20 of his new colleagues in the procedure. Thanks to their success, surgeries they perform are reimbursed by the French health insurance system. This is a good example where the government collaborates with an organization to support the health needs of these women. Madzou commented during the interview, saying the following—"What the sixteen women I operated on told me after the operation made me realize how important it was for them to get the surgery" (Bangre, 2008).

Dr. Marci Bowers

In the United States, clinics specializing in female genital cutting reconstructive surgery are very few. Some are located in Trinidad, Colorado, San Manteo, California, and Seattle, Washington. These clinics were established by Dr. Marci Bowers, a renowned American reconstructive surgeon specializing in Gynecology, Pelvic and Reconstructive Surgery, and a student of Dr. Pierre Foldes. She is not only a pioneer in the field of gender reassignment surgery, she is renowned as the first prominent transgender woman to perform the surgery and as one of the few U.S. doctors to perform female genital related reconstructive surgery. Bowers became the first American doctor to volunteer for Clitoraid after travelling to France through Clitoraid's sponsorship to train directly under Dr. Pierre Foldes. Due to her experience, she is empathetic with what her patients describe as a loss of identity, and "of not feeling whole" after female genital cutting. She explains how most of her patients have not had their entire clitoris removed. On March 27, 2009, she performed the first successful clitoral repair surgeries ever performed in the United States.

Before moving to Trinidad, Bowers had a successful practice at the Poly-Clinic in Seattle, where she helped deliver 2,000 babies. She has also served as Obstetrics and Gynecology Department Chairperson at Swedish (Providence) Medical Center and was named the only physician member of the Washington State Midwifery Board. During 2002–2003, she received America's Best Physicians Award, and is also recognized as a member of the European Academy of Sciences. In 2009, she established the clinic at Trinidad, Colorado, where she served before relocating to San Manteo, California and Seattle, Washington in 2010. Although she donates her services, patients pay their own hospital fees, travel, and lodging expenses. Those who are able, pay a fee for the procedure. She believes that if doctors receive training on how to perform this procedure, they will help many women who have been exposed to female genital cutting.

Other specialists in reconstructive surgery include Dr. Henning, a board-certified obstetrician and gynecologist who has owned a private practice since 1986. He currently lives and practices in the city of Fulton, New York. Born in Kansas, he possesses a PhD in medical training in the area of reproductive physiology. Dr. Henning also serves as a consultant with Clitoraid and looks forward to volunteering at their new facility in Burkina Faso (Clitoraid, 2013). Under Dr. Bowers, he received training in the clitoral restorative surgery and is responsible for serving the eastern coast communities where he lives. He explains how his eyes were opened to issues that plague women throughout the world after joining the Rae-lian Movement, a movement that advocates sexual freedom between con-senting adults. The movement is based on the belief that God, who is known as Elohim, is a benevolent creator who wishes for humans to enjoy fully the life they have been given (Beyer, 2013). This movement moti-vated him to be part of Clitoraid's humanitarian medical endeavor. Doc-tor Henning stresses the importance of community awareness, both in Western and other female genital-cutting communities. This is the only way to decrease the occurrence of female genital cutting. "Restoring the sexual pleasure that has been taken away from such victims is the beauty of the corrective surgery, and I look forward to helping these women," he says.

Another specialist is Dr. John Reid, also trained by Foldes, a specialist in general surgery. He works in England, in the Bristol area, and also vol-unteers for Clitoraid. Commenting on his work, he says, "I look forward to finding my role in the politics, media and therapy of an unfairly mutilated but vital human tissue" (Clitoraid, 2013). Dr. Larry Ashley, an associate professor at UNLV and Clinical Assistant Professor at the University of Nevada School of Medicine, joined the team at Clitoraid after recognizing the importance of post-operative patient education and counseling. He is a leading expert in sexual trauma, and an addictions specialist. His spe-cialty includes the treatment of combat and sexual traumas, with a primary focus on the training and mentoring of trauma and addiction profession-als. Dr. Betty Dodson, a famous sexologist and an international authority on women's sexuality, is renowned for her activism and public advocacy for women's sexual liberation. She helps provide guidance to women from female genital-cutting communities in order to help them regain some sense of pleasure. Dodson maintains a private practice in New York City and has an active website through which she interacts with her clients. She also volunteers for Clitoraid alongside other doctors to help expand these services to women who need their help (Clitoraid, 2013).

PATIENTS' EXPERIENCE

Patients who have been at her clinic express gratitude at a second chance. For instance, Massah, a patient who grew up in Sierra Leone and now lives in Australia, said the surgery "is like giving us a second life. Actually it's starting to live." Massah was circumcised at 11 years by a village woman. She felt ashamed, incomplete, and apprehensive toward sex and resisted going for pap smears in order to avoid embarrassment. "It's embarrassing going for pap smears . . . Just the look on people's faces," she says. Massah's hospital fee was US $1,700 and she does not regret it at all. She says, "I will spend my whole life saving . . . even if it's for one minute of feeling complete" (Tsai, 2010).

Fatou, in considering the surgery, observed, "It will enable me to take my revenge on those who did that to me . . . on those who wanted to take something from me" (Bangre, 2008). Diaryatou Bah, who was preparing for the procedure, observed, "The most important thing is to have female genital mutilation stopped, because what we will get after the operation may look like original clitoris but it will never be the same. . . . And the trauma of female genital cutting will always stay with us forever, no matter what we do" (Bangre, 2008).

Reconstructive surgery is not without criticism. Cultural relativists, such as Dr. Jacquis Wayneberg, the Director of the Paris Institute of Sexology, have described the procedure as "praiseworthy," but likely to promote neocolonial sentiments. He argues that "female circumcision, like male circumcision, is part of an anthropological process that makes an individual belong to his/her community or group . . . so the West can be suspected of neocolonialism when it says female circumcision is a mutilation without explaining or respecting its anthropological roots and without replacing it with a new identity marking" (Bangre, 2008).

Policy Enforcement and Guidelines

Most health care facilities do not have guidelines and trained personnel to deal with issues that continue to arise in their health facilities. Without guidelines on how to deal with health issues that these women face daily, it is difficult for these doctors to cope. In 1993, for instance, a doctor who was charged with contracting to perform female genital cutting in the United States was brought before the General Medical Council. Although he was found guilty of seven charges of serious misconduct, and had his license suspended, the Crown Prosecution Services did not proceed with the prosecution of the case, citing lack of evidence (Skaine, 2005: 251). With clear guidelines, prosecution of this doctor would have been ensured, and hence, the discouragement of such behavior.

Drastic measures are also needed to enforce policies against female genital cutting. For instance, it is also important that violations within the medical field are dealt with accordingly to ensure compliance. Although most European countries are trying to deal with the issue, it is difficult to determine the success rate. In the United Kingdom, for instance, it is illegal to perform female genital cutting under the Female Genital Mutilation Act 2003, and in Scotland, under the Prohibition of Female Genital Mutilation Act of 2005. Both Acts also make it illegal to perform the procedure abroad, to aid, abet, counsel, or procure the "carrying out of female genital mutilation abroad" (WHO/BMA, 2011: 5). Unfortunately, these prohibitions are not absolute since some doctors have succumbed to demand by some communities that their women be re-infibulated after each birth. Recognizing this as an issue, the Royal College of Obstetricians and Gynecologists produced clinical guidelines stating that:

> Any repair carried out after birth, whether following spontaneous laceration or deliberate defibulation, should be sufficient to oppose raw edges and control bleeding, but must not result in a vaginal opening that makes intercourse difficult or impossible. (WHO/BMA, 2011: 6)

This strict measure was arrived at because two doctors were found guilty of professional misconduct before the General Medical Council in 1993 and 2000. In 1993, a doctor performed female genital cutting while fully aware that it was illegal. Although he lost his license, the police refused to prosecute. In 2000, a doctor lost his license for offering to perform female genital cutting. Today, a person who is guilty of this offence can be imprisoned for up to 14 years.

In the *Working Together to Safeguard Children*, the United Kingdom government issues a set of guidelines for medical professionals on advice and policy regarding female genital cutting. Health organizations such as the British Medical Association, the Royal College of Obstetricians and Gynecologists, the Royal College of Nurses, and the Royal College of Midwifes have been given guidelines regarding the need to prohibit female genital cutting, including the need to prohibit medicalization of the procedure. The British Medical Association requires that medical professional should counsel parents of a girl regarding health and legal issues surrounding female genital cutting once a request for the procedure is made or if they suspect that the parents are likely to transport the child abroad for the procedure (Immigration Appellate Authority, 2000). The Royal College of Midwifes and the Royal College of Obstetricians and Gynecologists also prohibit re-infibulation after childbirth (Kwaak, 2003: 67).

The guidelines developed by the United Kingdom can be used as a model for ensuring a comprehensive address of the issue. Guidelines are provided as a support effort to frontline practitioners from health, education, and social care. Key points for doctors are outlined in the British Medical Association -BMA Ethics report.

- Deal with FGM in a sensitive and professional manner, and be sufficiently prepared so that they do not exhibit signs of shock, confusion, horror or revulsion when treating an individual affected by FGM.
- Always consider other girls and women in the family who may be at risk of FGM when dealing with a particular case. Ensure that mental health issues are considered when supporting girls and women affected by FGM.
- Health professionals, particularly nurses and midwives, need to be aware of how to care for women and girls who have undergone FGM, particularly when giving birth.
- All girls and women who have undergone FGM should be offered counseling to address how things will be different for them after de-infibulation procedures. Parents, boyfriends, partners and husbands should also be offered counseling. (BMA, 2004, 2011)

There should also be a clear display of health consequences of female genital cutting in women's clinics. Even if patients do not want to discuss their situation, they should have the opportunity to self-educate during patient waiting sessions. A list of possible consequences such as the one listed below should be on display in every examination room, including waiting rooms. They should read:

EFFECTS OF FEMALE GENITAL CUTTING

Short-term effects
- Hemorrhage
- Severe pain
- Urinary tract infection
- Injury to adjacent tissues
- Death
- Damage to other organs
- Fractures or dislocation due to restraint during the procedure

Long-term effects
- Haematocolpos
- Keloid formation
- Vulval abscess
- Sexual dysfunction

- Complications in pregnancy and childbirth
- Psychological damage: fear, anxiety, flashbacks, phobia, depression
- Penetration problems
- Lack of sexual response (Adapted from Momoh, 2010)

Where a medical examination is required, guidelines should be used by a consultant or pediatrician. As stated in the BMA Ethics Report, General Pediatricians should be encouraged to consider the following:

- Ask patients about female genital cutting as part of routine patient's history checkup.
- Give new patients information on female genital cutting as a "welcome pack."
- Find out about the possibility of performing the procedure overseas, especially during vaccinations/travel abroad.
- Ensure that health care centers have leaflets on the subject. (British Medical Association, 2011)

Guidelines for patients identified to be at risk
- Discuss concerns with "named nurse for child protection."
- If there are still concerns, refer to social services.
- Follow up referral in writing within 48 hours.
- Complete records and inform relevant people.
- First strategy meeting within two days of referral.
- Second strategy meeting within ten days of referral:
  o To evaluate information collected
  o To recommend if a child protection conference is necessary

Child Protection Conference
- A conference should be arranged to ensure the child is protected from exposure. The conference should ensure the following:
  o To determine allocation of social worker, management support and resources
  o To discuss and agree roles to implement the protection plan
  o To put child's name on child protection register
  o Therapeutic approach—safety and protection of the child/ren (Momoh, 2010)

These guidelines, which have improved health care services in the United Kingdom, could serve as a model for other countries to emulate.

NETWORKING WITH NGOs

It is important that nongovernmental organizations (NGOs) work hand-in-hand with health care departments in industrialized countries to promote awareness of these issues in order to identify needs and how to address them. While various departments of health in some industrialized countries have supported NGOs to carry out awareness campaigns about this practice, such as the United States, a lot needs to be done to ensure that health facilities take this issue seriously and that all doctors, nurses, and social workers are educated on this issue for effective address on these communities' concerns. In Australia, for instance, the government is not only involved in outreach programs that include the implementation of the National Education Program to prevent female genital cutting, minimization of health risk is central to the program. The Royal Australian College of Obstetricians and Gynecologists (RACOG) has established a powerful community education program. The main focus for health providers is to provide education, information, and support to women and girls who live with the risk and consequences of female genital cutting in order to access care and to minimize adverse health problems. Although the government promotes consistent health approach in the communities and facilitates support and access to health services, it also ensures that female genital cutting or any form of nonmedical genital modification is prohibited. It assists in developing materials to assist health professionals in this regard. For instance, it is unlawful to administer medical treatment to a child without the child's consent, or the consent of a person or court empowered to consent on the child's behalf. Although parents have the power to give consent on the child's behalf, they also have a duty of maintaining and protecting the child. Thus, the power they have can only be exercised in the interest of the child's welfare.

Also, the Supreme Court can overturn the parent's decision to consent to treatment if it deems the decision not to be in the interest of the child's welfare. While the law allows females over the age of 18 to consent to medical treatment which may include female genital cutting, the law ensures that medical practitioners cannot administer female genital-cutting procedures since it is an offence even if the child or adult consents (Matthews, 2011). Each state territory is required to report biennially on the work of health departments within communities on female genital cutting. Medical practitioners are encouraged to be culturally sensitive to values associated with the practice in order to provide adequate advice and to support members of the families involved. They are encouraged to consult with agencies that deal with female genital cutting in order to stay current on how to respond to girls and women who desire female genital cutting or medical assistance after the procedure.

In Canada, NGOs have been active in efforts to protect girls and women who live with the risk and consequences of female genital cutting. They work at providing education about the dangers of the practice and information about its illegality. The Society of Obstetricians and Gynecologists, Canadian Medical Association, and each provincial college of physicians and surgeons have adopted policies that prohibit medical professionals from performing female genital cutting (Skaine, 2005: 248). For instance, Save the Children Canada (SCC) focusses on promoting alternative traditional rite of passage for young girls known as "circumcision through words." The program which is described in the 1999 Canadian documentary *Circumcision through words* was first utilized successfully by PATH in Kenya, as discussed earlier, and has been used by medical associations in Kenya to educate health care professionals about the cultural beliefs of countries where female genital cutting is commonly practiced. The objective of the program in Canada is to utilize the alternative rites of passage program to educate younger women as well as involve the entire community in this alternative rite of passage, thus promoting awareness.

In France, the government has worked alongside private groups to launch campaigns to educate immigrant communities about the criminalization of the practice in the country since 1983. The Medical Ethics Code (1979), for instance, prohibits female genital cutting by medical doctors. The Code of Medical Deontology also prohibits physicians from performing female genital cutting. The French Medical Board is not aware of any breaches of the Code. Other groups include *Groupes des Femmes pour l'Abolition des Mutilations Sexuelles*, a group of African women in France who advise, support, and inform African women and families in France about the practice. *Commission International pour l'Abolition des Mutilations Sexuelles*, an associated member of UNICEF France, fights against this practice and also provides legal services. *Association Nationale des Medecins de Protection Matermelles et Infantiles* provides advice and medical treatment for women and children; *Prefecture d'Ile de France* is an organization concerned with women's rights in general, with programs focused on female genital-cutting prevention. Finally, *Movement Francais pour le Planning Familial* is also involved in this prevention campaign.

In Austria, like other industrialized countries, prevention of female genital cutting is considered a first priority. The medical profession is instructed through a special law (*Arztegesetz*), article 1, paragraph 54 (4), that if a doctor is suspicious that bodily harm or death of an individual is likely to be caused by an illegal act, he or she must immediately report to the police. Paragraph (5) of the same article adds that if a doctor is suspicious that a minor was "maltreated, tormented, neglected or sexually abused, he or she must report to the police immediately. If the injury or abuse is caused by a close relative as in the case of female genital cutting, the doctor may wait if the wellbeing of the minor depends on such an action" (Poldmans, 70).

Since female genital cutting is a health care issue, it is therefore important that health care professionals are educated on the needs of immigrant communities, particularly as relates to female genital cutting. They should be educated about cultural, physical, ethical, and legal ramifications of the practice to the patients they are likely to encounter and to their profession. It is important that they are aware of how to avoid insensitivity, disdain, and other negative emotions whenever they encounter women from female genital-cutting communities. The only way to be informed is to undergone serious training on the issue and to be provided with guidelines that cover this issue. As Leye et al. (2008) observe, it is probably necessary that a CD-Rom or other data medium should be produced covering all useful information on female genital cutting and made available to all gynecologists and trainees who are likely to encounter women who have undergone female genital cutting. A list of other services in various industrialized countries is provided in the Appendix.

Conclusion

The goal in this book has been to examine the prevalence of female genital cutting in industrialized countries and to explore the reasons for the current increase in the practice there. In the introduction, statistics are presented highlighting that female genital cutting is prevalent in industrialized nations such as the United States, the United Kingdom, France, Australia, Austria, the Netherlands, and Canada. The main reasons for this increase are globalization and immigration, which have caused cultural practices and values once considered foreign to assert themselves. The increase of this practice, which is generally associated with African, Middle Eastern, and some Asian countries, deserves attention since industrialized countries are renowned for protecting human and civil rights. It is important that girls and women in industrialized countries are assured of their civil rights in their own countries.

In order to contextualize the practice of female genital cutting, a description of the types of the practice, perceived origins, and the reasons for the practice have been presented. Clearly, female genital cutting is rooted in cultural and religious values. Where it is embraced, it began as a way for people to address moral concerns. A presentation of statistics and reasons for the practice are supplemented by a presentation of the voices of girls and women who live with the risk and consequences of the practice. Excerpts from these women's narratives add their own voice to the discussion. Experts' voices included in the discussion help affirm these women's views and demonstrate the unique dilemma that immigrants grapple with in industrialized countries. In highlighting these issues, it is hoped that policies can be put in place to help establish mechanisms to address their issues. While it is acknowledged that this process has begun at the highest levels, a lot more is yet to be done.

In the book, the health and moral concerns of the practice are high-lighted. It is noted that while health concerns draw from scientific evidence regarding harmful consequences of the practice on some girls and women, moral concerns are embedded in the value system embraced by both immigrants and industrialized countries. These concerns, it is argued, have been addressed from the perspectives of moral universalist as well as cultural relativist value systems, with universalist values providing the basis for human rights assertions and cultural relativist values promoting cultural rights claims. Although these competing perspectives seem to pose an irreconcilable dilemma in modern societies where multicultural-ism and cultural diversity are prized, I illuminate the ways in which both human rights and cultural rights can be negotiated and claimed.

Highlighted in this discussion is the role of world organizations such as the United Nations (UN) and the World Health Organizations (WHO). The UN, for example, sensitive to moral concerns related to gender discrimination, considers female genital cutting a violation of the human rights of the girls and women. Similarly, the WHO, concerned about health implications, has categorized the practice as genital mutilation. Consequently, countries and organizations affiliated with the UN and the WHO are required to comply with these two organizations' position on the practice. They must seek to discourage female genital cutting by any means possible, including putting laws into place that criminalize the practice. Although some countries have ratified covenants and stipulations established by the UN and WHO to discourage female genital cutting, others have been slow to do so, and the legal statutes that they do have are ambiguous, and therefore, difficult to enforce. This is one of the main reasons for the persistence of the practice. It is demonstrated that unenforced laws inhibit efforts to protect the rights of girls and women who live with the risk and consequences of the practice.

The emergence of postcolonial discourse and multicultural concerns has influenced attitudes toward female genital cutting. Calls for cultural diversity and groups' rights have shaped attitudes toward the practice in industrialized countries as in nonindustrialized countries. This has put pressure on medical organizations such as the American Academy of Pediatrics (AAP) to reconsider the practice, even to the point of considering the legalization of modified forms of the procedure. The central question of the book, then, is in some ways a response to recent calls from the perspectives of multiculturalism and cultural diversity. That is, can a nation embrace multiculturalism without undermining the human rights of its citizens? Should change be a concern or a consideration even where cultural diversity is embraced? Is it possible to be sensitive to cultural values without harming children, women, and any other individuals who are vulnerable in the society? Recognizing the need to negotiate the reality of social change within the moral milieu of contemporary society, recommendations are made toward promoting cultural appraisal of social values in light of social justice values, particularly those involving human rights.

Regarding the question of the double standard that emerges within cultural diversity discourses, it is argued that Western practices such as cosmetic surgery and male circumcision ought to be part of the discourse, but only insofar as human rights values are concerned. Cosmetic surgery is often cited as indicators of industrialized countries' double standard concerning genital cutting in general. In this book, I have argued for clear statutes requiring any cultural practice to be condemned if it qualifies as a human rights violation or a health hazard. Although it has been argued by some that both genital cutting and the Western practices mentioned above are done, among other reasons, for aesthetic reasons, it is important to acknowledge this important difference—the social pressure behind female genital cutting is immense. A woman in a community that embraces female genital cutting risks social ostracization, excommunication and social hostility if she declines to be cut. Clearly, the same is not true for women who do not undergo cosmetic surgery (or for uncircumcised men) in Western countries. As one of my respondents strongly asserted, individual choice should be the only reason for allowing any practice that is in violation of the health and human rights of any individual. I further argue that although patients' consent is often used to distinguish cosmetic surgery from female genital cutting, we should not allow consent to blind us to the possible harmful effects of cosmetic surgery as well. I recognize the difficulty of arguing for consent where procedures as potentially harmful as female genital cutting or cosmetic surgery are concerned. This is because informed consent is considered legitimate only when the patient is fully informed about the consequences of any given practice. In most female genital cutting communities, consent is often not an option. As a member of the indigenous community and culture, therefore, one is expected to comply. Often, initiates do not even know about the procedure until the day of initiation. With criminalization of the practice, young children, even babies are exposed to the practice at an age where they are unlikely to make an informed consent. True informed consent requires that one is capable of understanding implications of the practice and is able to make the decision based on the information received. While it is recognized that a respect for the rights of cultural groups is morally sound, in some ways, such respect is responsible for resistance to modern values and for the retention of, and possibly even renewed interest in cultural practices, some which may be harmful, such as female genital cutting.

It is also noted that although culture and religion remain significant factors in the persistence of female genital cutting in industrialized countries, modern values contribute to the persistence of the practice. In discussing the role of religion in the practice of female genital cutting, it is pointed out that indigenous, Jewish, Christian, and Islamic values are used to sanction female genital cutting, regardless of whether these values are found in the scriptures or not. The important point noted in this discussion is that religious and cultural values are difficult to distinguish, given the fact that both values reinforce each other. For instance, although indigenous values that legitimize female genital cutting are often misconstrued to be culture, it is important to note that religious values embedded in indigenous religions play a significant role in the persistence of the practice. In communities where female genital cutting persist, cultural and/or religious values tend to reinforce cultural identity, even among immigrants to industrialized countries. Also noted is the effect of social change on human attitudes and general behavior. It is argued that social norms and practices such as female genital cutting are human creations. They were formulated at some point in time to meet specific needs at the time. As times change, norms change as well to reflect contemporary needs.

It has also been argued that policy is a significant part to protecting the rights of girls and women from the risk and health consequences associated with female genital cutting. By reviewing efforts, policies, and intervention programs in various industrialized countries, it is argued that efforts have been made by some industrialized countries to establish and expand laws and policies that prohibit female genital cutting. It is noted in the study that most countries have some kind of legal policies in place intended to discourage female genital cutting. After analysis of the effectiveness of these policies, it is observed that there are loopholes or flaws in existing policies that are responsible for the persistence of the practice. It is argued that while policies and laws for the criminalization of female genital cutting are a necessary step to communicating that the practice is not tolerated, nonenforcement of existing laws make them ineffective. Nonenforcement is often as a result of flaws such as ambiguity, and lack of clarity of guidelines to follow. It is argued that policies and laws need not only be clear, they should be supplemented by localized strategies for effectiveness.

The need for elaborate intervention programs is argued for. Of particular interest is the need to develop community-based initiatives that are not only localized, but also broad in the identification of aspects of need with regard to this issue and the development of a specific strategy toward addressing each aspect of the identified need. Drawing from a community empowerment model, the need to involve local communities is advocated. Various successful community-based initiatives such as the Tostan case are cited to demonstrate how successful initiatives operate. It is argued that a successful initiative should include an educational and a religious component to capture the values and norms of socialization as these inform attitude formation.

Since health is a significant component to the controversy and the needs of girls and women who live with the risk and consequences, the book concludes by focusing on the need to expand the health care services in order to cater to specific needs of those affected. In order to address these risks, the chapter argues for medicalization of the procedure as the first step toward preventing girls from being exposed to unsterile and more dangerous forms of the procedure. Although this recommendation may be viewed by some as a way of condoning the practice, it is quickly noted that this should be viewed as a precautionary step to protect those who may not be convinced to abandon the practice. It is emphasized that medicalization guidelines should include informed consent just as it is required for any other surgical procedure. In the final section of health care intervention, the need for specialized forms of care is argued for in order to provide health services for women who live with the long-term consequences of the procedure. In order for this to be realized, the need for trained professionals is suggested in terms of ensuring that those in the medical profession are educated on the subject of female genital cutting, including how to identify those who have been cut. It is suggested that this topic be a significant section in the subject of reproductive health so that all in the medical profession who choose to specialize in the field can be aware of what to expect if they were to encounter patients with this issue. While controversial for some, the chapter ends by arguing for the need to encourage and provide services that include reconstructive surgery for those who choose to have these services. Girls and women who live in industrialized countries should be given the opportunity to make their own decision as to what kind of care they are entitled to and have the freedom to choose whether they want or do not want it.

In concluding remarks, it is noted that female genital cutting is gaining prominence in industrialized countries. It is observed that while globalization, immigration, and calls to embrace cultural diversity are modern, and therefore an acceptable reality, harmful cultural values and practices need not be condoned in the name of culture. The persistence of the practice in these countries, in spite of calls for protection of all from harmful cultural and social practice, is a concern. Since this practice affects permanent residents and even citizens in these countries, it should not be viewed as an exclusively immigrant issue. It is important, therefore, that industrialized countries acknowledge it as a national concern.

Although most industrialized countries have worked in conjunction with the WHO and the UN to establish and expand policies to discourage or prohibit female genital cutting, these policies are far from effective in protecting the rights of girls and women who live with the risk and consequences of the practice. As indicated in the study, existing intervention programs have serious flaws. While the criminalization of female genital cutting is a necessary first step toward communicating that the practice is not tolerated, enforcement of these laws is necessary if the practice is to be eradicated. To be effective, policies and laws need to be clear. In addition, they must be supplemented by localized, extralegal intervention strategies. Drawing from these findings, some recommendations are proposed below.

RECOMMENDATIONS

Zero Tolerance for Female Genital Cutting: As discussed in the findings, there are divergent voices on the subject of female genital cutting. While it is possible, as discussed in the findings, that the practice has possibly persisted due to convictions of some that it is a cultural or religious practice, those who view it as a human rights violation call for a zero tolerance of the practice. There must be zero tolerance of any form of genital cutting if attitudes toward the practice are to change. Allowing any form of the practice, whether modified or minor, is inimical to efforts to eradicate the practice. While it is recommended that informed consent be a factor in allowing mature individuals who insist on the procedure, there should be zero tolerance where informed consent is absent. And where informed consent is considered, there should be clear guidelines on how to legally follow the procedure of ensuring that there is no form of coercion as in the case of performing general surgery in these countries. This is because, it is difficult to monitor excisers or doctors who perform the practice to ensure that a minor, modified, or harmless form of the practice is performed. In other words, once a girl decides to be cut, what is done to her is left upon the whims of her exciser. The finality of the procedure makes it irreversible for many girls even if they were to protest after the event. Similarly, female genital cutting is a practice that is considered a taboo subject in communities where it is embraced. It is therefore very difficult for a girl or woman who has been subjected to it to talk about it without risking ostracization, excommunication, or even being killed in some communities. With sufficient political will to ensure eradication campaigns at national and international levels, the practice can and will be diminished.

Monitoring Female Genital Cutting: As illustrated in the findings, knowledge about the practice in industrialized countries is not only scarce, medical professionals are unaware of the existence of the practice, not to mention the health issues that it poses. In order to address the practice and to protect the rights of the girls and women who live with the risk and consequences of the practice, it is important that attitudes and behavior related to the practice are curbed. It therefore important that a serious data collection effort is undertaken in order to monitor the practice in order to identify declines and increases to effectively model intervention programs to statistical variables. Such an effort will allow scholars and policy makers to track the prevalence of female genital cutting and to monitor and understand changes in attitudes and behavior, both in individual countries and worldwide.

A central research center should be established to facilitate this. At present, statistical data on this practice in industrialized countries are either lacking or inadequate. One often-cited statistic—for example, 100–140 million girls have undergone female genital cutting—is over a decade old. A good model for the sort of statistical work that needs to be done is a project based in Israel, where researchers tracked the prevalence of the practice over a period of 10 years, showing the abandonment of the practice in that country over time (Belmaker, 2012). Similar work must be done in other countries. The first step is to track the number of immigrants from the countries where female genital cutting is traditionally practiced. Where the practice is established to be a problem, a serious form of monitoring of those involved should be part of the data collection efforts. Monitoring should also be extended to those who have acquired legal residency, including permanent immigrants and even citizens, as evidence suggests that the practice does not end when a person's immigration status changes.

Although, as indicated in the study, a number of people may be in a position to report the practice in early stages, most are ignorant about the practice and its consequences, and others do not know how to react when faced with evidence that a girl has been subjected to it. As noted earlier, in most nations, even medical professionals may not know what to do when they encounter patients who have been exposed to female genital cutting. Some medical professionals have chosen not to do anything, for fear of interfering with the private life of their patients.

Similarly, it is difficult to trace and to report female genital cutting to social and judicial authorities, mainly due to people's unwillingness. Efforts must be made to ensure the reporting of attitudes, intentions, and crimes related to the practice. It is, therefore, important that reporting procedures are clarified to ensure that all are held responsible for not reporting the practice. For instance, medical officials should be required to examine girls and women in order to identify signals and to report such cases to the authorities once they are discovered. This examination process should be extended to schools, such that school nurses are required to examine girls yearly, much as they examine them for pregnancy. This process will discourage parents from performing the practice, for fear of embarrassing their daughters or subjecting themselves to arrest. In addition to the approach adopted by France, where girls are examined, periodically to discourage the procedure among immigrants, industrialized countries need to ensure that reports of culprits are made and prosecuted where necessary. However, the responsibility to report the practice extends beyond the medical community. It is essential that all people who are in a position to signal or report the practice, including family members, neighbors, teachers, and religious leaders, be instructed in the crucial role they play in efforts to save girls and women from genital cutting and its lifelong consequences. They must be educated about choices they can make that will protect the life, health, and dignity of these women. By signaling to authorities that the practice is taking place, they can save lives. If they choose not to do so, they are implicated in all the possible negative effects that can result, and they should be held accountable in some form.

Community-Based Initiatives: Efforts to end the practice must emanate from within the community itself. This assumption draws from the community empowerment model. As illustrated above, community-based initiatives such as the Tostan case have been proven to be successful in ending female genital cutting (Dugger, 2011; Helmore, 2012). The need to improve community-based initiatives for effectiveness is crucial. Community initiatives are often successful because they address cultural values that promote the practice in an effort to transform the attitudes and behavior of those reluctant to abandon it. The purpose of prevention programs is to protect the vulnerable in society—children and women. It is for this reason that it is advised that intervention programs should integrate a human rights approach.

The Educational Component: These initiatives must also include an educational component. Female genital cutting is an international subject. It is important that this subject is taught at all levels of education as part of the empowerment process. While most countries recognize the need for awareness and the provision of information to communities regarding female genital cutting, most have not come through with the institution of these programs. As indicated earlier, effective education on this subject must be based on the human rights approach. Promoting social justice through the human rights approach is one way to ensure objective compliance. It is therefore important that the subject of female genital cutting should be included in all public education and national campaign programs. Teachers need to be trained in order to empower women. Textbooks on social studies should include the subject of female genital cutting to make it known to children in the early stage of life so they can watch out for signs of the practice. It is important that discussions are held among the immigrant communities in local and native languages in order to reach a wider audience. All schools and teachers should participate in intervention programs by passing across information to students to report concerns about the practice to authorities by calling hotline numbers on abuse.

Faith-Based Initiatives: Community-based intervention programs must seek to integrate faith-based initiatives in an effort to broaden attitude change toward the practice and to address values and socialization processes that inform attitude formation. Religious communities are in the best position to address issues that find justification in religious values. Since arguments opposing female genital cutting invoke the human rights, faith-based organizations, concerned as they are with human worth values, have an important role to play in the prevention of the practice.

Clarity of Laws: As discussed earlier, criminalization is a significant first step in discouraging female genital cutting. Indeed, as we have seen, various countries have turned to criminalization of female genital cutting as a means of intervention. If we are to end female genital cutting, criminalization is necessary. Although heavy-handed enforcement of the law may have the unintended consequence of driving the practice underground, laws remain tools for demarcating between right and wrong. Prosecution is essential to attitude change because criminal proceedings help raise public awareness. As Poldermans observes, each case that is prosecuted provides a warning signal to the families and communities, signaling to them that the practice is illegal. Nonbinding resolutions are not sufficient. Some countries have approved resolutions condemning the practice, such as those drafted by the Council of Europe (Parliamentary Assembly) and the European Union (Parliamentary). But resolutions are not binding and are difficult to enforce unless they become laws.[1]

Laws, then, seem essential. But are they desirable? Are they feasible? If it is agreed that they are, the question then becomes—which sort of law is most effective? As indicated earlier, nations can pass laws criminalizing female genital cutting; these laws often contain loopholes that can easily be exploited. Most of them, for example, tend to overlook certain aspects of the practice such as infibulation, which is often not specifically mentioned in the statutes passed by countries such as the United Kingdom and Austria, among others. Similarly, some of the laws found in industrialized countries do not specifically mention re-infibulation, piercing, and tattoos. Because these practices are clearly stipulated in the WHO documents as Type 4 female genital cutting, governments need to make sure that specific aspects of the practice are clearly defined in the legal documents as crimes that will be prosecuted. Neglecting to do so creates ambiguity in these laws, resulting in questions on the part of medical professionals about whether a given form of cutting is prohibited. If women are to be protected in industrialized countries, legislation must criminalize female genital cutting in all its forms.

The efficacy of any law lies in its enforcement. All countries must ensure that laws prohibiting female genital cutting are enforceable by removing all obstructive elements. An example of such a law is that about the principle of double criminality. In some countries, legal systems provide for the principle of double criminality. According to this principle, an individual is to be extradited only if two jurisdictions possess a law that criminalizes female genital cutting. This leaves a loophole in the case where one of the jurisdictions does not possess the law. The law must be clarified to include some kind of penalty even in countries that do not have the principle of double criminality in the books. It should be made clear that whether the principle of criminality exists in two jurisdictions or not, extradition should occur. Other procedures related to the gathering of evidence for the criminal proceedings need to be streamlined to ensure that protocol is clear. Where such procedure is not followed, a penalty must be imposed.

Extending Statutes of Limitation: It is essential that industrialized countries work at extending the statute of limitation governing female genital cutting. This will empower women who have suffered abuse as children to prosecute what they come to understand as criminal behavior. A broader time frame within which a woman can press criminal charges will ensure that those that are affected can sue their abuser at any time. In the Netherlands and Austria, women can sue their abusers any time after their 18th birthday, a policy that does not close the window within which they can press charges before they have had time to understand consequences of what has been done to them. As Poldermans (2005) observes, the likeliness of survivors to prosecute is increased when they have had ample time to deal with the psychological and physical effects of the procedure.

The Health Care Initiative: Since, the study identifies health as a factor in the categorization of female genital cutting as a human rights violation, it is important that intervention programs must also include a health component. As illustrated earlier, health care workers are poised to play a significant role in the prevention of female genital cutting. Yet, many of them are unprepared to treat and counsel the women who have undergone the procedure. There is therefore the need to expand health care services to minimize the health risks associated with female genital cutting and to address health issues that women who have undergone the practice deal with on a daily basis. In particular, it is important that issues surrounding female genital cutting be made a part of health care training programs so that health care workers will be equipped to treat patients who have suffered this violation of their human rights. It is important that health providers at all levels should receive training and financial support to treat female genital cutting-related complications if they are to assist in the prevention of the practice. By including in the health care training a component of reproductive health classes, with a specific topic on female genital cutting, all medical officials will have an opportunity to learn about this practice, specifically the health consequences they are likely to deal with. Thus, medical professionals will be trained on how to handle patients who have experienced female genital cutting and to address the unique needs of these women.

Networking Initiatives: Although it is important that real change must emanate from within communities themselves, governments and nongovernmental organizations must be involved in intervention processes. It is important that both the government and nongovernmental organizations have crucial roles to play. A networking initiative between the three bodies of the community must be ensured to promote effective intervention against female genital cutting. All governments should help to set up awareness programs among communities that live with the risk and consequences of female genital cutting. It is important that governments and nongovernmental organizations collaborate on various initiatives to discourage female genital cutting. Government support should be demonstrated through scaled-up successful community-based female genital cutting programs. Efforts by nongovernmental organizations should be supplemented by the continued enactment and enforcement of laws to protect girls who live with the risk of genital cutting.

All organizations dealing with female genital cutting should coordinate and cooperate with the government to help build statistics and improve intervention programs. Since nongovernmental organizations are often small and rely heavily on volunteers and donations, they should get financial support and technical assistance from governments, policy-making institutions, and other successful agencies. It is particularly important that advocacy organizations sharpen their advocacy skills. Organizations such as PHAROSD, GAMS, FORWARD, and the African Women's Organizations in Vienna should support awareness campaigns to help change attitudes toward the practice. With governmental support, such programs will contribute immensely toward protecting the rights of girls and women. For instance, programs such as Daphne Initiative (1997–1999), DAPHNE Program (2000–2003), and DAPHNE II (2004–2008), all of which are supported by the EU, have contributed a lot toward helping combat violence against women, youth, and children. Other programs such as EURONET, a European platform combining all organizations that deal with the prevention of female genital cutting, have also helped. Unfortunately, without funding, outreach efforts can be inhibited.

The goal of this book is to restate the need to protect the rights of girls and women from cultural abuse. Human rights of all should be respected, regardless of religion or cultural rights. While it is recognized that there are instances when individual and cultural rights are likely to conflict, where human rights are embraced, cultural rights ought to be reconciled to protect these rights. While cultural norms should be appreciated as markers of identity, harmful cultural values should be interrogated and transformed to reconcile them with moral values in order to promote social justice, good health and general welfare.

NOTE

1. Council of Europe, P.A. Resolution 1247, 2001; European Union, E.P. Resolution 2001/2035INI.

Appendix

❖

Contact List of
Specialized Centers

One of the goals in this book is to empower and to promote aware-ness. Awareness and knowledge must be followed with action. Access to resources is significant for empowerment to be realized. Below is a list of some specialized centers where survivors of female genital cutting can seek help.

Australia

The Women's: The Royal Women's Hospital
Victoria, Australia
193 Bluff Rd.
Sandringham VIC 3191
Australia
Phone: (03) 9076–1000/(03) 8345–3030/(03) 8345–3037

The Women's: The Royal Women's Hospital
Victoria, Australia
20 Flemington Rd.
Parkville VIC
Australia
Phone: (03) 9076–1000/(03) 8345–3030/(03) 8345–3037

The Women's: The Royal Women's Hospital
Locked Bag 300
Grattan St. & Flemington Rd
Parkville VIC 3052
Australia
Phone: (03) 8345–2000

Austria

Bright Future
Information Center for Women's Health and FGM
SchwarzspanierstraBe 15/1 Door 2 1090 Vienna
Austria
E-mail: afrikanisafrauenorganisation@chello.at
www.african-women.org

Desert Flower Foundation
Ungargasse 24
1030 Vienna
Austria
Phone: +43 1 4027916
E-mail: office@desertflowerfoundation.org
www.waris-dirie-foundation

FEM SUD
Health Center for Women in the Kaiser Franz Josef Spital Wien
KundratstraBe 3, 1100 Vienna
Austria
Phone: 01 601915212 or 5201
E-mail: femsued.post@wienkav.at
www.fem.at

Orient Express
Information Center for Women
HillerstraBe 6, 1020 Vienna
Phone: 01 7289725
E-mail: Office@orientexpress-wien.com
www.orientexpress-wien.com

Waris Dirie Foundation
Verein zur Förderung von Hilfsaktionen für Afrika
Millenium Tower 24th Floor
Handelskai 94–96

1200 Vienna
Phone: 0043 1 24 027 6351
E-mail: waris@utanet.at
www.waris-dirie-foundation.com

United Kingdom

Birmingham

Midlands Refugee Council
5th Floor, Smithfield House
Digbeth
Birmingham B5 6BS
Phone: 0121 242 2200

Princess of Wales Women's Unit Labour Ward
Birmingham Heartlands Hospital—Bordesley Green East
Birmingham, B9 5SS
Phone: 08000283550; 0121 424 3909/0121 424 0730/07817534274
(Mobile)
Contact: Alison bryne alison.byrne@heartofengland.nhs.uk

Women Can Self-Refer
Birmingham Heartlands Hospital
Princess of Wales Women's Unit
Labour Ward
Bordesley Green East
Birmingham
Phone: 0121 424 3514

Bristol

Minority Ethnic Women's & Girls Clinic
Charlotte Keel Health Centre
Seymour Road, Easton
Bristol, BS5 OUA
Phone: 0117 902 7111/0117 902 7100
Contact: Dr. Hilary Cooling

Ireland

Multi-Cultural Resource Centre (Northern Ireland)
9 Lower Crescent
Belfast BT7 1NR

Phone: 028 9024 4639
www.mcrc-ni.org

Northern Ireland Council for Ethnic Minorities (NICEM)
3rd Floor, Ascot House
24–31 Shaftesbury Square
Belfast
BT2 7DB
Phone: 028 9023 8645/028 90319666
www.nicem.org.uk

Leeds

FGM Clinic
St. James's University Hospital (St. JUH)
Antenatal Clinic
Level 4 Gledhow Wing
Leeds, LS9 7TF

Liverpool

Central Liverpool PCT
FGM Advocacy Worker Rahima Farah
Kuumba Imani Millennium Centre
4 Princes Street
Liverpool L8 1TH
Phone: 051 285 6370 (direct)

Multi-Cultural Antenatal Clinic
Liverpool Women's Hospital
Crown Street
Liverpool L8 7SS
Phone: 0151 702 4085/0771 751 6134/01517089988
Contact: Barbasa Valjelo@lwh.nhs.uk
Dorcas Akeju—Specialist Midwife

London

Acton African Well Woman Centre
(Acton Health Centre)
35–61 Church Road
London W3 8QE

Phone: 0208 383 8761/07956001065
Contact: Juliet Albert Juliet.albert@nhs.net
Hayat Arteh Hayat.arteh@nhs.net

African Well Women's Clinic
(Antenatal Clinic—Central Middlesex Hospital)
Acton Lane, Park Royal
London NW10 7NS
Phone: 020 8965 5733/020 8963 7177
Contact: Kamal Shehata Iskander kamal.shehataiskander@mwlh.nhs.uk
Jacky Deehan jacqueline.deehan@nwlh.nhs.uk

African Well Women's Clinic
(Guy's & St Thomas's Hospital)
8th Floor—c/o Antenatal Clinic
Lambeth Palace Rd
London SE1 7EH
Phone: 020 7188 6872
Mobile: 07956 542 576
Open: Mon–Fri 9 am–4 pm
Contact: Ms. Comfort Momoh MBE comfort.momoh@gstt.nhs.uk

African Well Women's Clinic
McNair Centre
Guy's and St Thomas' Hospital
St Thomas Street
London SE1 9RT
Phone: 020 7955 2381

African Well Women's Clinic
Northwick Park & St Mark's Hospital
Watford Road
Harrow
Middlesex HA1 3UJ
Phone: 020 8869 2870
Contact: Jeanette Carlson

African Women's Clinic
Elizabeth Garrett Anderson & Obstetric Hospital
Huntley Street
London WC1E 6DH

Phone: 020 7380 9300
Ext. 2531 (nurse practitioner)
Ext. 2538 (clinic coordinator)

African Women's Clinic—University College Hospital
Clinic 3; Elizabeth Garrett Anderson Wing
Euston Road, London NW1 2BU
Phone: 0845 155 5000
Contact: Maligaye Bikoo maligaye.bikoo@uclh.nhs.uk

African Women's Clinic—Women and Health
4 Carol Street
Camden, London NW1 OHU
Phone: 020 7482 2786
Contact: Maligaye Bikoo maligaye.bikoo@uclh.nhs.uk

African Women's Health Clinic
(Whittington Hospital)
Level 5, Highgate Hill
London N19 5NF
Tel: 020 7288 3482 Ext. 5954
Mobile: 0795 625 7992
Open: Last Wednesday of each month, 9am-5pm
Contacts: Joy Clarke joy.clarke@whittington.nhs.uk
or Shamsa Ahmed

AFRUCA (Africans United Against Child Abuse)
Unit 3D/F Leroy House
436 Essex Road
London N1 3QP
Phone: 020 7704 2261
www.afruca.org

Black Women's Health and Family Support
1st Floor, 62 Russia Lane
London E2 9LU
Phone: 020 8980 3503
www.bwhafs.com
bwhfs@btconnect.com

British Somali Community
Star House, 104–108 Grafton Road
London NW5 4BD

Phone: 020 7485 2963
www.britishsomali.org

Chelsea and Westminster Hospital
Gynaecology and Midwifery Depts.
369 Fulham Road
London SW10 9NH
Phone: 020 746 8000

Community Partnership Advisor Project
Voluntary Action Camden
293–299 Kentish Town Road
London NW5 2TJ
Phone: 020 7284 6575

Equality Now
5th Floor, 6 Buckingham Street
London WC2N 6BU
Phone: 020 7839 5456
E-mail: ukinfo@equalitynow.org

Eritrean Community in the UK
266/268 Holloway Road
London N7 6NE
Phone: 020 7700 7995
www.ericomuk.org.uk

Ethiopian Health Support Association
Priory House, Kingsgate Place
London NW6 4TA
Phone: 020 7419 1972
www.ethsa.co.uk

FGM National Clinical Group
C/o Institute of Women's Health
University College London Hospital NHS Trust
2nd Floor West, 250 Euston Road
London NW1 2PG
info@fgmnationalgroup.org
www.fgmnationalgroup.org

FORWARD
Unit 4

765–767 Harrow Road
London NW10 5NY
Phone: 020 8960 4000
www.FORWARDuk.org.uk
forward@forwarduk.org.uk

Foundation for Women's Research and Development (FORWARD)
Suite 2:1 Chandelier Building
2nd Floor, 8 Scrubs Lane
London NW10 6RB
Phone: +44(0)20 8960 4000
E-mail: forward@forwarduk.org.uk

Global Consultant on Public Health
FGM & Surgical Reversal (GCPH)
10a Russell Gardens
London N20 0TR
Phone: 0795 640 7063
comfort@fgmconsultancy.com
www.fgmconsultancy.com

Gynaecology & Midwifery Departments
Chelsea & Westminster Hospital
3rd Floor, 369 Fulham Rd.
London SW10 9NH
Phone: 0207 751 4488
Contact: Gubby Ayida

Gynecology & Midwifery Department
St. Mary's Hospital
Praed St.
London W1 1NY
Phone: 0207 886 6691/0207 886 1443/0207 886 6763
Contact: Judith Robbins or Sister Hany

International Planned Parenthood Federation
Newhams Row
London SEI 9LO
Phone: 020 8980 3503
E-mail: bwhafs@btconnect.com

Iskawaran Somali Mental Health Project
Unit 51—The Design Works

Park Parade, Harlesden
London NW10 4HT
Phone: 020 8838 6163

Leytonstone Community Health Project
Kirkdale House
7 Kirkdale Road
Leytonstone
London E11 1HP
Phone: 020 8928 2244

London Child Protection Committee
Association of London Government
59 1/2 Southwark Street
London SE1 0AL
Phone: 020 7934 9999
www.alg.gov.uk

Medical Ethics Department
British Medical Association
BMA House, Tavistock Square
London WC 1H 9JP
Phone: 020 7383 6286
E-mail: ethics@bma.org.uk

Project Azure
Metropolitan Police Child Abuse Investigation Command
Scd5mailbox-azure@met.police.uk
Phone: 020 7161 2888

RAINBO (Research, Action and Information Network for the Bodily Integrity of Women)
Queens Studios
121 Salisbury Road
London NW6 6RG
Phone: 020 7625 3400
www.rainbo.org
info@rainbo.org

Somali Welfare Association
33 Ladbroke Grove
London W10 5AA

Phone: 020 8968 1195
www.somwa.org

St. Mary's Hospital
(Gynecology & Midwifery Departments)
Praed Street
London W1 1NY
Phone: 020 7886 6691/020 7886 1443
Contacts: Judith Robbins or Sister Hany foong.han@imperial.nhs.uk

Waltham Forest Somali Women's Association
Greenleaf Road
Walthamstow, E17
Phone: 020 8503 7121

Waltham Forest African Well Women's Services
Oliver Road Polyclinics
Upper Ground Floor
75 Oliver Rd, Leyton
London E10 5LG
Phone: 0208 430 7381

West London African Women's Community Clinic
West London Centre for Sexual Health Caring Cross Hospital
(South Wing)
Fulham Palace Road
London W6 8RF
Phone: 0208 383 0827/07920450045/0203 315 3344
E-mail: fgmwestlondon@nhs.net
Contact: Lazara.DominguezGarcia@chelwest.nhs.uk

West London African Women's Hospital Clinic
Gynecology and Antenatal Clinics Chelsea and Westminster Hospital
369 Fulham Road, London, SW10 9NH
Phone: 0203 315 3344
E-mail: fgmwestlondon@nhs.net

WoMan Being Concern International
K405 Tower Bridge Business Complex
100 Clements Road
London SE16 4DG
Phone: 020 7740 1306
www.womanbeing.org

Women's and Young People's Services, Sylvia Pankhurst Health Centre
Mile End Hospital
Bancroft Road
London E1 4DG
Phone: 020 7377 7898/020 7377 7870
Contact: Dr. Geetha Subramanian
E-mail: geetha.subramanian@thpct.nhs.uk

Woodfield Medical Center
Antenatal Clinic
7e Woodfield Road
London W9 3XZ
Phone: 020 7266 8822
Contact: Miss Katy Clifford

AFRUCA (Africans Unite Against Child Abuse) Phoenix Mill
20 Piercy Street
Ancoats, Manchester M4 7HY
Phone: 01612059274
E-mail: info@afruca.org
www.afruca.org

BLACK Women's Health and Family Support
1st Floor, 82 Russia Lane
London E2 9LU
Phone: +440289803503
E-mail: bwhafs@btconnect.com
www.bwhafs.com

Manchester

St. Mary's Hospital
Hathersage Road, Manchester M13 0JH
Phone: 0161 276 6673
Contact: Dr. Fiona Reid—Consultant

Nottingham

Labour Ward City Campus
Nottingham University Hospitals
Hucknall Road
Nottingham NG5 1PB
Phone: 0115 969 1169 Ext. 55124/55127
Contact: Carol McCormick carol.mccormick@nuh.nhs.ukScotland

International Women's Centre
49 Lyon Street
Ground Floor Left
Dundee DD4 6RA
Phone: 01382 462058
www.diwc.co.uk

Save the Children Scotland
Haymarket House
8 Clifton Terrace
Edinburgh EH12 5DR
Phone: 0131 527 8200
www.savethechildren.org.uk/scotland

Scottish Refugee Council
5 Cadogan Square (170 Blythswood Court)
Glasgow G2 7PH
Phone: 0141 248 0799
www.scottishrefugeecouncil.org.uk

Sheffield

Agency for Culture & Change Management
The Old Corners Court
14/18 Nursery Street
Sheffield S3 8GG
Phone: 0114 275 0193
www.accmsheffield.org

Drop-in Service
Central Health Clinic
1 Mulberry Street
Sheffield 51 2PJ
Phone: 0114 271 8865

Wales

Central African Association
11 Richmond Road
Cardiff CF24 3AQ
Phone: 029 2045 9945
www.centralafrican.org.uk

MEWN Cymru—Minority Ethnic Women's Network
Wales 1st floor
Coal Exchange
Mount Start Square
Cardiff CF10 5EB
Phone: 029 2046 4445
www.mewn-cymru.org.uk

SPA Somali Advice & Information Office
68 James Street
Cardiff Bay
Cardiff
Phone: 029 2025 5526
www.switch-cymru.org.uk/html/SPA/contaus.htm

Welsh Refugee Council
Phoenix House
389 Newport Road
Cardiff CF24 1TP
Phone: 029 2048 9800
www.welshrefugeecouncil.org

United States

African Women's Health Care
Brigham and Women's Hospital
75 Francis Street
Boston, MA 02115
Contact: Nawal Nour, MD MPH
E-mail: Africanwomen@partners.org
Phone: (617) 732 4740/(617) 975 0966

Brigham and Women's Hospital
Development Office
116 Huntington Avenue
Boston, MA 02116

Dr. Marci Bowers
PO Box 1044
Trinidad, CO 81082
Phone: (719) 846 6300/(877) 439 2244
Fax: (719) 846 9500/(877) 439 9922
E-mail: mail@marcibowers.com

Dr. Marci Bowers
San Mateo, CA
(Consultations and Surgery)
Phone: (877) 439 2244
Fax: (877) 439 9922

Refugee Women's Health Clinic
Women's Care Center
2nd Floor, 25252 East Roosevelt Street
Phoenix, AZ 85008
Contact: Crista E. Johnson-Agbakwu, MD, MSc
Jeanne F. Nizigiyimana
E-mail: jeanne_nizigiyimana@dmgaz.org

Seattle Clinic
(Consults and GYN only)
Phone: (206) 328 3200
Fax: (206) 328 4636
E-mail: mail@marcibowers.com

Bibliography

Abbas-Shavazi, Muhammad Jalal and Peter McDonald. 2000. "Fertility and Multiculturalism: Immigrant Fertility in Australia: 1977–91." *International Migration Review*, Vol. 34, No. 1: 215–42.

Abu-Sahlieh, Sami Awad Aldeeb. 2001. *Male and Female Circumcision—Among Jews, Christians and Muslims: Religious, Medical, Social and Legal Debate.* Warren Center. PA: Shangri-La Publications.

Abu-Sahlieh, Sami Awad Aldeeb. 1999. "Muslims' Genitalia in the Hands of the Clergy: Religious Arguments about Male and Female Circumcision," in *Male and Female Circumcision: Medical, Legal and Ethical Considerations in Pediatric Practice*, edited by George C. Denniston, Frederick Mansfield Hodges, and Marilyn Fayre Milos. New York: Kluwer Academic/Plenum Publishers, 131–72.

Adhikari, Brinda and Lara Salahi. 2010. "Female Genital Cutting: Affecting Young Girls in America." *ABCNEWS.* www.abcnews.go.com.

Afkhami, M., and E. Fridi (eds.). 1997. "Introduction," in *Muslim Women and the Politics of Participation: Implementing the Beijing Platform.* Syracuse, NY: Syracuse University Press.

African Women's Health Center. 1999. Brigham and Women's Hospital: A Teaching Affiliate of Harvard Medical School. www.brighamandwomens.org.

Ahmadu, Fuambai. 2000. "Rites and Wrongs: An Insider/Outsider Reflects on Power and Excision," in *Female "Circumcision" in Africa: Culture, Controversy and Change*, edited by Bettina Shell-Duncan and Ylva Herlund. London: Lynne Reinne Publishers, 283–312.

Ahmed, Leila. 1992. *Women and Gender in Islam*. New Haven, CT: Yale University Press.

Ajisafe Moore, E. A. 2003. *The Laws and Customs of the Yoruba People*. Abeokuta Nigeria: Fola Bookshops.

Ake, Claude. 1987. "The African Context of Human Rights." *Africa Today*, Vol. 34, No. 142: 5–13.

Al-Amili, Muhammad ibn-Hasan Al-Hur. 1982. *Wasa'il al-shiah ila tehsil ila tehsil masa'il al-shariah*, Vol. 15. Teheran: Al-Maktabah al-Islamiyyah, 168.

Al-Jahiz, Abu-Uthman Umar Ibn-Bahr. 1996. *Kitab al-hayawan*, Vol. 7. Beirut: Dar al-jil, 27.

Al-Jamal, Suleyman. n.d. Hashiyat Al-Jamal, Vol. 5. Cairo: Al-Maktabah al-Tijariyyah, 174.

Ally, Muhammad Mashuq Ibn. 1992. *Theology of Islamic Liberation*. Maryknoll, NY: Orbis Books.

Amadiume, Ifi. 2000. *Daughters of the Goddess, Daughters of Imperialism: African Women Struggle for Culture, Power and Democracy*. London: Zed Books Ltd.

Ammah, Rabiatu. 1997. "Paradise Lies at the Feet of Muslim Women," in *The Will to Arise: Women, Tradition, and the Church in Africa*, edited by Mercy Amba Oduyoye and Musimbi R. A Kanyoro. Maryknoll, NY: Orbis Books, 74–86.

Amnesty International. 1997. "Female Genital Mutilation in Africa: Information by Country." www.amnestry.org/ailib/intcam/femgen/fgm9.htm.

Anderson, Barbara A. 2005. *Reproductive Health: Women and Men's Shared Responsibility*. Sudbury MA: Jones and Bartlett Publishers Inc.

An-Naim A., Abdullahi. 2000. "Islam and Human Rights: Beyond the Universality Debate." *American Society of International Law*, Proceedings of the 94th Annual Meeting, April 5–8, 95.

Archer, Margaret S. 1988. *Culture and Agency: The Place of Culture in Social Theory*. Cambridge, UK: Cambridge University Press, 1988.

Asali A., N. Khamaysi, Y. Aburabia, S. Letzer, B. Halihal, M. Sadovsky, et al. 1995. Ritual Female Genital Surgery among Bedouin in Israel. *Archival Sexual Behavior*, Vol. 24: 571–75.

Australian Government Department of Immigration and Citizenship. 2009. "Settler Arrivals 1998–99 to 2008–09." *Australia, States and Territories*, Canberra: DIC.

Australian National University. 2006. "Female Genital Mutilation Affects Birth: Study." *Science Daily*. www.sciencedaily.com.

Austrian Times. 2010. "Female Genital Mutilation Remains Problem, Group Warns." *Austrian Times*. www.austriantimes.

Ayorinde, Christine. 2004. "Santeria in Cuba: Tradition and Transformation," in *The Yoruba Diaspora in Atlantic World*, edited by Toyin Falola and Matt D. Childs. Bloomington: Indiana University Press, 209–30.

Bangre, Habibou. 2008. "An African Problem in the Heart of Europe: Female Genital Mutilation in Immigrant France." *The Root*. www.theroot.com.

Barstow, D.G. 1999. "Female Genital Mutilation: The Penultimate Gender Abuse." *Child Abuse Neglect*, Vol. 23: 501–10.

Bashir, Miller Layli.1996. "Female Genital Mutilation in the United States: an Examination of Criminal and Asylum Law." *American University Journal of Gender & the Law*, Vol. 4, No. 2: 415–54.

BBC News. 2007. "My Mother Held Me Down." *BBC News: One Minute World News*, July 10. http://news.bbc.co.uk.

Beckwith, Francis and Gregory Koukl. 1998. *Relativism: Feet Firmly Planted in Mid-Air*. Grand Rapids, MI: Baker Books.

Belluck, Pam. 2010. "Doctors Reverse Stand on Circumcision." *The New York Times*, May 26, 2010. www.nytimes.com.

Belluck, Pam. 2010. "Group Backs Ritual 'Nick' as Female Circumcision Option." *The New York Times*, May 6, 2010. www.nytimes.com.

Belmaker, R.H. 2012. "Successful Cultural Change: The Example of Female Circumcision among Israeli Bedouins and Israeli Jews from Ethiopia." *Isr J Psychiatry Relat Sci*, Vol. 49, No. 3: 178–83.

Berger, Peter. 1990. *The Sacred Canopy: Elements of a Sociological Theory of Religion*. New York: Anchor Books.

Berkowitz, Peter. 1999. "Feminism vs. Multiculturalism? The Liberal Project at Odds with Itself." *The Weekly Standard*, No. 1. www.peterberkowitz.com.

Beyer, Catherine. 2013. "Raelian Movement: An Introduction to Raelians for Beginners." *About.com: Alternative Religions*. http://altreligion.about.com.

Billet, Bret L. 2007. *Cultural Relativism in the Face of the West: The Plight of Women and Female Children*. Hampshire, UK: Palgrave Macmillan.

Bishai, David, Bonnenfant Yung-Ting, Manal Darwish, Taghreed Adam, Heli Balhija, Elise Johansen, and Dale Huntington. 2010. "Estimating the Obstetric Costs of Female Genital Mutilation in six African Countries." *Bulletin of the World Health Organization*, Vol. 88, No. 4: 281–88. http://www.who.int/bulletin/volumes/88/4/09-064808/en/.

Boddy, Janice. 1989. *Wombs and Alien Spirits: Women, Men and the Zar Cult in Northern Sudan*. Madison: The University of Wisconsin Press.

Bonvillain, Nancy. 2001. *Women and Men Cultural Constructs of Gender*. 3rd ed. Upper Saddle River, NJ: Pearson Prentice Hall.

Bourke, Emily. 2010. "Female Circumcision in Australia." *ABC News*, February 6. www.abc.net.au.

Boyer, Pascal. 2001. *Religion Explained: The Evolutionary Origins of Religious Thought*. New York: Basic Books.

Boyle, E. 2002. *Female Genital Cutting: Cultural Conflict in the Global Community*. Baltimore, MD: The John Hopkins University Press.

British Medical Association. 2004/2011. *Female Genital Mutilation, Caring for Patients and Child Protection: Guidance from the Ethics Department*. London, February 3. http://bma.org.uk/-/media/Files/PDFs/Practical%20 advice%20at%20work/Ethics/femalegenitalmutilation.pdf.

Bulbeck, Chilla. 1998. *Re-orienting Western Feminisms: Women's Diversity in a Postcolonial World*. Cambridge, UK: Cambridge University Press.

Burki, T. 2010. "Reports Focus on Female Genital Mutilation in Iraq Kurdistan." *The Lancet*, Vol. 375, No. 9717: 794.

Burstyn, Linda. 1995. "Female Circumcision Comes to America." *The Atlantic Monthly*, Vol. 276, No. 4: 28–35. http://www.theatlantic.com.

Burton, Sir Richard F. 1855 (1964). *Personal Narrative of a Pilgrimage to Al-Madinah and Meccah*. New York: Dover Publications, Vol. 1.

Butler, Judith. 1990. *Gender Trouble*. New York: Routledge.

Caldwell, John C., O.I. Orubuloye, and Pat Caldwell. 1997. "Male and Female Circumcision in Africa from a Regional to a Specific Nigerian Examination." *Social Science and Medicine*, Vol. 44, No. 8: 1181–93.

Carmody, Denise Lardner. 1989. *Women and World Religions*, 2nd ed. Englewood Cliff, NJ: Prenticehall.

Center for Reproductive Rights. 2004. "Legislation on Female Genital Mutilation in the United States." *Briefing Paper*, November 2004. www.reproductiverights.org.

Chen, Stephanie. 2010/2012. "Pressure for Female Genital Cutting Lingers in the U.S." http://edition.cnn.com/2010/health.

Clarke, L. 2004. "Women in Islam," in *Women and Religious Traditions*, edited by Leona M. Anderson and Pamela Dickey Young. Oxford: Oxford University Press.

Clitoraid. 2013. "Clitoraid's Head Surgeon Restores Clitoris for 4 Victims of Female Genital Mutilation." Clitoraid: Restoring a Sense of Dignity and Pleasure. www.clitoraid.org.

Coleman, Dorianne L. 1998. "The Seattle Compromise: Multicultural Sensitivity and Americanization." *Duke Law Review*, Vol. 47: 717–83.

Collins, James. 2010. "Beware! My Daughter was almost Circumcised Here in America!" *She Told Me: Lifestyle*. www.shetoldme.com.

Colorado Review Stat. 1999. Tit 18 Article 1 §105.

Committee on Bioethics. 2010. "Ritual Genital Cutting of Female Minors." *Pediatrics: Official Journal of the American Academy of Pediatrics*, Vol. 125, No. 5: 1088–93.

Coquery-vidrovitch, Catharine. 1997. *African Women: A Modern History.* Boulder, CO: West View Press.

Corbett, Sara. 2008. "A Cutting Tradition." *The New York Times*, January 20. www.nytimes.com.

Crosette, Barbara. 1995. "Female Genital Mutilation by Immigrants Is Becoming Cause for Concern in U.S." *New York Times*, December 10.

Crosset, Erin. 2012. "Eliminating Female Genital Mutilation Requires Individual State Solution." www.polymic.com.

Daly, Mary. 1978. *Gyn/Ecology: The Metaethics of Radical Feminism.* Boston: Beacon Press.

Davis, Anna. 2013. "Londoners Sign Fake Pro-Female Genital Petition out of 'Political Correctness,' Anti-FGM Advocate Says." *The World Post: A Partnership of The Huffington Post and Berggruen Institute on Governance*, October 28. http://www.huffingtonpost.com.

Delmar, Rosalind. 1986. "What Is Feminism?" in *What Is Feminism*, edited by Juliet Mitchell and Ann Oakley. New York: Pantheon Books, 8–33.

The Department of Health. 2004. CMO Estimates Update 37, cited in Pio (2011) West Lothian Female Genital Mutilation Protocal. www.childprotectionwestlithonian.org.uk.

Diesie. n.d. "Female Genital Mutilation." *Wiener Program Fur Franengesundheit.* www.diesie.at/English/FGM.

Dirie, Waris. 2005. *Onze Verborgen tranen.* Amsterdam: Sirene.

Dorkenoo, et al. 2007. "A Statistical Study to Estimate the Prevalence of Female Genital Cutting in England and Wales." *Forward: Safeguarding Rights and Dignity.* www.forwarduk.org.uk.

Dugger, Celia. 1996. "A Refugee's Body is Intact but her Family is Torn." *The New York Times*, A1–A9.

Dugger, Celia. 2011. "Senegal Curbs a Bloody Rite for Girls and Women." *New York Times*, October 15, 2011. http://www.nytimes.com.

Durkheim, Emile. 1982. *The Rules of Sociological Method and Selected Texts on Sociology and Its Method*, edited by Steven Lukes. New York: The Free Press.

Einstein, Gillian. 2008. "From Body to Brain: Considering the Neurobiological Effects of Female Genital Cutting." *Perspectives in Biology and Medicine*, Vol. 51, No. 1: 84–97. https://muse:jhu.edu.

Elchalal, U., B. Ben-Ami, R. Gillis, and A. Brzezinsk. 1997. "Ritualistic Female Genital Mutilation: Current Status and Future Outlook." *Obstet Gynecol Surv*, Vol. 52, No. 10: 643–51.

El Dareer, Asma. 1983. "Complications of Female Circumcision in the Sudan." *Tropical Doctor*, Vol. 13, No. 3: 131–33.

El Dareer, Asma. 1983. *Women, Why Do You Weep?* London: Zed Press.

Engineer, Asghar Ali. 1989. "Religion and Liberation," in *Religion and Liberation*, edited by Asghar Ali Engineer. Delhi: Ajanta Publications, 1989, 1–12.

Engineer, Asghar Ali. 1989. "Religion, Ideology and Liberation Theology—An Islamic Point of View," in *Religion and Liberation*, edited by Asghar Ali Engineer. Delhi: Ajanta Publications, 135–48.

Engineer, Asghar Ali. 1992. *The Rights of Women in Islam*. New York: St. Martin's Press.

Equality Now. 2012. "Female Genital Mutilation (FGM)." http://www.equalitynow.org/.

Essen, Birgitta, and Sara Johnsdotter. 2004. "Female Genital Mutilation in the West: Traditional Circumcision Versus Genital Cosmetic Surgery." *Acta Obstetricia et Gynecologica Scandinavia*, Vol. 83: 611–13.

European Institute for Gender Equality. n.d. "Current Situation of Female Genital Mutilation in France." www.europe.eu.

The European Parliamentary Estimates. The Amnesty International ENDFGM European Campaign. http://www.endfgm.eu/en/.

Exterkate, Marja. 2013. "Female Genital Mutilation in the Netherlands: Prevalence, Incidence and Determinants." *Pharos Center of Expertise on Health for Immigrants and Refugees*. www.awepa.org.

Farhat, Said Al-Munji. 2007. "Female Genital Mutilation is Part of the Sunna of the Prophet." *Excerpts of an Interview with Al-Azhar Cleric Farahat Said Al-Munji, aired on Al-Mihwar TV*, May 10, 2007. www.religiousforums.com.

Fazlur, Rahman. 1979. *Islam*. Chicago: University of Chicago Press.

Feldman-Jacobs, Charlotte and D. Clifton. 2010: Female Genital Mutilation/Cutting: Data and Trends—Update, Population Reference Bureau. http://www.prb.org/Publications/Datasheets/2010/fgm2010.aspx.

Fiorenza, Elisabeth Shussler. 1984. *Bread Not Stone: The Challenge of Feminist Biblical Interpretation*. Boston: Beacon Press.

Fiorenza, Elisabeth Shussler. 1998. *In Memory of Her*. New York: Crossroad.

Fleming, J. B. 1960. "Clitoridectomy: The Disastrous Downfall of Isaac Baker Brown FRCS (1867)." *Journal of Obstetrics and Gynecology of the British Empire*, Vol. 67: 1017–34.

Foster, Charles. 1994." On the Trail of a Taboo: Female Circumcision in the Islamic World." *Contemporary Review*, Vol. 264, No. 1540: 244.

Francouer, Robert T., et al. 1999. *Sexuality in America: Understanding our Sexual Values and Behavior*. New York: Continuum.

Francoeur, Robert T., R. J. Noonan, B. Opiyo-Omolo, and J. Pastoetter. 2004. "Female Sexuality Today: Challenging Cultural Repression." *Cross Currents*, 55–70, EBSCOHost database.

Freire, Paulo. 1987. *Education for Critical Consciousness*. New York: Continuum.

Freire, Paulo. 1970. "Concientization as a Way of Liberating," in *Liberation Theology: A Documentary History*, edited by Alfred T. Hennelly, S. J. Maryknoll. New York: Orbis Books, 5–13.

Gilbert, Jacqueline A. and John M. Ivancevich. 2002. "Valuing Diversity: A Tale of two Organizations." *The Academy of Management Executive*, Vol. 14, No. 1: 93–105.

Glazov, Jamie. 2011. "A Survivor's Battle against Female Genital Mutilation." *FrontPage Magazine*. www.frontpagemag.com.

Goldberg, Garey. 2012. "In Defense of Female Circumcision? Panel Presents Seven Facts." *Common Health Reform and Reality*. http://common health.wbur.org.

Goldscheider, C. and F. Goldscheider. 1987. "Moving Out of Marriage: What do Young Adults Expect?" *American Sociological Review*, Vol. 52: 278–85.

Goodwin, Jo-Ann and David Jones. 2008. "The Unspeakable Practice of Female Circumcision that is Destroying Young Women's Lives in Britain." *Mail Online*. www.dailymail.co.uk.

Gordon, D. A. 1964. "Female Circumcision and Genital Operations in Egypt and the Sudan: a Dilemma for Medical Anthropology." *Medical Anthropology Quarterly*, Vol. 5, No. 1: 3–14.

Grassie, William. 2007. "The Evolution of Religion: Memes, Spandrels, or Adaptations? How Evolutionary Psychology Explains Religion or Not." Lecture delivered at the Society for Integration of Science and Human Values (SiSHVa). www.metanexus.net.

Gregory, Sophronia Scott. 1994. "At Risk of Mutilation." *Time*, March 21, 46.

Griaule, Marcel. 1965/1970. *Conversations with Ogotemmeli*, International African Institute. New York: Oxford University Press.

Grillo, Ralph.1998. *Pluralism and the Politics of Difference: State, Culture, and Ethnicity in Comparative Perspective*. Oxford: Clarendon Press.

Gross, Rita M. 1966. *Feminism and Religion: An Introduction*. Boston: Beacon Press.

Gruenbaum, Ellen. 2001. *The Female Circumcision Controversy: An Anthropological Perspective*. Philadelphia: University of Pennsylvania Press.

Guy, Blake M. 1995. "Female Genital Excision and the Implications of Federal Prohibition." *William and Mary Journal of Women and the Law*, Vol. 2, No. 1, Art.7: 125–69. http://scholarship.law.wm.edu.

Gyekye, Kwame. 1995. *As Essay on African Philosophical Thought: The Akan Conceptual Scheme*. Philadelphia: Temple University Press.

Gyekye, Kwame. 1997. *Tradition and Modernity: Philosophical Reflections on the African Experience*. New York: Oxford University Press.

Halila, Sahil, R. H. Belmaker, Yunis Abu Rabia, Miron Froimocivi, and Julia Applebaum. 2009. "Disappearance of Female Genital Mutilation from the Bedouin Population of Southern Israel." *The Journal of Sexual Medicine*, Vol. 6, No. 1: 70–73.

Hamm, Lisa M. 2011. "Female Mutilation: A Model's Story of Ritual Torture." *South Coast Today*. http://archive.southcoasttday.com.

Hansen, Jane and Deborah Scroggins. 1992. "Female Circumcision: U.S. Georgia Forced to Face Medical Legal Issues." *Atlanta Journal and Constitution*, November 15, A. P1.

Harvey, Charlotte Bruce. 2002. "Doctor of Mercy." *Brown Alumni Magazine*. www.brownalumnimagazinecontentview1313/40/.

Hassan, Riffat. 1991. "An Islamic Perspective," in *Women, Religion and Sexuality: Studies on the Impact of Religious Teachings on Women*, edited by Jeanne Betcher. Philadelphia: Trinity Press International.

Hastings, Deborah. 2014. "Swedish Health Authorities Discover Every Girl in One Class had Undergone Genital Mutilation: Report." *New York Daily News*. www.nydailynews.com.

Helmore, Kristin. 2010. "Ending Harmful Practices through Community—Led Social Change in Senegal." UNFPA Feature Story. www.unfpa.org/public/news/pid/5181.

Hite, Shere. 1976. *The Hite Report: A Nationwide Study of Female Sexuality*. New York: Macmillan Publishing Co., Inc.

Holt, Tim. 2008. "Cultural Relativism." *Introduction to Moral and Cultural Relativism*. www.philosophyofreligion.info/culturalrelativism.html.

Honig, Bonnie. 1999. "My Culture Made Me Do It," in *Is Multiculturalism Bad for Women*, edited by Joshua Cohen, Matthew Howard, and Martha C. Nussbaum. Princeton: Princeton University Press.

Hundley, Tom. 2002. "Immigrants Bring Practice of Female Circumcision to Europe." Knight-Ridder/Tribune News Service, 23–43.

Ibn-Abd-al-Hakam. 1922. *The History of the Conquest of Egypt, North Africa and Spain, Known as the Futur Misr*, edited by Torrey CC. New Haven, CT: Yale University Press, 11–12.

Ibn-Qayyim, Al-Jawziyyah, Shams-al-Din. 1987. Tuhfat al-Wadud bi-ahkam al-mawlud, Cairo: Dar al Rayyan, 166.

Ierodiaconou, M. 1995. "'Listen to Us!' Female Genital Mutilation, Feminism and the Law in Australia." *Melbourne University Law Review*, Vol. 20: 562–71.

Israel, B. A., B. Checkoway, A. Schulz, and M. Zimmerman. 1994. "Health Education and Community Empowerment: Conceptualizing and Measuring Perceptions of Individual, Organizational and Community Control." *Health Educational Quarterly*, Vol. 21, No. 2: 149–70.

Jaggar, Alison M. 1988. *Feminist Politics and Human Nature*. Totowa, NJ: Rowman and Littlefied.

James, Stanlie M. 2005. "Female Genital Cutting," in *The Oxford Encyclopedia of Women in World History*, edited by Bonnie G. Smith. Oxford: Oxford University Press, 259–62.

James, Stanlie M. and Claire Robertson. 2002: *Genital Cutting and Transnational Sisterhood Disputing U.S. Polemics*. Urbana: University of Illinois Press.

Kahiga, Miriam. 1994. "One Rite, Too Many Wrongs." *Daily Nation*, April 3–5.

Kalev, Henriette Dahan. 2004. "Cultural Rights or Human Rights: the Case of Female Genital Mutilation." *Sex Roles*, Vol. 51, No. 5–6: 339–48.

Keaton, Sherri. 2010. "Female Mutilation Happens All Over the World, even in America." *Central Michigan Life*, April 21, 2010. http://www.cm-life.com.

Kegele, S., R. Hays, L. Pollack, T. Coates. 1996. "Community Mobilization Reduces HIV Risk among Gay Men: A Two Community Study." *11th International Conference on AIDS Vancouver* [Mo.D.581].

Kelton, W. Douglas. 1994. "Female Genital Mutilation." *Report of the Councils on Scientific Affairs, CSA Report*, 5-1-94 at line 11-12.

Kessler, David F. 1996. *The Falashas: A Short History of the Ethiopian Jews*. Oregon: Frank Cass & Co. Ltd.

Kukathas, Chandran. 1997. "Cultural Toleration," in *Ethnicity and Group Rights*, edited by W. Kymlicka and I. Shapiro. New York: New York University Press, 60–104.

Kwaak, Van der, Anke, et al. 2003. *Strategieen ter voorkoming van besnijdenis bij meisjes: Inventarisatie en aanbevelingen*, Amsterdam: Vrije Univeriteit and VU Medisch Centrum.

Kymlicka, W. 1995. "Multicultural Citizenship: A Liberal Theory of Minority Rights." *The Rights of Minority Cultures*. New York: Oxford University Press.

Kymlicka, W. and I. Shapiro. 1995. "Are There Any Cultural Rights?" in *The Rights of Minority Cultures*, edited by Kymlicka Will. Oxford: Oxford University Press, 228–55.

Lacey, Mark. 2004. "Genital Cutting Shows Signs of Losing Favor in Africa." *The New York Times*. http://query.nytimes.com.

Levy, Pema. 2010. "Female Genital Mutilation Performed at Cornell University." at *Change.org*. http://news.change.org.

Leye, Els and Jessika Deblonde. 2004. *Belgian Legislation Regarding FGM and the Implementation of the Law in Belgium*, ICRH Publications nr. 9 Lokeren: De Consulterij.

Leye, Els and Jessika Deblonde. 2004. "A Comparative Analysis of the Different Legal Approaches Toward Female Genital Mutilation in the 15th EU Member States, and the Respective Judicial Outcomes in Belgium, France, Spain, Sweden, and the United Kingdom." *International Centre for Reproductive Health (ICRH)*, Publication No.8, Ghent, *The Consolatory*, April 23–24.

Leye, Els, et al. 2006. "Health Care in Europe for Women with Genital Mutilation." *Health Care for Women International*, Vol. 27, No. 4: 362–78.

Leye, Els, Ilse Ysebaert, Jessika Deblonde, Patricia Claeys, Gert Vermeulen, Yves Jacquemyn, and Marleen Temmerman. 2008. "Female Genital Mutilation: Knowledge, Attitudes and Practices of Flemish Gynaecologists." *The European Journal of Contraception and Reproductive Health Care*, Vol.13, No. 2: 182–90.

Leye, Els, Ilse Ysebaert, Jessika Deblonde, Patricia Claeys, Gert Vermeulen, Yves Jacquemyn, and Marleen Temmerman. 2008. "Female Genital Mutilation: A Study of Health Services and Legislation in Some Countries of the European Union." Dissertation, ICRH Monographs.

Lightfoot-Klein, Hanny. 1989. *Prisoners of Ritual: An Odyssey into Female Genital Circumcision in Africa*. New York: Harrington Park.

Lightfoot-Klein, Hanny. 1989. "The Sexual Experience and Marital Adjustment of Genital Circumcised and Infibulated Females in the Sudan." *The Journal of Sex Research*, Vol. 26, No. 3: 375–92.

Livingston, James C. 1998. *Anatomy of the Sacred: An Introduction to Religion*, Upper Saddle River, NJ: Pearson Prentice Hall.

Longinotto, Kim. 2002. *The Day I Will Never Forget*, (Film) London: Women Make Movies.

Lopez, Claire. 2013. "Female Genital Mutilation on Rise in U.S." *The Clarion Project: Challenging Extremism, Promoting Dialogue*, March 18. http://www.clarionproject.org/analysis/female-genital-mutilation-rise-us.

MacIntyre, Alasdair C. 1984/2007. *After Virtue: A Study in Moral Theory*, 3rd edition, Notre Dame, IN: University of Notre Dame Press.

Mackie, Gerry. 1996. "Ending Foot binding and Infibulation: A Convention Account." *American Sociological Review*, Vol. 61, No. 6: 999–1017.

Mackie, Gerry. 1998. "A Way to End Female Genital Cutting." *The Female Genital Cutting Education and Networking Project*. www.fgmnetwork.org.

Magesa, Laurenti. 1997. *African Religion: The Moral Traditions of Abundant Life*. Maryknoll, NY: Orbis Books.

Mahran, Maher. 1981. *Les risques medicaux de l'excision (circoncision medi-cale)*, reprint of a paper published in *Bulletin Medicale de l'IPPF*, Vol. 15, No. 2: 1–2.

Maim, Sara. 2010. "Please Help Me: I Don't Want To Be Cut Like My Sister. . . ." www.dailymail.co.uk.

Mann, Judy. 1994. "Torturing Girls Is Not a Cultural Right." *The Washington Post*, February 23.

Matthews, Benjamin P. 2011. "Female Genital Mutilation: Australian Law, Policy and Practical Challenges for Doctors." *The Medical Journal of Australia*, Vol. 194, No. 3: 139–41.

Mehren, Elizabeth. 2004. "U.S Doc's Specialty is Women with Cut Genitals." *We-news: Covering Women's Issues-Changing Women's Lives*. www.women's.org.

Melching, Molly. 2012. "Honoring Maimouna Traore: Brave Pioneer of Abandonment of Female Genital Cutting in Senegal." *Half the Sky: Turning Oppression into Opportunity for Women Worldwide*. www.halftheskymovement.org.

Miller, Larry. 2007. "Barbaric Practice of Genital Mutilation on the Rise in Britain Mutilated Girls; U.K.'s Ignored Secret." *Doctor Bulldog and Ronin Conservative News, Views and Analysis of Events*. www.doctorbulldog.wordpress.com.

Miller, Michael. 2004. *Responses to Female Genital Mutilation/Cutting in Europe*, UNICEF Innocenti Research Centre, Florence, Italy, 6.

Mire, Soraya. 1993. "Genital Mutilation by Any Other Name. . . ." *NORCIC Newsletter*, Vol. 7 No.2. http://www.nocirc.org/publish/9–93.pdf.

Momoh, C. 2000. "Female Genital Mutilation, also known as Female Circumcision: Information for Health Care Professionals." London: Guy's and St. Thomas' Hospital NHS Trust.

Moore, Matthew and Karuni Rompies. 2004. "In the Cut." *Sydney Morning Herald*, Sydney, NSW January 13. http://www.cirp.org.

Morrison, Barbara S. 2008. "Feminist Theory and the Practice of Female Genital Mutilation (FGM)." http://uuair.lib.utsunomiya-u.ac.jp.

Najm, Kamaran. 2012. "The Situation of Children and Women in Iraq." *UNICEF Iraq*. http://www.unicef.org/iraq/MICS_highlights_ENGLISH_FINAL.pdf.

National Population Commission Federal Republic if Nigeria, 2004. *Nigeria Demographics and Health Survey 2003* http://dhsprogram.com/pubs/pdf/FR148/FR148.pdf.

New York Times Editorial. 2010. "Not Anyone's Daughter." *New York Times*. www.nytimes.com.

The Norwegian Ministry of Health and Social Affairs. 2002. "Information about the Act Relating to the Prohibition of Female Genital

Mutilation." www.regjeringen.no/upload/kilde/hd/bro2002/0002/ddd/ pdfv/155539-engels.pdf.

Nour, N.M. 2005. "Number of Women, Girls with or at risk for Female Genital Cutting on the rise in the United States." Press Release. Boston: African Women's Health Center, Brigham and Women's Hospital. www.brighamandwomens.org/africanwomenscenter/research.asp.

Nussbaum, Martha. 1995. "Objectification." *Philosophy and Public Affairs*, Vol. 24, No. 4: 249–91.

Obiora, Amede L. 1997. "Bridges and Barricades: Rethinking Polemics and Intransigence in the Campaign against Female Circumcision." *Case Western Reserve Law Review*, Vol. 47, No. 2: 275–78.

O'Connor, Colleen and John Yearwood. 1994. "Ancient Ritual Modern Dilemma." *Dallas Morning News*, May 22.

Odigie, Adesua. 2012. "New York Walk to End Ritual Cutting of Girls" in *We-News*, September 12, 2012, womensenews.org.

Okin, Susan Moller. 1997. "Is Multiculturalism Bad for Women?" *Boston Review: A Political and Literary Forum*, Vol. 22, October/November: 25–28.

Okin, Susan Moller. 1999. "Is Multiculturalism Bad for Women?" in *Is Multiculturalism Bad for Women*, edited by Joshua Cohen, Matthew Howard, and Martha C. Nussbaum. Princeton: Princeton University Press, 7–26.

Omayme, Gutbi. 1995. *Preliminary Report on Female Genital Mutilation (FGM)*. Ontario Violence Against Women Prevention Section of the Ontario Women's Directorate, April 10, Unpublished.

One Minute World News. 2007. "My Mother Held me Down." *BBC News*, July 10. http://news.bbc.co.uk.

Orubuloye, O.I., John. C. Caldwell, and Pat Caldwell. 1993. "African Women's Control Over Sexuality in an Era of AIDS: A study of the Yoruba of Nigeria." *Social Science and Medicine*, Vol. 37, No. 7: 859–72.

Parekh, Bhikkhu. 1997. "A Varied Moral World." *Boston Review: A Political and Literary Forum*. www.bostonreview.net.

Parker, R. 1996. Empowerment, Community Mobilization and Social Change in the Face of HIV/AIDS. *AIDS*, Vol. 10, suppl. 3: S27–S31.

Paula, Rapp. 2008. "Female Genital Mutilation Practices around the World." *Feminism and Women's Rights*. www.helium.com.

Poldermans, Sophie. 2005. "Combating Female Genital Mutilation in Europe: A Comparative Analysis of Legislative and Preventative Tools in the Netherlands, France the United Kingdom and Austria." MSc thesis, Vienna: University of Vienna.

Population Reference Bureau. 2001. "Abandoning Female Genital Cutting: Prevalence, Attitudes and Efforts to End the Practice." Population *Reference Bureau*. http://www.prb.org.

Poulter, Sebastian. 1986. *English Criminal Law and Ethnic Minority Customs*. London: Butterworths.

Powell, Richard A., Amanda Lawrence, Faith N. Mwangi-Powell, and Morrison Linda. 2002. "FGM, Asylum and Refugees: The Need for an Integrated U.K Policy Agenda." *Forced Migration Review*, Vol. 14: 35.

Powell, Richard A., et al. 2004. "Female Genital Mutilation, Asylum Seekers and Refugees: the Need for an Integrated European Union agenda." *Health Policy*, No. 70: 153–56.

Rahman, Anika and Nahid Toubia. (Eds.). 2001. *Female Genital Mutilation: A Guide to Worldwide Laws and Policies*. New York: Zed Books.

Ramsey, M. n.d. "Forward USA/Ethiopia: Assistance, education and support for women and girls affected by female genital mutilation." www.religioustolerance.org.

Rathmann, W.G. 1959. "Female Circumcision Indications and a New Technique." *General Practitioner*, Vol. 20, No. 3: 115–20.

Rausch, Katherine. 2011. "Phoenix Clinic Cares for Women with Cut Genitals." *WeNews* Correspondent, June 6. http://womensenews.org.

Rawls, John. 1971. *A Theory of Social Justice*. Cambridge, MA: Harvard University Press.

Reichert, E. 2006. *Understanding Human Rights: An Exercise Book*. London: Sage Publications.

Remondino, Peter Charles. 1891. *History of Circumcision: From the Earliest Times to the Present*. Philadelphia: F.A. Davis Publisher.

Renteln, A.D. 1990. *International Human Rights: Universalism versus Relativism*. Newbury Park, CA: Sage.

Richard F., D. Daniel, B. Ostynn, et al. 2000. *Technisch advise voor gezondheidspersoneel in Belgie. Vrouwelijke genital verminking (vrouwenbesnijdenis)—handleiding bij de bevalling*. Brussels: Belgian Ministry of Public Health.

Robert, Darby and J. Steven Svoboda. 2007. A Rose by any Other Name: Rethinking the Differences/Similarities between Male and Female Genital Cutting." *Medical Anthropology Quarterly*, Vol. 21, No. 3: 301–23.

Robert, Sue Lloyd. 2012. "Hidden World of Female Genital Cutting in the United Kingdom." *BBC News Night*, July 23. http://www.bbc.co.uk.

Robinet, Patricia. 2006. *The Rape of Innocence: One Woman's Story of Female Genital Mutilation in the U.S.A.* Eugene, OR: Aesculapius Nunzio Press.

Robinson, B. A. 2001. Female Genital Mutilation in Africa, the Middle East and Far East. http://www.religioustolerance.org/fem_cirm.htm.

Robinson, B. A. 2004. "Female Genital Mutilation and Female (Circumcision) in Africa, Middle East and Far East." *Religious Tolerance.org.* www.religious tolerance.org.

Robinson, Martin. 2013. "2000 Female Genital Mutilation Victims Seek Help at London Hospitals in Just Three Years but the True Figure Is 'Far More Than Figures Show.'" *Mail Online.* http://www.dailymail.co.uk/news/article-2414014/html.

Rodrigues, Yolanda and Tom Opdyke. 2007. "Slain Georgia Mom, Kids sought Asylum from Kenya." *The Atlanta Journal—Constitution.* www.freerepublic.com.

Rogers, E. M. 1983. *Diffusion of Innovations*, 3rd edition. New York: The Free Press.

Rosenberg, Tina. 2004. "Editorial Observer; Mutilating Africa's Daughters Laws Unenforced Practices Unchanged." *The New York Times.* www.nytimes.com.

Shaalan, M. 1982. Clitoris Envy: a Psycho-dynamic Construct Instrumental in Female Circumcision. Alexandria: WHO/EMRO Technical Publication, 271.

Sheehan, Elizabeth. 1997. *Victorian Clitoridectomy: Isaac Baker Brown and His HarmlessOperative Procedure, The Gender/Sexuality Reader.* R. N. Lancaster and M. di Leonardo, eds. New York: Routledge, 325–34.

Sheikyermami. 2007. "Egyptian Villagers Explain Why They Circumcise Their Daughters, Christians under Attack." http://mychristianblood.blogspirit.com; and www.egyptsearch.com.

Shell-Duncan, Bettina. 2001. "The Medicalization of Female 'Circumcision': Harm Reduction or Promotion of a Dangerous Practice?" *Social Science and Medicine*, Vol. 52, No. 7: 1013–28.

Shell-Duncan, Bettina and Ylva Hernlund. 2000. "'Female Circumcision' in Africa: Dimensions of the Practice and Debates," in *Female "Circumcision" in Africa: Culture Controversy and Change*, edited by Bettina Shell-Duncan and Ylva Hernlund. London: Lynne Reiner Publishers, 2000, 1–40.

Shryock, Harold. 1968. *On Becoming a Woman: A Book for Teen-Age Girls.* Victoria, Australia: Signs/Review and Herald.

Shweider, Richard. 2002. "'What About Female Genital Mutilation? and Why Understanding Culture Matters in the First Place," in *Engaging Cultural Differences: The Multicultural Challenge in Liberal Democracies*, edited by R. Shweider, M. Minow, and H. Markus. New York: Russell Sage Foundation Press, 216–51.

Simpson, Peter Viathagen. 2009. "Girl Receives Damages for Genital Mutilation." *The Local.* www.thelocal.se.

Skaine, Rosemarie. 2005. *Female Genital Mutilation: Legal, Cultural and Medical Issues.* Jefferson, NC: McFarland.

Sloan, R. D. 2001. "Out relativizing Relativism: A Liberal Defense of the Universality of International Human Rights." *Vanderbilt Journal of Transnational Law*, Vol. 34, No. 3: 527–95.

Smith, Christian. 1996. "Correcting a Curious Neglect or Bridging Religion Back," in *Disruptive Religion: The Force of Faith in Social Movement Activism*, edited by Christian Smith. New York: Routledge, 1996, 1–28.

Smith, Dorothy. 1999. *Writing the Social Critique: Theory and Investigations.* London: University of Toronto Press.

Spencer, Zara. 2002. "The Criminalization of Female Genital Mutilation in Queensland." *Murdoch University Electronic Journal of Law*, Vol. 9, No. 3. http://www.worldlii.org/au/journals/MurUEJL/2002/16.html.

Steiner, Henry J., and Philip Alston. 1996. *International Human Rights in Context: Law, Politics, Morals.* Oxford: Clarendon Press.

Sterns, Olivia. 2009. Operations Give Female Genital Mutilation Victims Hope on Reconstruction." *Human Rights and Culture*, Vol. 2, No. 23. http://newsletters.ahrchk.net.

Sterns, Olivia. 2011. "Pioneering OP Gives Female Circumcision Victims Hope." *CNN.* http://edition.cnn.com.

Synon, M. E. 2014. "Rise in Female Genital Mutilation: Inspectors Find Entire School Classes Victims." Breibert.com. www.breibart.com.

Tatnell, P. 2010. "Circumcising Young Girls is Child Abuse." *Goward, Sydney Morning Herald.* http:www.smh.au/lifestyle/wellbeing.

Thiam, Awa. 1989. *Black Sisters Speak Out: Feminism and Oppression in Africa.* London: Pluto Press.

Tilley, J. J. 2000. "Cultural Relativism." *Human Rights Quarterly*, Vol. 22, No. 2: 501–47.

Tostan. 1999. "Breakthrough in Senegal: The Process That Ended Female Genital Cutting in 31 Villages." Nairobi, Kenya: Population Council.

Tostan. 2012. "Celebrating the Movement to Abandon Female Genital Cutting (FGC) in Senegal." *Tostan Community-Led Development.* http://tostan.org.

Toubia, Nahid F. 1999. "Evolutionary Cultural Ethics and Circumcision of Children, *Male and Female Circumcision: Medical, Legal, Ethical Considerations in Pediatrics Practice*, edited by George C. Denniston, rederic Mansfield Hodges, New York: Kluwer Academic/Plenum Publishers.

Toubia, Nahid F. 1995. Female Genital Mutilation, *Women's Rights, Human Rights: International Feminist Perspectives*, edited by J.S. Peters and A. Wolper,. New York: Routledge, 224–37.

Tsai, Catherine. 2010. "Female Circumcision Victims Seek Out Colo Doctor." *U-T San Diego.* www.utsandiego.com.

Tuhus-Dubrow, Rebecca. 2007. "Rites and Wrongs: Is Outlawing Female Genital Mutilation Enough to Stop It from Happening Here?" *The Female Genital Cutting: Education and Networking Project*, February 11, 2007. www.fgmnetwork.org.

Tulloch, Teleta. 2009. "In Ethiopia, African Women Parliamentarians Condemn Female Genital Mutilations." UNICEF September 14. http://www.unicef.org/infobycountry/Ethiopia51122.html.

Turner, Diane. 2007. "Female Genital Cutting: Implications for Nurses." *Nursing For Women'sHealth*, Vol. 11, No. 4. http://nwh.awhonn.org.

UNESCO. 2003. "Convention for the Safeguarding of the Intangible Cultural Heritage." *United Nation's Educational Scientific and Cultural Organization: Legal Instruments*. http://portal.unesco.org.

UNICEF. 2005. "Multiple Indicator Cluster Survey Manual: Monitoring Situations of Women and Children." http://www.childinfo.org.

UNICEF. 2008. "Changing a Harmful Social Convention: Female Genital Mutilation/ Cutting." *Innocenti Digest*, Florence Italy. http://www.unicef-irc.org.

UNICEF. 2013. Female Genital Mutilation/Cutting: A Statistical Overview and Exploration of the Dynamics of Change, UNICEF, New York.

UNHR. 1998–2013. "What are Human Rights?" *United Nations Human Rights*. http://www.ohchr.org.

Vogel-Misicka, Susan. 2012. "Law Tightened on Female Genital Mutilation." *International Service of the Swiss Broadcasting Corporation*. www.swissinfo.ch.

Wade, Lisa. 2009. "Defining Gendered Oppression in U.S. Newspapers: The Strategic Value of 'Female Genital Mutilation.'" *Gender and Society*, Vol. 23, No. 3: 293–314.

Walker, A. and P. Parmar. 1993. *Warrior Marks: Female Genital Mutilation and the Sexual Blinding of Women*. London: Harcourt Brace.

Wangila, Mary Nyangweso. 2007. *Female Circumcision: The Interplay between Religion Gender and Culture*. Maryknoll, NY: Orbis Books.

Wangila, Mary Nyangweso. 2010. "Religion, the African Concept of the Individual and Human Rights Discourse: An Analysis." *Journal of Human Rights*, Vol. 9, No. 3: 326–43.

Walzer, Michael. 1988. *The Company of Critics: Social Criticism and Political Commitment in the Twentieth Century*. New York: Basic Books.

Wassuna, Angela. 2000. "Towards Redirecting the Female Circumcision Debate: Legal, Ethical and Cultural Considerations." *McGill Journal of Medicine*, Vol. 5: 104–10.

Webster, Paul. 2004. "Paris Court Convicts Mother of Genital Mutilation." *Observer*, February 1, 25.

Werner, D., D. Sanders, J. Weston, S. Babb, and B. Rodriguez. 1997. "Questioning the Solution: The Politics of Primary Health Care and Child Survival with an in-depth Critique of Oral Rehydration Therapy." *Healthwrights*, 967.

West Ann. 1996. *Cal. Health and Safety* Code § 124170.

West Ann. 1999. Colo. Legis. Serv. Ch. 216, §§ 2, 4 (99–96).

WHO Study Group. 2006. "Female Genital Mutilation and Obstetric Outcome in 28,393 Deliveries from Six African Countries: WHO collaborative Prospective Study." *The Lancet*, Vol. 367, No. 9525: 1835–41.

Winter, Sylvia. 1997. "'Genital Mutilation' or 'Symbolic Birth?' Female Circumcision, Lost Origins and the Aculturalism of Feminism/Western Thought." *Case Western Reserve Law Review*, Vol. 47, No. 2: 501–53.

World Health Organization (WHO). 1997. *Female Genital Mutilation*. A joint WHO/UNICEF/UNFPA Statement, Geneva: WHO.

World Health Organization (WHO). 2001. *Female Genital Mutilation: A Teacher's Guide*. WHO/FCH/GWH/01.3; WHO/RHR/01.16.31. www.who.int/frh-whd.

World Health Organization (WHO). 2010. "Female Genital Mutilation." www.who.int/mediacentre/factsheets/fs241/en/.

World Health Organization (WHO). 2014. "Female Genital Mutilation." http://www.who.int/mediacentre/factsheets/fs241/en/.

Yasin Berivan, A. Namir, G. Al-Tawil, Nazar P. Shabila, and Tariq S. Al-Hadithi. 2013. "Female Genital Mutilation among Iraq Kurdish Women: A Cross-Sectional Study from Erbil City." *BMC Public Health*, Vol. 13: 809.

Ye Hee Lee, Michelle. 2010. "Phoenix Health Clinic Volunteers Guide Connect with Refugee Women." *Arizona Republic*. www.azcentral.com.

Young, Marion Iris. 1990. *Justice and the Politics of Difference*. Princeton: Princeton University Press.

Young, Marion Iris. 1992. "Five Faces of Oppression," in *Rethinking Power*, edited by Thomas E. Wartenberg. Albany: State University of New York Press, 174–95.

Zero Tolerance. "Briefing Female Genital Mutilation/Cutting." www.zerotolerance.org.uk.

Index

About the Author

Mary Nyangweso, PhD, is Associate Professor of Religion and Peel Distinguished Chair of Religious Studies at East Carolina University, Greenville, NC. Her published works include *Female Circumcision: The Interplay of Religion, Gender and Culture in Kenya* (2007). She has also published articles in peer-reviewed journals and book chapters in a number of books in the area of gender and African religions. Nyangweso holds a doctorate in the Sociology of Religion from Drew University.